1988

A Guide to Oral Interpretation:
Solo and Group Performance

Second Edition

A Guide to Oral Interpretation:
Solo and Group Performance

Louise M. Scrivner
Berea College

Dan Robinette
Eastern Kentucky University

BOBBS-MERRILL EDUCATIONAL PUBLISHING   INDIANAPOLIS

Copyright © 1980 by The Bobbs-Merrill Company, Inc.

Printed in the United States of America

The Bobbs-Merrill Company, Inc.
4300 West 62nd Street
Indianapolis, Indiana 46206

Second Edition
First Printing 1980
Cover design by Richard Listenberger

Designed by David Stahl

Library of Congress Cataloging in Publication Data

Scrivner, Louise M.
  A guide to oral interpretation.

  Includes index.
  1. Oral interpretation.   I. Robinette, Dan,
joint author.   II. Title.
PN4145.S3   1979   808.5'45   79-11940
ISBN 0-672-61476-6

Contents

Preface

In the first edition of this text, the author acknowledged her debt to students: "The inspiration came from students whose encouragement and participation in the testing of exercises and methods in the classroom made much of the book a joint endeavor. Their questions, too, did much to direct the book's practical approach: 'Do we need to read so much about oral interpretation? Can't this be said in fewer words? How do I find the tone of a particular selection?' " *A Guide to Oral Interpretation* came as a response to this kind of questions.

Now, ten years later, we realize those questions were simply the tip of an iceberg. Students today are certainly concerned with those, but new questions have risen which imply a different thrust: "Is a poem little more than an object to be dissected and reassembled? Is not the experience, the 'moment' of a poem as important as the craftsmanship of a poem?" Furthermore, a change in the students' reading preferences is noted as students turn to new authors who are expressing simply and sincerely what they are experiencing—their loves, their fears, their disillusionments. John Malcolm Brinnin wrote, "Impatient with writers who saw literature as spiritual and cerebral discipline, they turned to writers who saw it as impulsive expression."[1]

Teachers and authors of oral interpretation textbooks, steeped largely in the discipline and tradition of the New Criticism, have been reluctant to adapt to the new demands of students who see the poetic experience not as static but as a dynamic process. As Richard Palmer, author of Hermeneutics, writes, "We have forgotten that the literary work is not a manipulatable object completely at our own disposal; it is a human voice out of the past, a voice which must somehow be brought to life."[2] It

---

[1] John Malcolm Brinnin. In *American Poets in 1976*. William Heyen, ed. Indianapolis: Bobbs-Merrill, 1976.

[2] Richard E. Palmer. *Hermeneutics*. Evanston, Ill.: Northwestern University Press, 1969.

was to this need that we addressed ourselves as we began the revision of the textbook.

We have retained the general practical approach which has thus far proved useful to students and teachers. So this text presents course content briefly and concretely, showing the student specific ways he or she may experience meaning in literature and suggesting specific ways the student may communicate this meaning effectively to an audience. But the hows, as the book's title implies, are presented not as mechanical processes but as guides which have been found workable.

We have emphasized a second point, which was implicit in the first edition, namely, that the text is a central concern of any oral interpretation experience. Thus, we try to understand the text by "standing under" the text—we acknowledge its primary importance, approaching it as a dynamic entity and asking, "What does *it* demand of *us*?"

This emphasis has prompted changes. Group performance of literature has been fully covered, making our text a first in this respect. We consider this part to be one of the best and most thorough coverages of interpreters theatre in any introductory text. We have retained the technical and psychological approaches to vocal and visual interpretation of the "moment" of literature. These are ways students can begin to embody literature. The technical aspects draw upon the basic theories most widely accepted in the field of oral interpretation. The psychological approach applies concentration, imagination, and identification specifically to interpretive reading. To these approaches we have added new illustrations from contemporary prose, poetry, and drama taken from students' experiences today. Finally, we have added new exercises in accordance with our philosophy that theory has more meaning when it is applied immediately. We feel that the exercises will aid students in heightening their sensitivity to and awareness of themselves, enabling them to identify with the experience of the literary selection.

Our thanks go to many friends and colleagues for their criticism and general support, in particular to Dr. James Conover of Ohio University. Our students, who have been our constant critics, always helped us to keep their point of view in mind. In particular, thanks go to Rick Robertson, a friend, and former student, but even more, an unrelenting critic.

There is, however, no one person we could choose who has been so closely involved with the project as to merit dedication. For indeed the close collaborative effort and warm professional relationship since we were student and teacher at Berea College was the single creative force responsible for this revision.

L. M. S.
D. R. R.

Part I

Solo Interpretive Reading: Principles and Methods

Chapter 1

Introducing Interpretive Reading

The Pasture[1]
Robert Frost

I'm going out to clean the pasture spring;
I'll only stop to rake the leaves away
(And wait to watch the water clear, I may):
I shan't be gone long.—You come too.

I'm going out to fetch the little calf
That's standing by the mother. It's so young,
It totters when she licks it with her tongue.
I shan't be gone long.—You come too.

Literally, the narrator in this poem invites us to come with him to perform a seemingly simple act, the clearing of the pasture spring. Of course, we know he figuratively asks much more of us. So does the poem, for it too is an invitation with more subtle meanings than the mere words on the page express. Its symbolism intrigues our mind, its rhythm compels our feelings; its syntax challenges our powers of interpretation; its imagery titilates our imagination. When we experience it as a whole, we see the poem not as a message or as an object, but as a living invitation—as MacLeish put it, "an action in the world"[2] which beckons us to become a part of that action, to respond to its movements so that we are a part of, as well as apart from, that poem.

But literature does not demand; it can only invite. And to the

---

[1] From *The Poetry of Robert Frost*, edited by Edward Connery Lathem. Copyright 1923, 1939, © 1967, 1969 by Holt, Rinehart and Winston. Copyright 1951 by Robert Frost. Reprinted by permission of Holt, Rinehart and Winston, Publishers.

[2] Archibald MacLeish. "Why Do We Teach Poetry?" *Atlantic Monthly*, April 1957.

interpreter who is not prepared to respond to this invitation, the trip will be short and superficial. In the following pages, we hope to increase the chance of a pleasant journey by introducing you to the art of interpretive reading, by looking at the place oral interpretation holds in the field of speech arts, and by investigating its goals.

Throughout this text, we will be focusing upon you as you become involved in the creative process of interpreting and performing literature—as a solo interpreter and as a member of a group performing literature. As you become a part of this creative process, you will become better able to respond, both intellectually and physically, to that invitation which literature offers.

Interpretive Reading—What Is It?

Broadly speaking, we could say that interpretive reading is simply oral reading. But of course it is much more. To say it is interpreting literature orally for the aesthetic pleasure of an audience is only to say the subject matter is literature and its purpose is to give aesthetic pleasure. No one statement can fully clarify or explain the subtleties of this performing art. But let us try.

Interpretive reading is discovering—discovering your perception of the meaning in an author's recorded experience and then finding means for performing that discovery, with all its dramatic immediacy, so that the audience may feel and respond to the author's truth.

Another way to introduce you to interpretive reading is to offer a process for experiencing it. Interpretive reading can be seen as a process, a fusion of creative acts on five levels: (1) you respond to an author's recorded experience during your initial reading; (2) you analyze the author's created work of art for understanding; (3) you relate this experience to your own experience; (4) you assimilate the total experience, the essence of its intellectual and emotional meaning; and (5) you make effective use of your mind, voice, and body to communicate the selection's meaning during a reading performance, to get a creative response.

When you experience the fusion of these creative acts, you will understand what interpretive reading is. Also, you will have become better prepared to respond to the invitation of literature. We discuss this creative process in some detail throughout the text. For the present, let us consider oral interpretation as a course of study.

Oral Interpretation of Literature: Course Content and Values

A course in oral interpretation of literature unites the two arts of literature and oral communication. Course content therefore is geared to aid you in the pursuit of two goals: understanding specific literary works and communicating that understanding effectively.

Oral interpretation was recognized as an art form by the ancient Greeks, and reached its zenith during the Golden Age of Latin literature, the Augustan Age, which lasted from 40 B.C. until 14 A.D.[3] The history of this area of the performing arts is interesting. Oral interpretation has known both high and low periods in popularity, and the low periods led to changes in the art. At the beginning of this century, oral performance was emphasized more than comprehension and interpretation of the literature. Today, the emphasis is on the subject matter—the literary text. Technique is no longer considered as an end in itself, but only as a means of communicating the thought and feeling within the literary work.

Because the interpreter is expected to communicate the author's meaning effectively, you cannot settle for a superficial understanding. When you study a literary selection with the intent of giving physical expression to it, you are motivated to share its meaning with the audience to the best of your ability. And what do you stand to gain from this?

Though some students may take a beginning course in interpretation for additional training in speech, few, if any, expect to be actively engaged as professional readers. All students, however, expect to be actively engaged in living; and oral interpretation can increase their awareness of life through their reading and understanding of literature.

The techniques of communicating literature can improve your speech skills and make you a more effective person in communicating your own feelings and thoughts. From a course stressing the study of literature, you should expect to improve your competence in recognizing, understanding, and appreciating good literature. Experiencing the world of literature more fully sharpens your sensory perceptions of the real world and gives you new insights into relationships and your own personality. In a speech, Dr. Robert Breen referred to experiencing literature as:

> . . . one of the most profoundly civilizing processes—the education of the senses and the pleasurable acquisition of that knowledge which is necessary for our understanding of human experience.

Relationship to Related Speech Activities

Oral interpretation is not public speaking, and it is not acting; yet at times it is very close to both. The interpreter's reading performance may take on the characteristics of the public speaker's. This occurs when the reader addresses the audience directly with introductory or transitional remarks. The reader's manner, at such times, is like that of the public speaker who "reaches out" to the audience to clarify a point. At such times the reader or speaker is usually relaxed and conversationally direct.

When an address or an essay is interpreted, the oral reader approaches the role of the public speaker, but there is a difference. The public speaker uses his or her own words, and the intent is to influence the

---

[3] Eugene and Margaret Bahn. *A History of Oral Interpretation.* Minneapolis: Burgess Publishing Company, 1970.

audience with these ideas in some way. The reader who interprets an address or essay orally is trying to stimulate the audience to appreciate someone else's ideas. Though the audience is addressed directly (as in public speaking), the reader's attitude is that of joining the audience in appreciating the ideas and attitudes of the author. The difference is a matter of attitude, which is brought about by the contrast in purposes.

An oral interpreter reading certain material approaches the role of the actor. How far into the acting area may a reader go in character interpretations? How closely may one identify with a character? Just what is the difference between the role of the actor and the role of the interpreter? Although these questions once fueled a controversy among teachers of oral interpretation, today they are no longer considered important enough to argue about, though some students continue to ask them. But the era when the reader was expected to restrain the use of physical and vocal animation to avoid slipping into acting is gone; one's performance style is no longer restricted by labels.

Since interpretive reading, like all art forms, is constantly in the process of change, we must expect to see changes in philosophy reflected in changes in style of performance. The accepted mode of communication in our time is realism—natural, conversational, and underplaying the emotion—yet we are aware of a new trend, as more attention is being given to sensory communication. Today's oral interpreter is being asked to respond more fully, both physically and vocally, to feelings inherent in the selection. What are the differences today between the actor and the interpreter?

Perhaps the primary difference arises from a very natural cause, the difference in the performing situations. The actor, with freedom to move about on stage, speaking the lines of one character and reacting to other live actors in their roles, works in a different environment from that of the oral interpreter. In the usual reading situation the interpreter may use a script. Your position may be somewhat confined: you have no costume, no set, no lighting effects, and no other live characters about.

The physical environment and the lines permit the actor to identify completely with the character—to be the character, but your environment discourages identification with the character or characters. You would find it impossible to be many people all at the same time, and you would find it difficult to perform your character's actions in your limited position. So what can you do when you must interpret several characters in a play or a story?

As interpreter, you present rather than represent your character. The actor portrays character; you suggest character. But there is always a middle ground between the extremes of suggestion and representation. You must be flexible; you may consider your manner of suggesting character acceptable so long as you observe one rule: you must never call attention to yourself. This aesthetic restriction applies to actor and interpreter alike. The application of this rule need not confine your movement or your speech. As interpreter, you may apply yourself fully to the material without calling attention to yourself. In the 1920s Ralph Dennis, then head of the speech department at Northwestern University, stated a sensible philosophy of the interpreter's role:

> How can we measure platform art? . . . By this: does it appeal, does it get over to *the judicious few as well as to the many?* That's a high standard, a practical standard. . . . If we accept such measurements what care we about personation or impersonation, characterization, or acting, except as they be good or bad mediums for the individual under discussion. . . .
>
> If a reader . . . shows me life through his personal slant, his concept, his vision; if he is sincere, true, honest, does not offend, if he moves me, makes me think, I am for him. . . . Let's not quibble over terms, over methods. . . . Let's learn how to retranslate, into living words and actions that will be understood by all, the thoughts, the life values, the life interpretations which men have put into books.[4]

So Frost's poem—and, by extension, all literature—is but a record of the thoughts, values, and experiences, embedded in language by the author and frozen on a page by the typesetter. Still, the poem invites the interpreter to make the journey. And the interpreter, skilled in understanding and communicating meaning, can participate fully in that journey, permitting the audience to become a part of that creative act of sharing we call interpretive reading.

---

[4] Ralph Dennis. "One Imperative Plus," *The Quarterly Journal of Speech,* June 1922, p. 223.

Chapter 2

Overview of Principles and Methods

What Is the Nature of Meaning?

The principle upon which interpretive reading is based is this: **The essence of meaning is the response an organism makes to a stimulus.**

Oral interpretation is involved with meaning, discovering meaning and conveying meaning, impression and expression. The meaning we find in a passage comes from our responses to stimuli. But what triggers our responses? Why does a child, having once felt pain from touching a hot stove, continue to attach the meaning "hurt" to the stove? The reason is that the child has learned through experiencing. A student reading printed words on the page receives meaning from these symbols (stimuli) according to his or her experience; understanding and feeling are a possible response only if the words have meaningful associations for the reader.

We can discover literary meaning through experiencing literature and share it through interpretation. The nature of meaning, as it is involved in oral interpretation, is complicated and cannot be fully explained. Because it is always personal and ever changing, meaning must remain an unmeasurable element in communication. Richard Palmer, an authority on interpretation theory, says the meaning of each written phrase must be grasped in order to interpret meaning:

> How does this mysterious grasping of meaning take place? The process is a puzzling paradox: in order to read it, it is necessary to understand in advance what will be said; and yet this understanding must come from the reading. . . . Oral interpretation has two sides: it is necessary to understand something in order to express it, yet understanding itself comes from an interpretive reading—expression.[1]

---

[1] Palmer, *Hermeneutics.*

Other writers have stressed that the meanings of literature are realized in the act of oral reading, both practicing and performing.

Now let us take a closer look at the five-level interpretive process outlined in Chapter 1 to see if it will serve you in experiencing and interpreting literature. The first two levels, (1) responding initially to recorded experience and (2) analyzing a created work of art, offer methods for discovering meaning. The next two levels, (3) relating the author's experience to your own and (4) assimilating the whole experience, reinforce your discovered meaning. Together, these steps should enable you to embody the meaning and spirit of the selection. On the fifth level, (5) making effective use of your mind, voice, and body to communicate meaning and feeling, you share your interpretation with your audience.

This five-level process serves primarily as a study guide. Actually, the five acts merge and something more is added in the final creative performance. The interpreter is more than the sum of his or her attributes, just as the literary selection is more than the sum of its parts. This approach calls attention to one of the most important principles of interpretive reading: **Major emphasis is given to the literary text.**

An Interpretive Process

Responding to Total Experience

You are asked to respond to an author's recorded experience in an initial reading. Why? "The author's recorded experience" is the key phrase. **Discovering the Author's Recorded Experience.** We are saying that **what the author extends, transforms, and shapes into prose, poetry, or drama is human experience—either the author's own or what has been experienced vicariously.**

In "Robert Frost: The Way of the Poem," John Ciardi reports:

> Once at Bread Loaf, however, I heard him add one very essential piece to the discussion of how it "just came." One night, he said he had sat down after supper to work at a long piece of blank verse. The piece never worked out, but Mr. Frost found himself so absorbed in it that, when next he looked up, dawn was at his window. He rose, crossed to the window, stood looking out for a few seconds, and *then* it was that "Stopping by Woods" suddenly "just came," so that all he had to do was cross the room and write it down.[2]

The author, then, through sensitive use of language and some special talent for perceiving the meaning of human experience, transforms his or her experience into literary art. And the author's recorded experience is what you seek to embody in a reading performance.

But you may ask why you are expected to respond in an initial

---

[2] From "Robert Frost: The Way to the Poem" by John Ciardi. *Saturday Review,* April 12, 1958. Reprinted by permission.

reading. Well, if you are to be possessed of this piece of literature, you must get an overall feel for it—what happens to you as you read it, how and why you identify with it, what qualities of the whole piece appeal to you.

Discovering Mystery. Sometimes the first thing we sense about a literary selection is hard to put into words. About the short story, Eudora Welty says:

> The first thing we see about a story is its mystery. And in the best stories, we return at the last to see mystery again. Every good story has mystery—not the puzzle kind, but the mystery of allurement. As we understand the story better, it is likely that the mystery does not necessarily decrease; rather, it simply grows more beautiful.[3]

As an example of this, if we are familiar with Hemingway's writing, we may be aware that he is telling us over and over that the only way to live in this world of pain and violence is to be brave, courageous, and tough. He expresses this with such gusto and terseness that the effect works on the reader like magic. In contrast, we see Eudora Welty's stories completely lacking in violence and never offering a moral. She takes us into a simple situation and shows us life in a setting. Her magic lies in how exactly she catches the atmosphere—the sound, the smell, the feel of a place—and in how rightly she catches the tone and rhythm of the people she places in the setting.

Responding on Your Level. Reading a selection for the first time, you may respond only superficially, but usually you will have some awareness of why the material holds your attention and appeals to you. You should begin where you are, expressing your honest response as best you can, not being concerned if your response differs from those of your classmates. Your own response to the creation is as right as anyone else's; few writers intend their work to have only a single reading response or interpretation.

But why should you start with a response to the whole selection? Because the whole should always be kept in mind as you analyze the parts, you will be considering each part not as itself but rather as it fits together with the rest of the selection to produce the total experience.

Analyzing a Created Art Form

Following your initial response to a literary selection as a whole, you analyze it. In the first step, your attention was focused on the selection as a whole; now, your attention turns to the parts of the selection.

Approach to Analysis. The dictionary defines "analyze" as "to examine critically so as to bring out the essential elements or give the essence of... "[4] This might suggest that we are now viewing the literary text as an object to

---

[3] Eudora Welty, *The Reading and Writing of Short Stories.* Copyright © 1949, by Eudora Welty.

[4] *The American College Dictionary,* C. L. Barnhart and Jess Stein, eds. New York: Random House, 1963.

be dissected, taken apart in order that we may examine each part objectively and critically. This is not our intention.

The authors of this text **see a selection or passage of literature as an action, a speech act, or a performance in itself.** We see a poem or story as something alive, moving sometimes with sharp clashes, sometimes in quiet reflection. With this philosophy we do not approach the literary selection as an inert object to be examined objectively, without passion.

Focus for Analysis. When we analyze a selection, we are looking at the means the author has used to mold human experience into a work of literary art and, in so doing, extended our responses. By examining the situation the author has created, the movement of the chosen form, how the language is used, etc., we become aware of elements that spark our active responses. We also form a more accurate appreciation of the author's literary skill. In analyzing literature, you further your understanding of intellectual meaning, improve your ability to evaluate writing skills, and you develop your sensory awareness and capacity for responding to emotional meaning.

Relating the Author's Experience to Your Own

Using Your Inner Resources. What do you have that can reinforce your interpretation and help you embody the meaning and spirit of a selection? You have your own background of experiences, both real and imagined. Charles McGaw's comment in *Acting is Believing* regarding the actor's inner resources applies as well to the interpreter. "What the actor has in him is his own experience. His *inner* resources are everything that he has ever seen and felt and thought."

But is it possible to share another's experience? We must possess something before we can share it. But is it possible to possess another's experience? Even when two people have approximately the same experience, the interpretations of the experience differ because of differences between the individuals. Each interpretation is colored by your personal response to the piece of art, because you are influenced by your own background and knowledge. Each response is also influenced by time and mood. A good piece of literature can be read again and again and still hold something new to be found in the next reading. With every reading, you have changed, and you will never be in exactly the same mood twice. So it is that the meaning of literature is always on the wing, and no one can expect to capture the exact experience of the author. You can never possess the experience in the usual sense of the word, but you can be made alive to or be possessed of the author's experience. When you relate your own experiences to another's, you become more personally involved; when you feel closer to another's experience, you are more in possession of that person's experience.

Relating Your Experience. It is a very natural thing to relate your personal experiences to fictional experiences. An author's imagery may suddenly remind you of a scene you have witnessed or a sound you have heard. While walking across campus, reflecting on the relationship of certain characters in the material you are preparing, you may recall an occasion when you experienced a similar relationship. When or where this relating process takes place is not important.

Through imagery, an author hopes to stimulate you to share in an experience. In life, we experience the sensory responses of sight, sound, taste, smell, touch, movement, and so on directly; in reading, we experience them indirectly. If you can recall an experience, a time when you actually stood at a distance and sensed the beauty, the calm, the majesty of a city in the early morning light, you probably will respond more fully to this imagery from Wordsworth's poem "Composed upon Westminster Bridge":

> This City now doth, like a garment, wear
> The beauty of the morning: silent, bare,
> Ships, towers, domes, theatres, and temples lie
> Open unto the fields, and to the sky;
> All bright and glittering in the smokeless air.
> Never did sun more beautifully steep
> In his first splendour, valley, rock, or hill;
> Ne'er saw I, never felt, a calm so deep!

We are more likely to respond to any recorded sensory experience when we have been emotionally involved in a comparable one.

Assimilating the Whole

Reinforcing Meaning. In the fourth interpretive step, you look again at the entire selection, and you reinforce your interpretation by assimilating the whole through many oral readings. During these practice sessions, you may further your understanding of the author's experience. Reverberations accumulate; sometimes a sudden discovery of new meaning, either from what is spoken or from what is left unsaid, takes your breath. You become a different interpreter every time you go through this process. You learn more about what you didn't know you knew and felt.

Considering Aesthetic Effect. It is here, too, that you should pause to consider the aesthetic effect of the whole selection. What makes it a work of art? After analyzing the piece, you may have a new respect for the author's craftsmanship—how he or she has created a harmonious whole, with unified, complete ideas and form. But does this make it a work of art? Certainly, idea and form united in harmony are necessary for this. But is this enough? Whether the piece is art depends upon the essence of its meaning, what it has caused you to understand in a new way, a truth, a new world opened. This is something you want to share. This becomes your experience, created by you, based on the author's original experience, now assimilated and yours in a very real sense, yours to share.

13

Communicating: Use of Mind, Voice, and Body

Writers on oral interpretation approach the communicative act from various directions: a few, viewing oral interpretation mainly as a means of understanding literature, neglect communication. Others, while giving central place to the literary text, stress communication as well. The majority of writers, viewing oral interpretation both as a means of understanding literature and as a performing art, give communication secondary attention. All writers recognize the unity of vocal and bodily expression, but most give this topic limited attention and space. The authors of this book also view the text itself as central, but we do not emphasize the text at the expense of the mind, voice, and body control of the interpreter.

We believe that success in communicating the essence of meaning and feeling in a literary selection depends upon the use the interpreter makes of voice, body, and mind. We offer a possible way to aid communication with two approaches, technical and psychological. Chapter 4 amplifies the psychological approach; Chapters 5 and 6 are devoted to theory and exercise material for body and voice.

Technical Approach. Techniques are the hows of learning something: playing the piano, playing football, playing tennis, or painting a portrait, making a cake, or writing a story. Art forms and other activities require skills. In this case, the techniques are tools for learning how to use the voice and body effectively and how to employ controls to aid in projecting logical and emotional meanings in literature.

There are certain principles that you should keep in mind while working on techniques. As we said earlier, the interpreter's techniques should never intrude, offend, or interfere with the communication of meaning and feeling. In other words, they should never draw attention to themselves as techniques, and they should never be used to merely display the interpreter's ability.

Sometimes the listener is made aware of techniques, not because they have been exhibited as effects, but simply because the reader seems to be aware of using them. Communication becomes art when there is sufficient refinement of techniques and when they are used without apparent effort.

The hows for voice and body should never be considered as rules that must be followed by every student, every time. They are, rather, possible means, but the extent of their use should be determined by where the student is and wants to go. In any case the student should learn, with the teacher's guidance, where lies the greatest need for acquired techniques, and plan practice exercises accordingly. Concentrated effort on a few significant points is usually the best way to get results.

As you begin to work on exercises, you become overly conscious of the hows. To avoid this awareness of mechanics in performance, you should work on techniques only in practice sessions. You should use prescribed exercises with short reading passages, concentrating on one problem at a time. In performance and performance rehearsal you should forget techniques, put the problems aside, and concentrate only on the author's ideas and feelings.

Your attitude toward technique is important in determining your success. Because changing a habit is slow and hard to measure, you may become discouraged and discredit the whole process. This can be avoided if you realize at the beginning that mastery of a technique takes discipline, patience, and effort. What Stanislavski, the well-known director of the Moscow Art Theatre, had to say about the actor's work applies as well to students in any of the speech arts:

> Let someone explain to me why the violinist who plays in an orchestra on the tenth violin must daily perform hour-long exercises or lose his power to play? Why does the dancer work daily over every muscle of his body? Why do the painter, the sculptor, the writer practice their art each day and count that day lost when they do not work? And why may the dramatic artist do nothing, spend his day in coffee houses and hope for the gift of Apollo in the evening? . . . There is no art that does not demand virtuosity.[5]

Any noticeable improvement in the use of voice and speech depends upon knowledge and artistic application of technique. This demands work.

Psychological Approach. The psychological approach is based on the simple theory that, if you think about the meaning of the passage as you read it aloud, your expression of the thoughts will be good. The basic validity of the theory has long been recognized in the interpretation field. Though the general theory is reasonable, it is usually recommended with reservation, and the hows of such an approach remain rather mystical and undefined. To argue which is better—the technical or the psychological approach—is useless. Both methods can be useful. It is a matter of individual needs and talents.

It is true that concentration on the thoughts and feelings may bring about a marked improvement in control of voice and body, but the method cannot correct a lisp or a flat vowel sound. And how does one discipline oneself to concentrate, to use the imagination, and to relate one's own experience?

In Chapter 4, we will draw upon some aspects of the Stanislavski method in acting to aid in the application of concentration, imagination, and identification, and attempt to adapt these acting techniques to the practical needs of the interpreter.

Applying Aesthetic Principles

The final test for an interpretive performance is that it be aesthetically pleasing. There are four general criteria that must be considered here:

---

[5] *My Life in Art.* Copyright 1948 by Elizabeth Reynolds Hapgood. Reprinted by permission of the publisher, Theatre Arts Books, New York.

appropriateness of speech level, empathy, aesthetic distance, and aesthetic standards for selecting material.

Appropriateness of Speech Level

Different material makes different demands on the interpreter. What degree of naturalness can we use and still stay within the bounds of propriety? The poetic and elegant language of the Bible, of Shakespeare, or of the Greek classics must be lifted above ordinary speech and be given appropriate dignity and beauty. Our aesthetic sense might well be offended if we heard Medea's passionate lines read with the flavor of colloquial speech.

On the other hand, when we try to speak such lines with the correct dignity, we always fear overdoing it, and rightly so. Nothing is more offensive than affected, artificial speech. Somehow the interpreter must sense the right level for the selection. Listening to others in class, you become aware of the underplay or overplay of precision and beauty of speech in relation to the demands of the material. Listening to professional readers, you become sensitive to the artistic demands of literary material.

Empathy

The American College Dictionary defines empathy as "the imaginative projection of one's own consciousness into another being." Like most dictionary definitions, this is accurate so far as it goes. But empathy includes a kind of physical sympathy with another person or with a situation in which we are not actually participating. We have all experienced that human tendency to unconsciously feel into a situation: to laugh or cry at the movies, to pucker our lips when we see someone eating a lemon, to move our bodies to follow the ball down the basketball court. We respond in this way because, in each case, we are feeling into the action or situation we are observing, and, as a result, the body tends to imitate the observed action.

As you read aloud for an audience, you become involved to the extent you feel your way into the author's experience and your body responds to the action implicit in the ideas and feelings expressed by the words. If successful, you also arouse such a response in your listeners: you cause them to feel into the author's experience. Whether the listener's response is physical—leaning forward, for example—or spiritual—the impression of mind meeting mind—you sense the response. When this happens, a magic circle is completed, and communication is at its highest. How to arouse empathy is an important concern of all artists. Aesthetic distance is one means of arousing the right empathic response.

Aesthetic Distance

Aesthetic distance may be a physical or figurative distance, detachment, or a degree of disinterest that permits interest in the immediate activity. The principle of aesthetic distance is the artist's tool in arousing the audience to appreciate the significance of a situation or the beauty of an object. When an object is too near, aesthetic pleasure may be destroyed: a painting may fail to give aesthetic pleasure when you stand too close; loud music in a small room may offend a person's aesthetic taste; the nearness of the actors in a play-in-the-round may destroy the illusion; a dramatic reading given in a small room may embarrass the listeners.

Reading various types of material in the classroom, you sense that highly emotional material needs to be somewhat removed from the audience. What can you do? Arranging chairs to increase the distance between yourself and the listeners can help. The lectern serves to increase the distance. In addition, you can control the distance by using the level of restraint that fits the physical nearness.

To determine the right degree of physical detachment, you should consider the audience's role. When the audience is to be directly involved, as in public speaking, you try to reduce aesthetic distance in order to draw your listeners in. This is the *open stance*. But when the listeners' role is to overhear, as in drama, you withdraw, increasing aesthetic distance. This is the *closed stance*. For the interpreter, aesthetic distance often helps maintain an illusion.

Aesthetic Criteria for Selecting Material

Within each literary form, you have almost an unlimited amount of material from which to choose. To some extent, you can be guided by your own tastes, but you must also consider the literary worth of your choice and its suitability for the audience.

Guides for choice. Audience response is a good proving ground for standards. When selecting material to share with a particular audience, it is wise to consider details regarding the group, the place and time, age, sex, level of intelligence, interests, and mood of the occasion. Just as no song is beautiful in a place where persons desire quiet, so no serious poem, however beautiful, will be appropriate for a group which at that moment desires only light entertainment. Then, too, if the material is beyond or below the comprehension level of the listeners, they will be bored or offended by the choice. Each selection must be chosen with the particular audience for which it is intended kept in mind. The interpreter should ask, "Will this selection be interesting, understandable, suitable, and worth the listening time of this group at this time?"

In the classroom the student is influenced by what passages classmates select to read aloud. A student with a weak background in literature makes discoveries through listening and is challenged by the highest level of knowledge, intelligence, and sensitivity in the class. Accepting this challenge helps the student's own values and tastes in literature grow, and his or her choices, as a result, will contribute to the growth and interest of the entire group. You are wise to select material that can be easily followed by the ear. These points should be kept in mind:

Vivid and emotional action will hold the attention; abstract philosophical thought will not.

The ear prefers simplicity to complexity, concreteness to abstraction, and vivid imagery to vague generality.

Some authors have an ear attuned to the sounds of words, phrases, and sentences; their writing seems to flow with the natural cadence of human speech.

Guides for literary value. Three qualities—universality, individuality, and suggestion—have been identified as "the extrinsic factors of literary skill that take the reader beyond the bounds of the selection and relate him to a range of human experience."[6]

Universality describes motives and experiences that all people share. Written words may cause you to remember an experience or may evoke an idea, and may prompt you to say, "This is true; I've always known this." Because you can relate to the experience or to the idea, you believe and respond to it emotionally. We identify with Mark Twain's Huck Finn and with Doug in Ray Bradbury's *Dandelion Wine,* because much of what they think and experience is what all boys think and experience in the process of growing up. *Jonathan Livingston Seagull* is about the aspirations of the young—and not only of the young—for a fuller, freer participation in life; we relate to this theme because we ourselves have experienced such a desire.

Individuality is evident in the manner in which the author treats the subject. What makes the selection unique and fresh? What makes it more effective than the treatment of the same subject by another author? Perhaps *Jonathan Livingston Seagull*'s individuality comes from the author's juxtaposition of fantasy and truth, mystery and adventure, in the talking seagull's story. An author's individuality is usually apparent in the use of language for a given effect. Notice how, in the following lines, images of sight, sound, and movement create the atmosphere of a coal camp:

> . . . *step easy, Plant tender leather feet with care—*
> *For here are slate streets, coal dusted,*
> *Water washed to every grey shade.*
>
> *Here are coal roads that twist you by dark houses,*
> *Brown rotting fences and raucous creeks,*
> *By young wet noses standing at gates . . .*[7]

The third of the extrinsic factors to consider is **suggestion.** This is demonstrated in each of the above examples. The author of *Jonathan Livingston Seagull* does not specifically tell the reader to dare to follow his dreams and aspirations; the reader finds this, or another meaning, independently of the author. Ray Bradbury's words on the cover indicate the story's power of suggestion for him: "Richard Bach with this book does two things: he gives me flight; he makes me young." In the quotation from *Slatefall,* did the words "young wet noses" evoke a sharp visual image?

---

[6] Charlotte Lee and Frank Galati. *Oral Interpretation.* Boston: Houghton Mifflin Company, 1977, pp. 9–10.

[7] Billy Edd Wheeler, *Slatefall.*

Have you known roads that "twist you," or have you heard a "raucous creek"?

Characters may be symbolic, suggesting the central theme of a literary work: *Jonathan Livingston Seagull* might be considered as a symbol of youth in search of a full and free life; in Thornton Wilder's play *Skin of Our Teeth*, Mr. Antrobus is a symbol of man picking up the pieces of civilization to start again; and the pigs in George Orwell's *Animal Farm* behave much like human beings. Interpretive reading is a suggestive art form, and material that suggests—rather than demands—a response is what you are looking for.

When you have carefully considered the literary value of your selection of literature, you have your interpretation of the text under way. Having surveyed the basic principles and methods of interpretive reading and the application of certain aesthetic principles, we are ready to consider the creative art of literary interpretation.

Chapter 3

Literary Interpretation

Theory of Interpretation

> Reading a work, then, is not a gaining of conceptual knowledge through
> observation or reflection; it is an "experience," a breaking down and breaking
> open of one's old way of seeing. It is not the interpreter who manipulates the work,
> for the work remains fixed; rather, the work has impressed itself on him and he is
> so changed he can never regain the innocence lost through experience.[1]

The above quotation expresses a theory of interpretation long respected in
oral interpretation. This books seeks to illuminate the theory through its
practical application. On each level of study, you will use this experiential
mode of literary study; in each encounter with a literary selection in
practice performance, you discover meaning through experiencing the
selection.

To give permanence to your response and to your way of seeing
each literary work, we suggest that you keep a journal in which you record
your responses—sometimes maybe only random, spontaneous notes,
sometimes answers to questions we pose. Perhaps, too, you may want to
record syntheses of your literary interpretations and reading performances.

Discovering Through Initial Responses

As we said earlier, in your first oral reading you gain an overall impression
of the authors' recorded experience and recognize your own responses.
You may also come up against the mystery of its appeal for you.

---

[1] Palmer, *Hermeneutics.*

As you approach your initial reading, open your mind to the work's subject matter and let it speak to you through its language. Read the selection aloud several times and jot down notes describing your response. Then consider these questions: What happened to you as you read the selection? Did you discover new meaning as you read it? Why does the selection appeal to you? Does the author's experience seem to be primarily one of thought, feeling, character, or action?

You will want to find an answer to the question, "What is the author saying?" You may have found an answer in the first reading. The essence of what the author is saying may come to you quickly or slowly; you may find an answer entirely different from what another person may find.

Discovering Through Analysis

As we said in Chapter 2, in the act of analysis, we look at ways the author has shaped human experience into literary art. You look at the author's use of language and point of view—the situation and its movement—to understand and experience the intended meaning.

Perhaps during your initial reading or earlier, when choosing the text, your response was blocked by words and allusions you did not understand or by complicated sentence constructions which failed, when first read aloud, to convey logical sense. These matters should receive immediate attention.

Removing Blocks to Comprehension

Find the meaning of unfamiliar words and allusions by consulting proper sources. Let us illustrate this by referring to a single verse of a poem, "Safe in Their Alabaster Chambers," by Emily Dickinson.

> *Safe in their Alabaster Chambers—*
> *Untouched by Morning—*
> *And untouched by Noon—*
> *Sleep the meek members of the Resurrection,*
> *Rafter of Satin—and Roof of Stone—* [2]

Simply by using the dictionary, you would find that alabaster is a cold, hard, white, and smooth substance. Consulting a reliable source to clarify the allusion "meek members of the Resurrection," you would find that this refers to the Puritan belief in a literal resurrection of the body after death. Further investigation would clarify this verse; the whole poem would require an extended study of symbolic meanings for full understanding.

---

[2] Reprinted by permission of the publishers and the Trustees of Amherst College from *The Poems of Emily Dickinson*, edited by Thomas H. Johnson, Cambridge, Mass.: The Belknap Press of Harvard University Press, Copyright © 1951, 1955 by the President and Fellows of Harvard College.

Find the subject, verb, and object in difficult sentence construction in order to clarify the relationship of word and phrases. You can have comprehension difficulties even when individual word meanings are clear. In some cases sensitivity to the relationship of words and phrases is needed, for the use of inversion and long complex or compound arrangements may obstruct meaning. Unless you have the knack for unraveling a twisted sentence, you may have difficulty with Shakespeare's meaning in this speech from Act I, Scene 2 of *Julius Caesar:*

> CASSIUS. . . . I will this night,
> In several hands, in at his windows throw,
> As if they came from several citizens,
> Writings, all tending to the great opinion
> That Rome holds of his name; wherein obscurely
> Caesar's ambition shall be glancèd at.
> And after this, let Caesar seat him sure,
> For we will shake him, or worse days endure.

To clarify this difficult passage, find the subject and verb of the main clause; that is, ask yourself what is the main action and who is doing that action. Cassius says, "I will . . . " do something. What will he do? "I will throw . . . " What will Cassius throw? Look at the passage to see what Cassius could throw; the only reasonable possibility seems to be that he "will throw writings." Now go on asking yourself questions about the passage: when? what kind of writings? why? where? etc. Eventually you can fill in all the information given in the speech, and you might put Cassius's words in ordinary form, something like this: "This night I will throw in at his window writings in several hands, as if they came from several citizens, all tending to the great opinion that Rome holds of his name, wherein Caesar's ambition shall be glanced at obscurely. And after this, let Caesar seat him sure, for we will shake him, or endure worse days."

Once the sentences are in more or less familiar order, you can go over the unfamiliar words and the words used with meanings different from their usual ones, such as "hands" for "handwritings," etc.

Exercise.

How does analyzing the grammatical construction of each of the following sentences help the oral reader project the author's meaning?

1   Histories make men wise; poets, witty; the mathematics, subtile; natural philosophy, deep; moral, grave; logic and rhetoric, able to contend. *Abeunt studia in mores* [studies form manners.] (Francis Bacon, *Of Studies*)
2   It was as if the boy had already divined what his senses and intellect had not encompassed yet: that doomed wilderness whose edges were being constantly and punily gnawed at by men with plows and axes who feared it because it was wilderness, men myriad and nameless even to one another in the land where the old bear had earned a name, and through which ran not even a mortal beast but an anachronism indomitable and invincible out of an old, dead time, a phantom, epitome and apotheosis of the old, wild life which the little puny humans swarmed and hacked at in a fury of abhorrence and fear, like pygmies about the ankles of a drowsing elephant;—the old bear, solitary, indomitable, and alone; widowered,

childless, and absolved of mortality—old Priam reft of his old wife and outlived all his sons.[3]

Situation: Point of View

The situation (the circumstances that exist at the beginning of an action) and its movement (what happens) are important aspects of any piece of literary art. These matters comprise the content, the substance of a selection. In any literary work a situation exists, even though it may be only implied, and something is happening or has happened or is going to happen, and this is the dramatic action.

Answers to the two questions "Who is speaking?" and "To whom?" help the oral interpreter understand the manner in which the author uses a narrator. The interpreter's oral style must be right for the author's written style. The interpreter must know the nature of the storyteller in order to project appropriate attitudes and degrees of characterization; you must recognize the listener so that you may establish proper speaker-audience relationships.

An author may choose one of three points of view: exterior omniscient, exterior third-person observer, or interior first person. Having chosen the point of view, the author creates a narrator, who tells the story to us, the audience.

Omniscient Point of View. The author who has chosen the omniscient point of view may create a third-person narrator who may enter the consciousness of any of the characters, who knows and may express the thoughts and feelings of the characters. Here is an example of the narrator's using this omniscient power not only to see into the consciousness of all the characters, but also to comment and judge as well:

> "Come, come, sir, walk downstairs with Miss Sharp, and I will follow with these two young women," said the father, and he took an arm of wife and daughter and walked merrily off.
>
> If Miss Rebecca Sharp had determined in her heart upon making the conquest of this big beau, I don't think, ladies, we have any right to blame her; for though the task of husband-hunting is generally, and with becoming modesty, entrusted by young persons to their mammas, recollect that Miss Sharp had no kind parent to arrange these delicate matters for her, and that if she did not get a husband for herself, there was no one else in the wide world who would take the trouble off her hands.
>
> (William Makepeace Thackeray, *Vanity Fair*)

A variant of the omniscient is a limited view where the narrator enters into the thoughts of only one of the characters, and reports just from that character's or his or her own point of view. In "The Marriages," by Henry James, the narrator's omniscient power extends only into the character of Adela:

> "Won't you stay a little longer?" the hostess said, holding the girl's hand and smiling. "It's too early for everyone to go; it's too absurd." Mrs. Churchley

---

[3] Lines from "The Bear" by William Faulkner in *Go Down Moses,* copyright 1942. Reprinted by permission of Random House.

inclined her head to one side and looked gracious; she held up to her face, in a vague, protecting, sheltering way, an enormous fan of red feathers. Everything about her, to Adela Chart, was enormous. She had big eyes, big teeth, big shoulders, big hands, big rings and bracelets, big jewels of every sort and many of them.. . . . Was Mrs. Churchley's fortune also large, to account for so many immensities? Of this Adela could know nothing, but she reflected, while she smiled sweetly back at their entertainer, that she had better try to find out.

Third-Person Observer Point of View. The third-person narrator who does not enter the thoughts and feelings of a character simply relates what he or she has seen and heard. In some cases the narrator's presence almost goes unnoticed by the reader: the narrator becomes a mere reporter of scenes, and the reader is shown rather than told the story, through the dramatic interplay between the characters or the thoughts in a character's mind. But seldom is the narrator's attitude toward the character and the situation completely lost. This is the objective use of the third-person view which allows the situation to unfold dramatically, as in a play. In Erskine Caldwell's story "Daughter," the sense of the situation and of what is happening is sharply focused through the dialogue of Jim, a sharecropper who has shot his daughter because he could not bear to see her starve; the sheriff; and various unidentified persons in the crowd. Though the third-person narrator briefly addresses the reader, the story is told dramatically; an illusion of an actual occurrence is created.

> "You ought to have sent her over to my house, Jim. Me and my wife could have fed her something, somehow. It don't look right to kill a little girl like her."
> "I'd made enough for all of us," Jim said. "I just couldn't stand it no longer. Daughter'd been hungry all the past months."
> "Take it easy, Jim boy," the sheriff said, trying to push forward.
> The crowd swayed from side to side.
> "And so you just picked up the gun this morning and shot her?" somebody asked.
> "When she woke up this morning saying she was hungry, I just couldn't stand it."[4]

Obviously, there is a difference in the degree of personality authors allow third-person narrators to develop. In *Vanity Fair,* the narrator is very subjective. The characterization of such a narrator usually is not fully developed, but she or he is recognized as a product of the same place and time as the characters in the story. The direct speeches of the other characters are reported by the narrator, whose voice colors the character interpretations.

In the story "Daughter" the objective point of view lessens the importance of the narrator, who is presented as an unidentified observer, without personality. You would address the narrator's brief remarks to the audience and characterize the other speakers as they address each other. **Interior First-Person Point of View.** If an author uses the interior

---

[4] From *Jackpot,* copyright, 1940, by Erskine Caldwell; by permission of Duell, Sloan and Pearce, Inc.

25

first-person point of view, you must determine whether the "I" of the narrative is a character telling his or her own story, a minor character involved in the action, telling the story of a leading character, or a narrator reporting everything observed or heard. In Mark Twain's *The Adventures of Huckleberry Finn,* Huck tells his own story and, in the telling, reveals himself and the adults seen through his eyes. In the following passage, Huck, to relieve his troubled mind, has just written a letter to Miss Watson to report the whereabouts of Jim, her runaway slave. He says:

> I felt good and all washed clean of sin for the first time I had ever felt so in my life, and I knowed I could pray now. But I didn't do it straight off, but laid the paper down and set there thinking—thinking how good it was all this happened so, and how near I come to being lost and going to hell. And went on thinking. And got to thinking over our trip down the river; and I see Jim before me all the time: in the day and in the nighttime, sometimes moonlight, sometimes storms, and we a-floating along, talking and singing and laughing. But somehow I couldn't seem to strike no place to harden me against him, but only the other kind. I'd see him standing my watch on top of his'n 'stead of calling me, so I could go on sleeping; and see him how glad he was when I came back out of the fog; and when I come to him again in the swamp, up there where the feud was; and such-like times; and would always call me honey, and pet me, and do everything he could think of for me, and how good he always was; and at last I struck the time I saved him by telling the men we had smallpox aboard, and he was so grateful, and said I was the best friend old Jim ever had in the world, and the *only* one he's got now; and then I happened to look around and see that paper.
> It was a close place. I took it up, and held it in my hand. I was a-trembling, because I'd got to decide, forever, betwixt two things, and I knowed it. I studied a minute, sort of holding my breath, and then says to myself:
> "All right, then I'll *go* to hell"—and tore it up. . . .

But the first-person narrator does not always tell his own story. In *The Great Gatsby,* a character who is closely involved in the action tells the story of the leading character. We see Gatsby through the eyes of Nick Carraway. Nick gives us a close-up view of Gatsby, and his view is credible because the author places him in a position to observe closely, to receive reports from others, and to participate in Gatsby's experience.

> . . . my eyes fell on Gatsby, standing alone on the marble steps and looking from one group to another with approving eyes. His tanned skin was drawn attractively tight on his face and his short hair looked as though it were trimmed every day. I could see nothing sinister about him. I wondered if the fact that he was not drinking helped to set him off from his guests, for it seemed to me that he grew more correct as the fraternal hilarity increased. When the "Jazz History of the World" was over, girls were putting their heads on men's shoulders in a puppyish, convivial way, girls were swooning backward playfully into men's arms, even into groups, knowing that some one would arrest their fall—but no one swooned backward on Gatsby, and no French bob touched Gatsby's shoulder. . . .[5]

The first-person point of view gives the oral interpreter the opportunity to characterize the narrator fully. The narrator's personality and

---

[5] Lines from *The Great Gatsby* by F. Scott Fitzgerald, copyright 1925, 1953. Reprinted by permission of Charles Scribner's Sons.

relationship with other characters should be discovered by the interpreter and projected to the audience. When the narrator's direct speech is broken by dialogue, your eye focus and your characterization of the speakers should suggest who is speaking to whom. (See Differentiation.)

Point of View in Poetry. The point of view in a poem is similar to that in fiction: a narrator tells a story either from an external third-person view (omniscient or observer) or from an interior first-person view. In both narrative fiction and poetry a narrator's presence may be clearly established and maintained, or it may be only vaguely evident. But there are a few distinctions in the way a short-story writer and a poet handle point of view. In fictional prose a narrator is created by the author; the narrator's voice should not be assumed to be the author's voice. In poetry the speaker's may or may not be the poet's voice. Furthermore, in narrative poetry a story may be told through face-to-face dialogue between characters without the use of a narrator. Let us cite these distinctions as evidenced in particular poems.

The unknown author of the ballad "Lord Randal" uses the dialogue of the mother and son to tell the story; there is no narrator who addresses the reader directly.

Lord Randal
Anonymous

"O where hae ye been, Lord Randal, my son?
O where hae ye been, my handsome young man?"
"I hae been to the wild wood; mother, make my bed soon,
For I'm weary wi hunting, and fain wald lie down."

"Where gat ye your dinner, Lord Randal, my son?
Where gat ye your dinner, my handsome young man?"
"I din'd wi my true-love; mother, make my bed soon,
For I'm weary wi hunting, and fain wald lie down."

"What gat ye to your dinner, Lord Randal, my son?
What gat ye to your dinner, my handsome young man?"
"I gat eels boiled in broo; mother, make my bed soon,
For I'm weary wi hunting, and fain wald lie down."

"What became of your bloodhounds, Lord Randal, my son?
What became of your bloodhounds, my handsome young man?"
"O they swelld and they died; mother, make my bed soon,
For I'm weary wi hunting, and fain wald lie down."

"O I fear ye are poisond, Lord Randal, my son!
O I fear ye are poisond, my handsome young man!"
"O yes! I am poisond; mother, make my bed soon,
For I'm sick at the heart, and I fain wald lie down."

This little drama in one scene takes place after the real action, and we learn what has happened through the dialogue. We are *told* nothing;

27

we are allowed to overhear the conversation and to infer the meaning. The realization of what has happened comes to us through simple questions that build in intensity, creating suspense. The poem has more to say than it states; the bare details given may suggest a complicated relationship among the three people: the mother, the son, and his true-love. Suggestion is usually more effective in arousing an emotional response than facts given by a narrator. A story is often presented through dialogue in the old ballads, and Robert Frost and other modern poets have continued to use this method effectively.

The dramatic monologue and the soliloquy are two forms of poetry in which a story is told or implied without the assistance of a formal narrator. In the dramatic monologue the speaker is always a character, clearly identified, who speaks in the first person and reveals the situation (past and *present*) through words directed to a silent character. (See "The Laboratory," by Robert Browning.) The soliloquy differs from the dramatic monologue only in that the speaker is not talking with or to anyone. In both forms the narrator is a fictional character outside the personality of the author.

In interpreting these or similar dramatic forms, you would characterize the speaker and indicate through eye focus and other means that the character is speaking either to another character, to a silent character, or to himself or herself. In each case, you would not let the speaker be aware of the audience.

A lyric poem may be close to the soliloquy in that a speaker expresses his or her thoughts (implying a dramatic action). But the speaker in the lyric may be the poet, and not necessarily a fictional character created outside the personality of the poet, as the speaker in the soliloquy is. In the lyric it is not always possible to be sure whether the author or the narrator is speaking, and, on first reading, the listener may not be easily identified:

A Deep-Sworn Vow[6]
William Butler Yeats

Others because you did not keep
That deep-sworn vow have been friends of mine;
Yet always when I look death in the face,
When I clamber to the heights of sleep,
Or when I grow excited with wine,
Suddenly I meet your face.

Here we have no sure way of knowing whether Yeats or his narrator is speaking. The situation—what has happened between two people—might lead one to believe that either the man or the woman is speaking, but, since the author is a man, we are inclined to think that the narrator is a man. The speaker appears to be addressing his words to a

---

[6] Copyright 1919 by Macmillan Publishing Co., Inc., renewed 1947 by Bertha Georgie Yeats.

specific listener, but on second reading we sense that the "you" of the poem is not actually there. The narrator is reflecting on a past experience, and the "you" of the poem is present only in his memory.

The reader may find narrative writers and poets who use combinations or shifts in point of view, but even from this discussion of the most obvious problems, it is evident that point of view affects oral reading considerably and that in some cases it is no easy matter to discover and project the qualities of the narrator of a story or poem.

Movement of Situation

To chart the movement of the situation, that is, to show what happens, we need to examine how the author has put together the basic material of the work, how the selection is structured.

Structure of Plot. Some authors of narrative fiction stay close to such traditional plot forms as the beginning-middle-end pattern. They insist on satisfying resolutions, on answering for the reader all the questions aroused by the conflict. Other writers direct the reader's interest through conflict and actions, but they force the reader to use the imagination to find answers to the questions raised. Modern writers deviate from the traditional patterns, finding new shapes for narrative fiction. But even the most nonconventional form may be said to have a pattern influenced by and itself influencing the author's purpose. In his *Aspects of the Novel,* E. M. Forster points the distinction between story and plot.

> Let us define a plot. We have defined a story as a narrative of events arranged in their time-sequence. A plot is also a narrative of events, the emphasis falling on causality. "The king died and then the queen died" is a story. "The king died, and then the queen died of grief" is a plot. The time-sequence is preserved, but the sense of causality overshadows it. . . . If it is in a story we say "and then?" If it is in a plot we ask "why?"[7]

A plot line can be evident in narrative or dramatic poetry; lyric poetry, too, can be seen as an action with narrative elements (story) and dramatic conflict (plot) implied.

The plot structure can be charted simply by asking, "What happens next?" and "Why?" We can see these divisions as motivational units or acts.

Rhythm of Content. The rhythm of content is the increase and decrease of tension throughout a selection. High points are usually followed by low.

Generally speaking, within each major structural division of a work, there is a high point (minor climax). The highest point of the whole work is usually the structural climax, the highest peak of interest or the turning point in the situation. The minor climaxes may build in intensity to the climax of the entire piece and then release their tension quickly, or the climax may come early, with a slow release; there are countless variations

---

[7] E. M. Forster, *Aspects of the Novel* (New York: Harvest Books, Harcourt, Brace & World, Inc., 1927), p. 86. By permission of the publishers.

of these basic forms. When the emotional peak comes at a different point than the structural climax, it may be helpful if you consider the work as having two climaxes: structural (or logical) and emotional. In *Oral Interpretation*, Lee and Galati say:

> Sometimes the highest emotional intensity will come at the logical climax. Often, however, this is not the case. The logical climax may precede the emotional high point and prepare for it. This will be true, for instance, when the emotional climax depends upon a character's or a writer's response to a completed cycle of events. On the other hand, if the outcome of events depends upon a character's emotional reaction, the emotional climax will precede the logical one. . . .[8]

In the poem "Bredon Hill," by A. E. Housman, the rhythm changes abruptly in the fifth stanza of the poem, and the structural climax follows almost immediately:

> *My love rose up so early*
> *And stole out unbeknown*
> *And went to church alone.*

The highest emotional peak, however, comes in the last lines, two stanzas later:

> *Oh, noisy bells, be dumb;*
> *I hear you, I will come.*[9]

Place and Time

Huck Finn would not be Huck Finn in a modern setting. Believable fictional characters seem to belong to a certain place and time, which act upon them. So these two elements are keys to understanding characters. Thomas Hardy's settings act upon the characters in his stories and influence their actions. It seems that the characters do what they do and are what they are at least partly because of where they are in place and time. In Joseph Conrad's "Heart of Darkness," setting is the source of a character's destruction: the character, Kurtz, identifies with the African jungle, and in the end, this destroys him. William Faulkner's characters are believable because they spring from their place—Yoknapatawpha County, Mississippi: though the Snopeses are found everywhere, they belong to this particular place. Hemingway's places sometimes take on symbolic meanings: in the story "A Clean Well Lighted Place," the place, a cafe in Paris, well lighted and clean, is a symbol of what one character is searching for in his fellow man and, perhaps, what all men are searching for in life.

From the study of literary works set in a world separated from our

---

[8] Lines from *Oral Interpretation* by Charlotte Lee and Frank Galati, copyright 1977. Reprinted by permission of Houghton Mifflin Co.

[9] From "A Shropshire Lad"—Authorized Edition—from *The Collected Poems of A. E. Housman.* Copyright 1939, 1940, © 1965 by Holt, Rinehart and Winston. Copyright © 1967, 1968 by Robert E. Symons. Reprinted by permission of Holt, Rinehart and Winston, Publishers.

time, we gain an understanding of attitude and values of a past era, which enables us to see the present in light of the past. Our understanding of what an author is saying in a literary work may depend upon this kind of historical awareness or connectiveness.

Pervading Tone

The word "tone" can have many meanings: it can refer to vocal sound, the intonation of voice that expresses a particular attitude; it can refer to the feeling or attitude created by a word or word arrangement in a certain context; or it can be used in a larger sense to refer to the prevailing attitude or predominant spirit of a piece of writing, an effect produced by the author's handling of language and expression of mood. In this text, it will be used in all of these ways.

We may recognize the prevailing tone or atmosphere of a piece of literature as being dark, light, serious, playful, intimate, approving, disapproving, or any of many other possible attitudes.

To determine the prevailing tone, you may need to give first consideration to a literary work's position in time. Your recognition of attitudes may be blocked because you do not understand the sort of language used, the attitudes and values of a past era. Usually, however, tonal effect is due to an author's attitude toward the subject or toward the readers, or to the way the author combines these.

Author's attitude toward the subject. While recording his or her own or another's experience, an author reveals an emotional response to that experience. This emotional response is the mood of the piece. An author seldom tells us about these feelings directly, but rather shows us through the description of the setting, through the movement of the situation, and through the choice and arrangement of words. Responding to these, we are made to feel the author's response: sadness, joy, anger, happiness, bitterness, indignation, acceptance—or any of the whole range of emotions. Within a selection, an author's moods may vary from light to dark, from comic to tragic, but in the material as a whole we can find a dominant mood.

Even in a short poem, changes in attitude may be evident. In "A Deep-Sworn Vow," the speaker seems at the beginning to have a casual attitude toward his subject ("others" has an impersonal connotation), but in five short lines the simple words build up a deeply personal tone. The general mood evoked is reflective; the speaker is not bitter, but he is deeply concerned. In interpreting the poem, you would project changes in attitude, but at the same time maintain the dominant reflective mood.

Author's attitude toward the audience. An author's attitude toward the audience may be in tune with that toward the subject—lightly playful or satirical. In such cases, the attitude simply invites the reader to share the author's mood. But the author's attitude toward the subject and toward the audience can be quite distinct. An author may express an attitude of sympathy for a subject and at the same time convey a tone of warning or condemnation of the reader or listening audience. John Steinbeck in *The*

Grapes of Wrath, for example, expresses an attitude of sympathy for a dislocated group of Americans. At the same time, he is pointing an accusing finger at the American reader, who he says is responsible for the plight of the group.

In narrative fiction, dramatic poetry, and the drama, imaginary characters are often the chief means through which the author's attitudes are disclosed. In the brief passage from Caldwell's "Daughter," there is sympathy for the prisoner Jim. Fellow sharecroppers, addressing Jim, express regret for this, but they are in sympathy with Jim because they understand what has led him to do what he has. The characters reveal Caldwell's attitudes toward injustice. Caldwell's attitude toward his subject is one of sympathy; his attitude toward his readers is one of accusation. Together these say what the author wishes to say.

In life we reveal our attitudes toward individuals and situations by tonal inflections and our bodily reactions. An author must attempt to convey by words alone all the subtleties that vocal tone and bodily gestures may express in direct communication. So to discover subtle attitudes, the interpreter must become aware of the tonal quality or the tonal gestures suggested by words—words alone and words in combination—in their emotional environment. The scientist attempts to hold words to their denotative, literal meanings, abstracting meaning. The literary artist, on the other hand, selects words to connote, to evoke emotional meanings. Words have the power to awaken in the reader an intimate sense of things and relationships. So now we will consider the author's most important means of projecting attitudes—language.

Discovering Meaning Through Language

Connotation and Imagery. To read poetry and descriptive prose effectively, you must be aware of the emotional association words take on in a particular context (connotative meaning) and you must be sensitive to the sensory appeals made through imagery.

In "A Deep-Sworn Vow," the simple words imply meanings that to some extent can be shared by all. Our common knowledge of marriage vows leads us to believe that the "deep-sworn vow" implies a spiritual bond, one outside the bonds of law, between a man and a woman; "friends," as it is used with "others" in this context, seems to suggest a casual relationship; "clamber to the heights of sleep" suggests a dream state between consciousness and unconsciousness; and "suddenly I meet your face" suggests an impact of realization with some deep emotional connotations.

Images can call all the senses to memory. This sentence from Thoreau's *Walden* may awaken your sense of sound:

> Late in the evening I heard the distant rumbling of wagons over bridges—a sound heard farther than almost any other at night,—the baying of dogs, and sometimes again the lowing of some disconsolate cow in a distant barn-yard.

Notice how another author unites the senses of color, movement, and smell:

Night Watch[10]
Richard Mason

The winter has fallen heavy.
Outside the succubus night in her frail glory
Has left the streets in black,
And stained the stagnant air
With wretched dreams of doom.

In front the valley heaves,
And each brittle light
Paints an image of death before
The altar of the mind.
Tremors of dance across
A pregnant river;
Delicate all the while,
Conducting feigned curtsies—
On, then, on again—
Will of the wisp faint;
   Tragic
Even as the mists extend a lucid hand
To silence these demure lamps of despair . . .

Irony. The presence of irony is marked by a sort of grim humor. It is lighter and less direct than sarcasm, but it is often more biting, precisely because it is indirect. An ironic statement contains an element of contrast; it has a double significance. Its intent is the opposite of what is said. There are many devices through which irony may be achieved, among them overstatement, understatement, and paradox.

Overstatement is exaggeration. Mark Anthony's funeral oration is the classic example: "Brutus is an honourable man." The speaker intends to have his audience believe not what he says, but the direct opposite of it.

Understatement is an ironical statement that appears to be less than it actually is; what is left unsaid is the real statement. Underplay has the effect of emphasizing and making the audience more aware of the reality. Notice in these lines from Marvell's "To His Coy Mistress" the effect obtained because the poet says less than he could:

The grave's a fine and private place,
But none I think do there embrace.

Paradox may be considered a statement which, though it seems contradictory, reveals a truth. It often suggests a mixture of attitude, as Juliet's "Parting is such sweet sorrow."

Metaphor and Simile. A *simile* is a figure of speech in which a similarity

---

[10] "Night Watch" by Richard J. Mason. Reprinted by permission of author.

between two objects is pointed out with the use of "as" or "like." "March came in like a lion" is a common simile: the primary term of the comparison, March, acquires from the secondary term, lion, the qualities of "the king of beasts." In the *metaphor* the likeness between two objects is not pointed out. It is a figure which imaginatively identifies one object with another, and the reader must figure out how two seemingly unrelated things relate. When Shakespeare says, "All the world's a stage," the relationship is clear. But when he compares old age to the season of late fall or early winter,

> That time of year thou mayst in me behold
> When yellow leaves, or none, or few, do hang
> Upon those boughs which shake against the cold,
> Bare ruin'd choirs, where late the sweet birds sang,

the meaning is not so evident, because the comparison is conveyed through a group of complex images. In the modern poem "Auto Wreck," by Karl Shapiro, we see metaphors and similes at work conveying a powerful emotional impact: the ambulance is "the little hospital" (metaphor); its warning light is a "ruby flare pulsing out red light like an artery" (simile); and the wrecks are "empty husks of locusts" (metaphor).

Personification is a metaphor which gives human qualities to lifeless objects, animals, or abstractions: Keats refers to the Grecian urn as an "unravished bride of quietness," and an urn takes on the human quality of purity; Donne refers to the sun as "Busy old fool, unruly Sun," and the sun takes on the human qualities of a meddlesome old man.

Symbolism. On a literal level, a symbol is someone or something tangible that stands for something intangible: a lion is an animal which stands for courage; a flag is a piece of cloth which stands for a nation. The tangible object (lion or flag) has within itself the suggestion of a universal meaning. The language is rich in such symbols; they come into our daily conversation with perfect naturalness.

Another type of symbol suggests meaning only because of the way it is used in a given text. For example, in Carl Sandburg's poem "Prayers of Steel,"

> Let me pry loose old walls.
> Let me lift and loosen old foundations.

"old walls" and "old foundations" might be thought to stand for an outdated institution, convention, or conformity in general. Usually many associations are attached to a symbol. Objects, people, and events may take on symbolic meanings because of the way they are handled in a piece of literature: rain in a novel by Hemingway, snow in a poem by Emily Dickinson, and the apple tree in Arthur Miller's *All My Sons* are all used as symbols of death.

To understand an author's symbolism, you must first of all recognize certain details as symbols and then discover what meaning the author attaches to them.

Sound Symbolism. Recognizing the way the author has used sound to reinforce meaning is a means of understanding subtle emotional connotations. An author may select words with soft, smooth sounds [l, ō, au] to suggest beauty, or choose words with sharper, harder sounds to suggest harshness or abruptness [p, b, t, k, g]. *Onomatopoeia* is the imitation of actual sounds; the sound of the word suggests the sense, as in "hiss" and "bubble." *Alliteration* is the repetition of identical consonant sounds: "What a tale their terror tells . . . " and *assonance* is the repetition of vowel sounds: "To the moaning and the groaning of the bells."

Rhythmic Patterns

Rhythm is an especially important element in poetry. But rhythmic patterns of recurrent beat or stress lend pleasure and heightened emotional response to both prose and poetry. The rhythm of poetry, like that of music, is based upon repetition, a turning from and returning to basic patterns.

How to recognize and handle verse patterns when reading poetry aloud will be discussed in Chapter 8. Here we will only say that unless there is an evident reason for using heavily stressed rhythm (such as a humorous effect depending upon exaggeration of beat), you should find a way to de-emphasize meter and rhyme.

When we read a poem naturally, as if we were engaged in lively conversation, stress takes care of itself. To de-emphasize meter and all regular patterns, we simply let the time elements of pause and duration play over the patterns. (See Chapter 8, "Stopping by Woods on a Snowy Evening.") A person may do this instinctively, without giving any thought to metrics, simply reading the phrases for sense, as in animated talk— pausing, giving some sounds more time, some less. In such reading, the poem's rhythm is generally maintained, but it remains a kind of under-flow, with the meaning on top.

Now let us move on to the last question in the analyzing process: What is the author saying?

Essence of Meaning: Theme

The theme of a selection is not the subject, but what the author is saying about the subject. It is both the point of the whole piece and the reason the author wrote it.

General themes concern conflicts: a character's search for identity, love, real-life values, and the like may be blocked by personal frustrations, man's inhumanity to man, fate, and so forth. The theme may be seen as the result of such a conflict. But sometimes a conflict is only implied. In a poem or in a modern short story an author's theme may be nothing more than a comment on life. In modern literature the theme more often points out some aspect of truth rather than a moral. In "A Deep-Sworn Vow," Yeats is simply recounting a life experience and saying that it is possible for a past love affair to make a lasting impression on the unconscious mind. His theme is highly colored by emotional connotations. This reminds us that, in considering the theme of a piece of literature, thought and feeling can seldom be divorced.

Study of a selection itself is the best way to find the underlying central meaning. Everything in the selection helps to point out the theme, but the conflict, the emphasis given to certain words or phrases, and the title are all important clues.

Illustrating Analysis

To illustrate our full discussion of both understanding and experiencing a literary work, we will use the following poem:

Bredon Hill[11]
A. E. Housman

In summertime on Bredon
  The bells they sound so clear;
Round both the shires they ring them
  In steeples far and near,
  A happy noise to hear.

Here of a Sunday morning
  My love and I would lie,
And see the coloured counties,
  And hear the larks so high
  About us in the sky.

The bells would ring to call her
  In valleys miles away;
"Come all to church, good people;
  Good people, come and pray."
  But here my love would stay.

And I would turn and answer
  Among the springing thyme,
"Oh, peal upon our wedding,
  And we will hear the chime,
  And come to church in time."

But when the snows at Christmas
  On Bredon top were strown,
My love rose up so early
  And stole out unbeknown
  And went to church alone.

They tolled the one bell only,
  Groom there was none to see,

The mourners followed after,
And so to church went she,
And would not wait for me.

The bells they sound on Bredon,
And still the steeples hum.
"Come all to church, good people,"
Oh, noisy bells, be dumb;
I hear you, I will come.

Situation. Who is speaking, to whom, where, and when? The speaker is one of the lovers in the poem; from the first line of the third stanza, we know this to be the boy. We can assume that he is a character outside the personality of the author. The speaker is not addressing any specific person; he simply tells his story. Yet, in characterizing the speaker, you may feel his desire to recall a past experience. This would suggest a degree of withdrawal from a listening audience. At times, you might suggest that the narrator is thinking aloud, remembering. At the end, when he addresses the bells directly, he wishes to withdraw completely; thus, the interpreter would use a closed stance and would establish no eye contact with the audience.

Place and passage of time in this poem are extremely important. Through the imagery of the changing seasons, we are made to feel sharp contrasts in mood.

What happens? We can view the movement of the situation in three "acts." Act 1—The speaker recalls the situation as it existed and was experienced in the summer: lovers lie on Bredon Hill, seeing and hearing, experiencing this place; church bells call; the girl stays with her lover; and in the high point in this act he responds to the bells. Act 2—The boy recalls a change in the season; the girl goes to church alone; one bell tolls; mourners follow (the structural climax of the poem). Act 3—Bells call people to church; the boy responds to the bells. (His answer is the emotional climax.)

How does the author's language reveal the changes in mood? How does it reveal the changes in the attitude of the speaker and of the author? In the first "act" of the poem the narrator's attitude toward the scene is evident through the visual and sound imagery: the sound of the bells is a "happy noise to hear"; the sounds of the larks are "about us in the sky"; and the couple lies among "springing thyme" looking down on "coloured counties." No elaborate description could make us sense so vividly the peace and beauty of the English countryside and the narrator's and the author's feeling for this place. Here, too, the youth's attitude toward what is happening is confident and carefree: the bells call "her," "but here my love would stay"; and he answers the bells in a rather light, merry tone: "Oh, peal upon our wedding,/And we will hear the chime,/And come to church in time."

But at the beginning of the second "act" there is an abrupt change in time and mood, it is winter and the mood is dark, for the beloved has been snatched away by death. The author's economy of language emphasizes the emotional connotations of the simple words: in contrast to the short vowel sounds in the previous stanzas, the long vowel sounds (especially long o) are dominant in the terse descriptive phrases: "stole out unbeknown," "went to church alone," "tolled the one bell only." The youth's feelings of dejection and aloneness are strikingly evident in "groom there was none to see," and "And would not wait for me." The contrast in his attitude toward the bells in the first part of the poem and in the last part is significant: their "happy noise" is now a "noisy sound." His answer to the bells at the end, a cry of bitterness, tells us that the youth is not consoled.

We respond to both light and dark moods in "Bredon Hill." Though the speaker of the poem knows the unhappy outcome of the situation as he begins his story, through recalling a happy time now gone, he is allowed to escape the present reality of death. In the quick transition from past to present, your oral interpretation should reflect the author's change in sound symbolism and you should project the impact of emotion-charged words with the appropriate timing. The light tone experienced in the past gives stress to the dark tone of the present and to the essence of truth revealed at the end. The intensity of the ending shows the poem to be primarily dark in tone.

What is the author saying? In "Bredon Hill," young lovers are separated by death. What is the outcome of this conflict? From only an initial reading, one might impose a moral theme because at the end the speaker's attitude toward the experience is not immediately clear. Is Housman pointing a moral? No, he is not saying that the boy, having learned a lesson, will now go to church, as all good people do! The tone of the boy's words at the end is angry and bitter, for he suddenly sees the world as a dark riddle and life as intolerably cruel. What is the meaning of his cry, "Oh, noisy bells, be dumb; I hear you, I will come"? Is he expressing a wish to die, to follow his love to the church in death? Or is he expressing his indignation that death is inevitable? The church bells call all the good people to church as before; daily life goes on and the dead are forgotten. If this latter interpretation is accepted, the poet is pointing out the inconstancy of the human heart, a bitter discovery. While expressing sympathy for his subject, the author leaves us with a troubled sense of human inconstancy.

The question method is valid and helpful, but in an oral interpretation class it can never stand alone. Each question must be asked in the context of how it leads you to realize visual and aural response in performance.

Below is a class exercise project designed to bring literary interpretation and oral interpretation into some perspective early in the course. From twelve poems, or short prose selections found in other parts of the text, you are asked to select, interpret, and share your interpretation with the class in oral reading. Sharing these experiences can generate class discussion and serve to prepare you for reading performance assignments to follow.

Class Project

In an initial reading:
1   Discover what happens to you as you read this? Why does the selection have appeal for you? Can you relate this experience to your own?

Does the author's experience seem to be primarily one of thought, action, feeling, character, or fantasy?

2 Having cleared any blocks to comprehension, analyze the selection, asking who is speaking, to whom, where, and when? What happens? What are the high points of tension? How does the language reveal mood and attitudes? What is the prevailing tone? What is the author saying?

3 In class, consider problems in communicating your selection. Share your preparatory experiences with the class; share your interpretation in an oral performance; add a question for class discussion.

Poems for Study and Oral Interpretation

The Scoffers
William Blake

Mock on, mock on, Voltaire, Rousseau;
Mock on, mock on, 'tis all in vain!
You throw the sand against the wind,
And the wind blows it back again.

And every sand becomes a gem
Reflected in the beams divine;
Blown back, they blind the mocking eye,
But still in Israel's paths they shine.

The atoms of Democritus
And Newton's particles of light
Are sands upon the Red Sea shore,
Where Israel's tents do shine so bright.

A Primer of the Daily Round[12]
Howard Nemerov

A peels an apple, while B kneels to God,
C telephones to D, who has a hand
On E's knee, F coughs, G turns up the sod
For H's grave, I do not understand
But J is bringing one clay pigeon down
While K brings down a nightstick on L's head,
And M takes mustard, N drives into town,
O goes to bed with P, and Q drops dead,
R lies to S, but happens to be heard
By T, who tells U not to fire V
For having to give W the word
That X is now deceiving Y with Z,
Who happens just now to remember A
Peeling an apple somewhere far away.

---

[12] "A Primer of the Daily Round" by Howard Nemerov, copyright 1975, University of Chicago Press. Reprinted by permission of author.

one winter afternoon[13]
e. e. cummings

one winter afternoon

(at the magical hour
when is becomes if)

a bespangled clown
standing on eighth street
handed me a flower.

Nobody,it's safe
to say,observed him but

myself;and why?because

without any doubt he was
whatever(first and last)

mostpeople fear most:
a mystery for which i've
no word except alive

—that is,completely alert
and miraculously whole;

with not merely a mind and a heart

but unquestionably a soul—
by no means funereally hilarious

(or otherwise democratic)
but essentially poetic
or ethereally serious:

a fine not a coarse clown
(no mob,but a person)

and while never saying a word

who was anything but dumb;
since the silence of him

self sang like a bird.
Mostpeople have been heard
screaming for international

---

measures that render hell rational
—i thank heaven somebody's crazy

enough to give me a daisy

Auto Wreck[14]
Karl Shapiro

Its quick soft silver bell beating, beating,
And down the dark one ruby flare
Pulsing out red light like an artery,
The ambulance at top speed floating down
Past beacons and illuminated clocks
Wings in a heavy curve, dips down,
And brakes speed, entering the crowd.

The doors leap open, emptying light;
Stretchers are laid out, the mangled lifted
And stowed into the little hospital.
The bell, breaking the hush, tolls once,
And the ambulance with its terrible cargo
Rocking, slightly rocking, moves away,
As the doors, an afterthought, are closed.

We are deranged, walking among the cops
Who sweep glass and are large and composed.
One is still making notes under the light.
One with a bucket douches ponds of blood
Into the street and gutter.
One hangs lanterns on the wrecks that cling,
Empty husks of locusts, to iron poles.

Our throats were tight as tourniquets,
Our feet were bound with splints, but now
Like convalescents intimate and gauche,
We speak through sickly smiles and warn
With the stubborn saw of common sense,
The grim joke and the banal resolution.
The traffic moves around with care,
But we remain, touching a wound
That opens to our richest horror.

Already old, the question Who is innocent?
For death in war is done by hands;
Suicide has cause and stillbirth, logic.
But this invites the occult mind,
Cancels our physics with a sneer,
And spatters all we know of dénouement
Across the expedient and wicked stones.

Oak Spring[15]
William Heyen

OAK SPRING
Does not resist
its own leaves. These
appear, as easily as
snow, when winter snows,
or rain, when the sky rains,
or all the birds
it is always blind to.
But this blossoming, this
fulfillment, this
green explosion
every year of even its old age,
this different dimension
of miracle: snow, rain, birds,
yes, but imagine
all the sap of your own
wooden body beginning
to warm, your skin
breaking to bud and leaf;
imagine, coming
to everything you are,
without second, or third, or fourth,
or fifth thoughts
that each time you utter
this language of tongues,
you're living closer
to your last spring.

Alice's Sister and the Breakfast Dishes[16]
for Alice
Joan Moore

We were a green and common lot,
but hadn't thought to be treated like
wet litters of unwanted cats—
thrown like that into the sack
and dragged with a fury new in her
across—how many—stoney miles
of new england pasture.
When woods of a sudden undered us
we felt how it must dearly be,
after hurricane at sea,
to pull one's bellies on the beach.

But Alice's sister, sweet by sour,
did not intend our pieces peace.
She'd grown blacker, if anything.
seeing, as she reached the trees,
her rowdy army lose its grit—
those brothers sisters cousins dogs
who, whenever she struck, appeared
in numbers like the pitiful poor
from every cranny on the place—
damn bunch of rabbits all turned tail,
hopping to hide, running to tell,
the biggest tattle gone downwind
to sing to the plowing Irishman.

Assigning with her devilish bell
the miniscule pisspots to hell,
she disappeared in Big Deepwoods,
dragging the goods in after.
So began the second aeon
of our execution.

Us crashing behind her, Alice's sister
stormed up a creekbed sloshed with spring
whose miles of ripper snake at last
oozed to a slow meandering.
Here, her ire calmed a wee,
she fell upon some poetry,
hummed a Bach, whistled for rocs,
saluted wyverns overhead,
cursed the church, blessed the celts.
and set her sleek, pink unicorns
on some fat-assed centaurs.
Bringing up the rear, of course,
our presto-presto pizzicato
to her squalling "Hear, Hear,
Lord give ear to me fine drum corps—
the best in all connecticut!"

Late afternoon, the trip got done—
hunger alone could stop that one.
She holed into the muddy bank,
there put the limp and tattered sack;
kicked it; crossed her forehead; spat;
then, like a bloody crook or cat
who needs to hide its dirty tracks,
she daubed some soggy leaves thereon;
without a rat tat tat was gone.

Alice, later, finding us here
in these shatters of ourselves,
named it The Vale of China Tears.
Alice was our recompense.
For though she'd not restore us,

her taking care to find out grave
and dignifying our debasement
with that lovely name redeemed us.
And Alice brought us back her face
which, loved so much before the wreck,
we'd despaired of seeing again.
When she untied the sack, looked in,
why, it was like the sun come there
golden through her yellow hair.
And we awoke to miracle:
for where she'd been but one before,
she now was more: the integer
our integer could make of her;
this new equation ever solved
when we reflect and multiply
the loving face of Alice
to prove the grace of God.

Since There's No Help
Michael Drayton

Since there's no help, come let us kiss and part,
Nay, I have done: you get no more of me,
And I am glad, yea glad with all my heart,
That thus so cleanly, I myself can free,
Shake hands for ever, cancel all our vows,
And when we meet at any time again,
Be it not seen in either of our brows,
That we one jot of former love retain;
Now at the last gasp of Love's latest breath,
When his pulse failing, Passion speechless lies,
When Faith is kneeling by his bed of death,
And Innocence is closing up his eyes,
Now if thou wouldst, when all have given him over,
From death to life, thou might'st him yet recover.

To His Coy Mistress
Andrew Marvell

Had we but world enough, and time,
This coyness, Lady, were no crime.
We would sit down, and think which way
To walk, and pass our long love's day.
Thou by the Indian Ganges' side
Shouldst rubies find; I by the tide
Of Humber would complain. I would
Love you ten years before the Flood,
And you should, if you please, refuse
Till the conversion of the Jews.
My vegetable love should grow
Vaster than empires, and more slow;
An hundred years should go to praise

Thine eyes, and on thy forehead gaze;
Two hundred to adore each breast,
But thirty thousand to the rest;
An age at least to every part,
And the last age should show your heart.
For, Lady, you deserve this state,
Nor would I love at lower rate.
  But at my back I always hear
Time's wingèd chariot hurrying near;
And yonder all before us lie
Deserts of vast eternity.
Thy beauty shall no more be found,
Nor, in thy marble vault, shall sound
My echoing song; then worms shall try
That long preserved virginity,
And your quaint honour turn to dust,
And into ashes all my lust:
The grave's a fine and private place,
But none, I think, do there embrace.
  Now therefore, while the youthful hue
Sits on thy skin like morning dew,
And while thy willing soul transpires
At every pore with instant fires,
Now let us sport us while we may,
And now, like amorous birds of prey,
Rather at once our time devour
Than languish in his slow-chapt power.
Let us roll all our strength and all
Our sweetness up into one ball,
And tear our pleasures with rough strife
Thorough the iron gates of life:
Thus, though we cannot make our sun
Stand still, yet we will make him run.

Old Christmas Morning[17]
Roy Helton

"Where you coming from, Lomey Carter,
  So airly over the snow?
And what's them pretties you got in your hand,
  And where you aiming to go?

"Step in, Honey: Old Christmas morning
  I ain't got nothing much;
Maybe a bite of sweetness and corn bread,
  A little ham meat and such.

"But come in, Honey! Sally Anne Barton's
  Hungering after your face.

Wait till I light my candle up.
  Set down! There's your old place.

"Now where you been so airly this morning?"
  "Graveyard, Sally Anne.
Up by the trace in the salt lick meadows
  Where Taulbe kilt my man."

"Taulbe ain't to home this morning . . .
  I can't scratch up a light;
Dampness get on the heads of the matches;
  But I'll blow up the embers bright."

"Needn't trouble, I won't be stopping:
  Going a long ways still."
"You didn't see nothing, Lomey Carter,
  Up on the Graveyard hill?"

"What should I see there, Sally Anne Barton?"
  "Well, sperits do walk last night."
"There were an elder bush a-blooming
  Where the moon still give some light."

"Yes, elder bushes, they bloom, Old Christmas,
  And critters kneel down in their straw.
Anything else up in the graveyard?"
  "One thing more I saw:

I saw my man with his head all bleeding
  Where Taulbe's shot went through."
"What did he say?"
                "He stopped and kissed me."
  "What did he say to you?"

"Said, Lord Jesus forguv your Taulbe;
  But he told me another word;
He said it soft when he stooped and kissed me.
  That were the last I heard."

"Taulbe ain't to home this morning."
  "I know that, Sally Anne,
For I kilt him, coming down through the meadow
  Where Taulbe kilt my man.

"I met him upon the meadow trace
  When the moon were fainting fast,
And I had my dead man's rifle gun
  And kilt him as he come past."

"But I heard two shots."
                " 'Twas his was second:
  He shot me 'fore he died;
You'll find us at daybreak, Sally Anne Barton;
  I'm laying there dead at his side."

Fiddler Jones[18]
Edgar Lee Masters

The earth keeps some vibration going
There in your heart, and that is you.
And if the people find you can fiddle,
Why, fiddle you must, for all your life.
What do you see, a harvest of clover?
Or a meadow to walk through to the river?
The wind's in the corn; you rub your hands
For beeves hereafter ready for market;
Or else you hear the rustle of skirts
Like the girls when dancing at Little Grove.
To Cooney Potter a pillar of dust
Or whirling leaves meant ruinous drouth;
They looked to me like Red-Head Sammy
Stepping it off, to "Toot-a-Loor."
How could I till my forty acres
Not to speak of getting more,
With a medley of horns, bassoons and piccolos
Stirred in my brain by crows and robins
And the creak of a wind-mill—only these?
And I never started to plow in my life
That some one did not stop in the road
And take me away to a dance or picnic.
I ended up with forty acres;
I ended up with a broken fiddle—
And a broken laugh, and a thousand memories,
And not a single regret.

Mrs. Williams[19]
Edgar Lee Masters

I was the milliner
Talked about, lied about,
Mother of Dora,
Whose strange disappearance
Was charged to her rearing.
My eye quick to beauty
Saw much beside ribbons
And buckles and feathers
And leghorns and felts,
To set off sweet faces,
And dark hair and gold.
One thing I will tell you . . .
The stealers of husbands
Wear powder and trinkets,
And fashionable hats.

---

[18] "Fiddler Jones" by Edgar Lee Masters in Spoon River Anthology. Reprinted by permission of Mrs. Ellen C. Masters.

[19] "Mrs. Williams" by Edgar Lee Masters in Spoon River Anthology. Reprinted by permission of Mrs. Ellen C. Masters.

Wives, wear them yourselves.
Hats may make divorces—
They also prevent them . . .

Porphyria's Lover
Robert Browning

The rain set early in tonight,
  The sullen wind was soon awake,
It tore the elm-tops down for spite.
  And did its worst to vex the lake:
  I listened with heart fit to break.
When glided in Porphyria; straight
  She shut the cold out and the storm,
And kneeled and made the cheerless grate
  Blaze up, and all the cottage warm;
  Which done, she rose, and from her form
Withdrew the dripping cloak and shawl,
  And laid her soiled gloves by, untied
Her hat and let the damp hair fall,
  And, last, she sat down by my side
  And called me. When no voice replied,
She put my arm about her waist,
  And made her smooth white shoulder bare,
And all her yellow hair displaced,
  And, stooping, made my cheek lie there,
  And spread, o'er all, her yellow hair,
Murmuring how she loved me—she
  Too weak, for all her heart's endeavor,
To set its struggling passion free
  From pride, and vainer ties dissever,
  And give herself to me forever.
But passion sometimes would prevail,
  Nor could tonight's gay feast restrain
A sudden thought of one so pale
  For love of her, and all in vain:
  So, she was come through wind and rain.
Be sure I looked up at her eyes
  Happy and proud; at last I knew
Porphyria worshipped me; surprise
  Made my heart swell, and still it grew
  While I debated what to do.
That moment she was mine, mine, fair,
  Perfectly pure and good: I found
A thing to do, and all her hair
  In one long yellow string I wound
  Three times her little throat around,
And strangled her. No pain felt she;
  I am quite sure she felt no pain.
As a shut bud that holds a bee,
  I warily oped her lids: again
  Laughed the blue eyes without a stain.

And I untightened the tress
  About her neck; her cheek once more
Blushed bright beneath my burning kiss:
  I propped her head up as before,
  Only this time my shoulder bore
Her head, which droops upon it still:
  The smiling rosy little head,
So glad it has its utmost will,
  That all it scorned at once is fled,
  And I, its love, am gained instead!
Porphyria's love: she guessed not how
  Her darling one wish would be heard.
And thus we sit together now,
  And all night long we have not stirred,
  And yet God has not said a word!

Aunt Jennifer's Tigers[20]
Adrienne Rich

Aunt Jennifer's tigers stride across a screen,
Bright topaz denizens of a world of green.
They do not fear the men beneath the tree;
They pace in sleek chivalric certainty.

Aunt Jennifer's fingers fluttering through her wool
Find even the ivory needle hard to pull.
The massive weight of Uncle's wedding band
Sits heavily upon Aunt Jennifer's hand

When Aunt is dead, her terrified hands will lie
Still ringed with ordeals she was mastered by.
The tigers in the panel that she made.
Will go on striding, proud and unafraid.

The Mountain Woman[21]
DuBose Heyward

Among the sullen peaks she stood at bay
And paid life's hard account from her small store.
Knowing the code of mountain wives, she bore
The burden of the days without a sigh;
And sharp against the somber winter sky,
I saw her drive her steers afield each day.

Hers was the hand that sunk the furrows deep
Across the rocky, grudging southern slope.

---

[20] "Aunt Jennifer's Tigers" is reprinted from *Poems, Selected and New, 1950–1974*, by Adrienne Rich, with the permission of W. W. Norton & Company, Inc. Copyright © 1975, 1973, 1971, 1969, 1966 by W. W. Norton & Co., Inc. No. 91 Copyright © 1967, 1963, 1962, 1961, 1960, 1959, 1958, 1957, 1956, 1955, 1954, 1953, 1952, 1951 by Adrienne Rich.

[21] From *Skylines and Horizons* by DuBose Heyward. Copyright 1924 by DuBose Heyward. Copyright 1952 by Dorothy Heyward. Reprinted by permission of Holt, Rinehart and Winston, Publishers.

At first youth left her face, and later hope;
Yet through each mocking spring and barren fall,
She reared her lusty brood, and gave them all
That gladder wives and mothers love to keep.

And when the sherriff shot her eldest son
Beside his still, so well she knew her part,
She gave no healing tears to ease her heart;
But took the blow upstanding, with her eyes
As drear and bitter as the winter skies.
Seeing her then, I thought that she had won.

But yesterday her man returned too soon
And found her tending, with a reverent touch,
One scarlet bloom; and, having drunk too much,
He snatched its flame and quenched it in the dirt.
Then, like a creature with a mortal hurt,
She fell, and wept away the afternoon.

Winter Fantasy[22]
Jonathan Aldrich

This for my-lady's neckpiece:—
they have let the red fox go,
and the bell on his collar
tinkles out of the morning, over the snow.

Picture five hunters riding
brown horses with black tails who, at a horn,
turn from the center of the morning
into the yellow sun

(one hunter remembering hills of the home
he cursed), the low hounds nosing ahead
where the fox has clipped the bright crust, his track
a skitter of beads;

and a faraway sled
glides down a hill, its trail
curved like an elephant's tusk (one hunter remembers the curl
of his dead child) as they pass through a dwindling brake
—its gray twigs turned like spokes of an ignited wheel—
to an etched hollow, and hard lake, maintaining
a simple tree, with limbs fringe-white
above and black below, suitable for hanging,
as the pack, all prinked and singing,
swerves to a call.

Fur bristling,
their quarry holds at a bush,

---

[22] "Winter Fantasy" by Jonathan Aldrich, Reprinted by permission of author.

50

compact, his collar bell
still tinkling, trying with a paw
to shake it off—too late!—
They are leaping the last hedge, crying—
as he goes, in a flash, abstract,
his eyes blown white.

Suggested Readings

Bacon, Wallace. "The Act of Interpretation," *Oral English*, Spring 1972, pp. 1–6.

———. *The Art of Interpretation*. New York: Holt, Rinehart and Winston, Inc., 1972.

Bahn, Eugene and Margaret L. *A History of Oral Interpretation*. Minneapolis: Burgess Publishing Company, 1970.

Bowen, Elbert R., *et al.* "Expressing Responses to Meaning," *Communicative Reading*. New York: MacMillan Publishing Co., 1978.

Campbell, Paul. "Communication Aesthetics," *Today's Speech,* Summer 1971, pp. 7–19.

Ciardi, John. *How Does a Poem Mean?* Boston: Houghton Mifflin Company, 1959.

Danziger, Marlier K., and W. Stacy Johnson. *Introduction to the Study of Literature.* Boston: Heath Publishing Co., 1965.

Forrest, W. C. "Poem as Summons to Performance," *British Journal of Aesthetics,* July 1969, pp. 298–305.

Geiger, Don. "The Oral Interpreter as Creator," *The Speech Teacher,* November 1954, pp. 260–277.

———. *The Sound, Sense, and Performance of Literature.* Chicago: Scott, Foresman and Company, 1963.

Guerin, Wilfred L., *et al. A Handbook of Critical Approaches to Literature.* New York: Harper and Row, 1966.

Haas, Richard, and David A. Williams, eds. *The Study of Oral Interpretation: Theory and Comment.* Indianapolis: The Bobbs-Merrill Company, Inc., 1975.

Hudson, Lee. "Oral Interpretation as Metaphorical Expression," *The Speech Teacher,* January 1973, pp. 27–32.

Marconx, J. P. "Current Trends in Literary Analysis for Oral Interpretation," *The Speech Teacher,* November 1966, pp. 324–327.

Ohmann, Richard. "Speech Acts and the Definition of Literature," *Philosophy and Rhetoric,* Winter 1971, pp. 1–20.

Palmer, Richard E. *Hermeneutics.* Evanston, Ill.: Northwestern University Press, 1969.

Richards, I. A. *Principles of Literary Criticism.* New York: Harcourt, Brace, Jovanovich, 1925.

Rickert, William E. "Communication Models for Teaching of Oral Interpretation," *The Speech Teacher,* March 1973, pp. 133–140.

Valentine, K. B. *Interlocking Pieces: 20 Questions for Understanding Literature.* Dubuque, Iowa: Kendall Hunt Publishers, 1977.

Wellek, Rene, and Austin Warren. *Theory of Literature.* New York: Harcourt, Brace, Jovanovich, 1966.

Part II

Communicating Guides: Mind, Body, Voice

Chapter 4

Guides for Psychological Control

The Psychological Approach for Communicating Meaning

The basis of the psychological approach for oral interpretation is that a person's own psychology, one's own thinking, affected by actual and vicarious experience, can be used to stimulate personal involvement in an author's recorded experience.

    Earlier we recognized the interpreter's inner resources as a way to stimulate responses to literary meanings. As a professional actress and an inspiring teacher of theatre, Uta Hagen is well aware of her inner resources and how to use them:

> I realize that I have endless sources within myself to put to use in the illumination of endless characters in dramatic literature; that I am compounded of endless human beings, depending on the events moving in on me, my surroundings, circumstances, relationships with a variety of people, what I want and what's in my way at a given moment: all within the context of my identity.[1]

This means, among other things, that in learning to use your inner resources to interpret and perform literature, you become better acquainted with your inner self, and better understand who you are. But the application of the psychological approach may seem vaguer for you, the interpreter, than it does for the actor. From students we hear, "When a teacher says, 'Just imagine the scene,' do I just stand there and hope it will appear? And directors are constantly saying, 'Just relax and concentrate,' How?" In this chapter we will offer some answers to such questions.

---

[1] Uta Hagen. *Respect for Acting.* New York: Macmillan Publishing Company, 1973, p. 25.

Imagination

The American College Dictionary defines imagination as "the act of forming mental images of what is not actually present to the senses," or as "the power of reproducing images stored in the memory under suggestion of associated images." When you imagine something, you see it in your mind's eye, you hear sounds in your mind's ear. We imagine through sensory recall.

People vary in their ability to use imagination. As children, we are quite imaginative, but our imagination is often dulled along the way to adulthood. A child at play is in dead earnest: believing in being a policeman, with a certain tree as the culprit. For a moment, the child creates a magic spell, at the same time knowing this is only play. Both the actor and the oral interpreter also create such illusions. In interpreting literature orally, we use the creative faculty of imagination to re-experience feelings and emotions. An interpreter who can use the imagination to call up images while reading has a valuable and artistic skill. The ability can be cultivated.

This text identifies two types of sensory recall. Sense memory is recalling physical sensations of sight, sound, smell, and touch, including movement, temperature, pain, hunger, etc. Emotional memory is the recall of psychological or emotional responses you have experienced in emotional moments or occurrences. For example, if you have always been sensitive to sounds, you have stored sounds in your memory. When you read these lines from Matthew Arnold's poem "Dover Beach,"

> *Listen! you hear the grating roar*
> *Of pebbles which the waves draw back, and fling,*

the poet's imagery evokes the sound in your mind's ear. On the other hand, if your sense perceptions are dull, you might need to associate the sound imagery with a particular event, a time when you were emotionally aroused by a comparable sound. In such a case, you would be using emotional memory to trigger a response, stimulating your creative imagination by means of identification.

Identification

The American College Dictionary defines this term as "an act of recognizing a point of sameness—making associations in feeling." Have you ever entered a small-town bus station at a late hour, when only a few sleepy travelers, tired waitresses, and idle noise-seekers remained, and suddenly become aware of the sounds and the visual details of this American scene? If so, the remembered experience could be related to the following passage:

> "You can do ennythang, but keep offa mah blue suede shoes!" shouts the man in the jukebox. "You can burn down mah house, you can steal mah cah, you can drink mah lickah fum a ole fruit jah!"
> It is a song: he shouts it from a tight, excited throat against the frantic drumming of the rural guitars. The hidden record spinning in the bloated,

winking jukebox blasts the walls of the bus station cafe, walls and ceiling shiny with old white enamel and the congealed grease given off by a million hamburgers; the sound bursts along the counters and booms and rattles in the glass cases of dead pie slices, crusted cake segments and soggy, oily sweet rolls.[2]

When recalling such a scene, you should not try to remember how you felt at the time; instead, you should activate your memory by asking questions regarding the details: Who was with you? Was it a cold night? How many people were there? What did you do? In this way it is possible to bring the past experience back into your consciousness and to arouse toward the scene an attitude comparable to the attitude the author expresses in the selection.

Concentration

The American College Dictionary defines concentration as "the act or process of directing attention on a single object." Concentration is a powerful force, requiring discipline. We sense this power in a period of concentrated study, in a speaker intent on an idea, in an actor concentrating on the thoughts of the character, and in a reader concentrating on the thoughts of an author, narrator, or character. Concentration brings about a kind of selflessness; it makes the genius.

Uta Hagen presents a very good example of the effectiveness of concentration when she asks why an animal, a cat stalking a moth, for example, is able to preempt the best actors on stage. Her answer, of course, is concentration. The cat is not aware of the audience or the actors. Its prime concern is the moth and its involvement with that moth. As members of an audience, we are drawn to the activity because of the cat's unity of purpose, its concentration.

The ability to concentrate comes partly through an innate talent and partly through developing the skill. To develop the skill, a person should first of all learn to relax. Lee Strasberg, the renowned teacher and director of Actor's Studio, asks his students to relax physically and then to concentrate on three specific areas for *mental* relaxation, which Strasberg has discovered through experience to be "indicators of mental tensions":

> After he is physically relaxed, he then goes through these three areas. He tries to relax the temple area. Then he tries to relax the eyes. Finally he tries to relax the whole mouth area so that the tension is as much as possible reduced.[3]

How does one concentrate? First try a simple exercise of concentration not involving the emotions. Pick an object in the room and concentrate on it. Suppose you take a classroom chair. To force your mind to stay

[2] From *My Escape from the C.I.A.* by Hughes Rudd (New York: E. P. Dutton & Co. Inc., 1966). Reprinted by permission of the publisher.

[3] From *Strasberg at the Actor's Studio* by Lee Strasberg and Robert H. Hethmon. Copyright © 1965 by Lee Strasberg and Robert H. Hethmon. Reprinted by permission of The Viking Press, Inc.

focused on this concrete object, ask yourself questions and find answers to your questions. Try something like this, orally or silently:

How many wooden parts does this chair have? Well . . . there is the seat, and there is the back, and the arm—three. What about the height? I'd say the seat is about 18 inches from the floor and the back another 18 inches. What about the legs? . . . and so on.

This exercise points out two fundamental guides for concentration: **Find concrete objects on which to concentrate.**

Focus on details that concern the object in order to keep the concentration going.

When we read literature aloud, where do we concentrate?

Concentrating on Physical Objects. At times you must suggest the presence of physical objects. In reading Juliet's lines in the vial scene, for example, on one level, you should concentrate on the vial of poison. To make this possible, answer questions: How large is this vial? To what could I compare it? How heavy is it? How much liquid does it hold? etc. So you become more aware of the object, and when you read the line "Come vial," you can imagine the actual object and the feel of it in your hand.

Concentrating on Reflective Thoughts. In reading lyric poetry or inner monologues within selections of prose and poetry, you concentrate on the speaker's reflective thoughts. Here your emotional response to the thoughts is important. Your ability to use your imagination and to identify a personal experience with the author's will serve you well.

In the lyric "A Deep-Sworn Vow," the speaker's emotion results from reflective thoughts concerning a past love affair. Perhaps you have had no such experience, but you have had an emotional reaction of some kind resulting from a relationship with another person. Asking yourself questions in order to recall the details of your experience would help to arouse the emotion that you felt in the past. After this, you should be more successful in projecting the speaker's emotion.

Concentrating on Imagery. In reading a descriptive passage such as Thomas Wolfe's "Circus at Dawn," your concentration should be on the imagery, the sensory experience. Here, too, you should try to find an experience comparable to the scene described. You may not have witnessed the movement of a circus train, but in all probability you have viewed some scene with a similar sense of wonder and excitement. It is the attitude toward the scene that it is important to recapture, through identification and emotional memory.

Concentrating on the Desire of a Character. Similar emotional desires from your own life experience can be found to relate to a character's desire. If you were reading "The Laboratory," you might think your experiences far removed from this character's desire to murder her rival. In his book, *Acting: The First Six Lessons,* Richard Boleslavsky gives the classic example of how seemingly unrelated experiences may be related through imaginative thinking. (The creature is the pupil; the "I" is the teacher.)

Creature. All right, suppose I have to play a murderer. I have never murdered anybody. How shall I find it?

"I". Oh, why do actors always ask me about murder? The younger they are, the more intense they want to act. All right, you have never murdered anybody. Have you ever camped?

Creature. Yes.

"I". Were there any mosquitoes around?

Creature. It was in New Jersey.

"I". Did they annoy you? Did you follow one among them with your eyes and ears and hate until the beast landed on your forearm? And did you slap your forearm cruelly without thinking of the hurt to yourself—with only the wish to . . .

Creature. To kill the beast.

"I". There you are. A good sensitive artist doesn't need any more than that to play Othello in Desdemona's final scene. The rest is the work of magnification, imagination and belief.[4]

Notice that the teacher does not ask the pupil to remember the hate felt, but instead, to remember following the mosquito with "eyes, ears, and hate" until the chance came to kill it. In remembering the desire to kill the mosquito, the interpreter arouses an emotion of hate which can be used to relate to a character's desire to murder.

Concentrating on Multiple Levels. In the sleep-walking scene, Lady Macbeth's concentration is on her hands and on her desire to be free of guilt. Juliet's concentration in the vial scene shifts from her desire to escape an arranged marriage, to her fearful thoughts of the tomb, to two physical objects—the vial and the dagger. In the mother's lines from *Long Day's Journey into Night,* Mary Tyrone's concentration is vague and shifting. In her drugged state, her mind shifts quickly from her hands, to the desires of her youth, to her desire to remember why she came into the room.

In summary, identification and concentration are means by which we use emotional memory for imagining and becoming closer to an author's experience. Physiological sensations—seeing, hearing, touching, smelling, tasting, and sensations of movement, etc.—can be realized imaginatively through sense memory alone.

Exercises for Imagination, Identification, and Concentration

1 Relax:

a Take a relaxing exercise. With your body in a relaxed position, concentrate on relaxing (1) the temples, (2) the bridge of the nose and the eyes, and (3) the mouth area.

b Play cat, and since relaxation comes from concentration, stretch, arch your back, extend your limbs, drop your jaw, yawn, and settle down.

2 Imagine:

a the sound of a train whistle far away, moving nearer; a strange sound outside the house at night; a symphony orchestra; a rock concert; the sounds of the environment.

---

[4] *Acting: The First Six Lessons:* Copyright 1949 by Norma Boleslavsky. Reprinted by permission of Theatre Arts Books.

b the taste of an orange, a hot pepper, raw oysters, cool lemonade.

c the smell of garlic, a fish market, a summer evening, sweat.

3   Sense:

a extreme hot or cold water on your body; a blow to your body; sharp pain.

b walking on a sandy beach; through air as though in molasses; in the rain.

c lifting a weight; heavy or light space; playing ball—ball is normal, heavy, light.

d the feel of fur; the feel of a hand on yours; a wind storm.

4   Concentrate:

a You are in: a jail; a dungeon; a child's room; your own room; a tree house; a dentist's office; a church; a library. Describe it orally.

b Concentrate on each part of your body; let your concentration skip from one part to another; feel your body.

5   Respond to Shakespeare's imagery in *As You Like It* through sense memory:

The Seven Ages of Man

All the world's a stage,
And all the men and women merely players:
They have their exits and their entrances;
And one man in his time plays many parts,
His acts being seven ages. At first the infant,
Mewling and puking in the nurse's arms.
And then the whining schoolboy, with his satchel,
And shining morning face, creeping like snail
Unwillingly to school. And then the lover,
Sighing like furnace, with a woeful ballad
Made to his mistress' eyebrow. Then a soldier,
Full of strange oaths, and bearded like the pard,
Jealous in honour, sudden and quick in quarrel,
Seeking the bubble reputation
Even in the cannon's mouth. And then the justice,
In fair round belly with good capon lin'd,
With eyes severe, and beard of formal cut,
Full of wise saws and modern instances;
And so he plays his part. The sixth age shifts
Into the lean and slipper'd pantaloon,
With spectacles on nose and pouch on side,
His youthful hose, well sav'd, a world too wide
For his shrunk shank; and his big manly voice,
Turning again towards childish treble, pipes
And whistles in his sound. Last scene of all,
That ends this strange eventful history,
Is second childishness and mere oblivion,
Sans teeth, sans eyes, sans taste, sans everything.

6   Read one of the following poems aloud. Try to identify the speaker's emotional experience with a personal experience of your own, in order to project the speaker's attitude toward the experience.

War Song[5]
Dorothy Parker

Soldier, in a curious land
  All across a swaying sea,
Take her smile and lift her hand—
  Have no guilt of me.

Soldier, when were soldiers true?
  If she's kind and sweet and gay,
Use the wish I send to you—
  Lie not lone till day!

Only, for the nights that were,
  Soldier, and the dawns that came,
When in sleep you turn to her
  Call her by my name.

from Non Sum Qualis Eram Bonae Sub Regno Cynarae
Ernest Dowson

Last night, ah, yesternight, betwixt her lips and mine
There fell thy shadow, Cynara! thy breath was shed
Upon my soul between the kisses and the wine;
And I was desolate and sick of an old passion,
  Yea, I was desolate and bowed my head:
I have been faithful to thee, Cynara! in my fashion.

All night upon mine heart I felt her warm heart beat,
Night-long within mine arms in love and sleep she lay;
Surely the kisses of her bought red mouth were sweet;
But I was desolate and sick of an old passion,
  When I awoke and found the dawn was grey:
I have been faithful to thee, Cynara! in my fashion.

Techniques for Projecting Emotional Meaning

Emotional Responses Through Overt Actions

If you have difficulty feeling a certain emotion, you can deliberately arouse it by using your body as if you were experiencing that emotion. If the mood is anger, then look, stand, move, gesture, and speak angrily. Use your whole body and exaggerate the mood in any way you can think of. Grip the floor with your toes, bang the lectern, stamp your foot, and spit out the lines, making the sounds in the words harsh and biting. After this deliberate focus on the emotion, gradually change your focus to the cause of the

[5] From *The Portable Dorothy Parker* Copyright 1944, renewed © 1972 by The Viking Press Inc. Originally appeared in *The New Yorker* Reprinted by permission of The Viking Press.

emotion. The following dramatic monologue offers an opportunity for powerful emotional responses:

The Laboratory
Ancien Régime
Robert Browning

Now that I, tying thy glass mask tightly,
May gaze through these faint smokes curling whitely,
As thou pliest thy trade in this devil's-smithy—
Which is the poison to poison her, prithee?

He is with her, and they know that I know
Where they are, what they do: they believe my tears flow
While they laugh, laugh at me, at me fled to the drear
Empty church, to pray God in, for them!—I am here.

Grind away, moisten and mash up thy paste,
Pound at thy powder,—I am not in haste!
Better sit thus, and observe thy strange things,
Than go where men wait me and dance at the King's.

That in the mortar—you call it a gum?
Ah, the brave tree whence such gold oozings come!
And yonder soft phial, the exquisite blue,
Sure to taste sweetly,—is that poison too?

Had I but all of them, thee and thy treasures,
What a wild crowd of invisible pleasures!
To carry pure death in an earring, a casket,
A signet, a fan-mount, a filigree basket!

Soon, at the King's, a mere lozenge to give,
And Pauline should have just thirty minutes to live!
But to light a pastille, and Elise, with her head
And her breast and her arms and her hands, should drop dead!

Quick—is it finished? The color's too grim!
Why not soft like the phial's, enticing and dim?
Let it brighten her drink, let her turn it and stir,
And try it and taste, ere she fix and prefer!

What a drop! She's not little, no minion like me!
That's why she ensnared him: this never will free
The soul from those masculine eyes,—say, "no!"
To that pulse's magnificent come-and-go.

For only last night, as they whispered, I brought
My own eyes to bear on her so, that I thought
Could I keep them one half minute fixed, she would fall
Shrivelled; she fell not; yet this does it all!

Not that I bid you spare her the pain;
Let death be felt and the proof remain:

Brand, burn up, bite into its grace—
He is sure to remember her dying face!

Is it done? Take my mask off! Nay, be not morose;
It kills her, and this prevents seeing it close:
The delicate droplet, my whole fortune's fee!
If it hurts her, beside, can it ever hurt me?

Now, take all my jewels, gorge gold to your fill,
You may kiss me, old man, on my mouth if you will!
But brush this dust off me, lest horror it brings
Ere I know it—next moment I dance at the King's!

Arousing Emotional Responses Through Playacting

Let us use the character from "The Laboratory" to illustrate this exercise. An analysis of the character reveals a complex creature of medieval times, a lady who, in a jealous rage, is plotting the murder of her rival. Her hatred has been intensified by her jealousy of the other woman's beauty and by the mocking attitude of the lovers toward her. You should first try physically to get a feel for the proud and cruel little woman, then go through the lines with overt movements and gestures to show, both her outward appearance and inner state of mind. With the text as your guide, find specific actions: tying on the mask, moving about the shop inspecting the "devil's-smithy," moving toward the old man when speaking to him, sitting and rising, removing jewels, etc. Working this way, you get a clear external image of the speaker and a feel for the character that will be useful later when you only suggest the character.

Arousing Emotional Responses Through Paraphrase

Start with a part in the selection where the emotional response is difficult for you. Talk about it in emotional terms, then read the part immediately. The tone you use in your paraphrase should be transferred, when you read, to the lines in the text. Read "A Deep Sworn Vow" again, supplying these oral paraphrases or additions.

Yet always [yes, it's happened every time!] when I look death in the face
*   [your face—I saw it so clearly]*
When I clamber to the heights of sleep [it was as though I had to reach
*   you],*
Or when I grow excited with wine [how impassioned I was!],
Suddenly [a flash] I meet your face [and I know].

These additions should make your pauses longer and more meaningful and help to convey the emotional overtones. First, as you rehearse, say the additions aloud, and then say them silently between the lines.

Arousing Emotional Response Through Word Coloring

Charles A. Dana, the renowned nineteenth-century journalist, said this about words:

> Words seem to be little vessels that hold in some puzzling fashion exactly what is put into them. You can put tears into them, as though they were so many little buckets; and you can hang smiles along them, like Monday's clothes on the line; or you can starch them with facts and stand them up like a picket fence; but you won't get the tears out unless you first put them in.

If you have trouble coloring words with their emotional meanings, take the time to consider them separately. In rehearsal, exaggerate the feeling in the words: let the happy words laugh, the sad words cry, the sarcastic words mock, and the angry words pierce.

In the following poem color the words and sounds to suggest the surf, tow, and wind.

Foreboding[6]
Don Blanding

. . . zoom . . . zoom . . . zoom . . .
that is the sound of the surf . . .
as the great green waves rush up the shore
with a murderous thundering ominous roar
and leave drowned dead things at my door
. . . zoom . . . zoom . . . zoom

. . . suish . . . suish . . . shui-s-h . . .
that is the sound of the tow
as it slips and slithers along the sands
with terrible groping formless hands
that drag at my beach house where it stands
. . . suish . . . shis-s-h . . . shuis-s-sh . . .

eeeie . . . eeeie-u-u . . . eeeie-u-u . . .
that is the sound of the wind
it wails like a banshee adrift in space
and threatens to scatter my driftwood place
it slashes the sand like spite in my face
eeie-u-u-u . . . eeie-u-u . . . eeie-u-u . . .

Surf . . . tow . . . or the wind . . .
which of the three will it be . . .
the surf . . . will it bludgeon and beat me dead
or the tow drag me down to its ocean bed . . .
or the wind wail a dirge above my head . . .
zoom . . . suis-s-h . . . eeie-u-u . . .

---

[6] Reprinted by permission of Dodd, Mead and Company, Inc. from *Vagabond's House* by Don Blanding. Copyright 1928, 1956 by Don Blanding.

Chapter 5

Guides for Visual Communication

Earlier in the book, the accepted mode of communication in the 20th century was characterized as natural, conversational, and emotionally underplayed.

Change in Accepted Mode of Communication

Now, in the last quarter of the century, aware of what up-tight people we Americans have become, we are removing many of the restraints on our emotions. Perhaps we are too close to dramatic and disturbing changes to make objective judgments about where this is leading us, yet we are aware of some healthy signs. We are airing our problems, attempting to discover ourselves, and, more important, we are communicating more openly and honestly. In the last few decades, our poets have also been writing about feelings everyone knows and events of a kind everyone has experienced.

How have these changes affected our manner of communicating? More specifically, how have the changes affected visual communication?

Stress on Nonverbal Communication

For some time we have been aware of the stress given to nonverbal communication. Encounter groups began springing up where people could free themselves to make contact with others, to play together, to touch each other, and to awaken dulled senses. Kinesics, the study of body movement in relation to speech, has made us more aware of emotional and empathetic responses and how all movement extends the spoken language.

Movement classes in college theatre departments have been filled to overflowing; teachers have been in demand to lead movement workshops; and scores of books have appeared, mapping ways to free one's body and express one's feelings creatively. Yes, at every turn we have been made aware that more visible expression of emotion is becoming the accepted mode. Modern writers, adhering to the same philosophy, seem to call for this style of oral communication; the interpreter's oral-visual style is always affected by the literary style of the material at hand.

Visual Style and Literary Style

The interpreter's body should aid in expressing the style and tone of the writing. To realize how great are the extremes in the tone of literary texts, we need only to contrast the bigger-than-life characters of a Greek tragedy to the weak, disillusioned characters often found in the modern realistic play. Obviously communication of such widely varying literary tones needs to be expressed in the stance and body rhythm of both the actor, who is representing the character, and the oral interpreter, who is presenting the speakers. The actor creating a role and the interpreter suggesting many roles must see the literary text in its historical environment and give physical expression to the appropriate cultural attitudes of the author.

Aesthetic Principles

Body techniques should not be obvious as techniques: posture, movement, and gestures should seem natural and effortless, as though they result from a spontaneous response to the meaning of the material.

Physical Response

We are aware that a close relationship exists among body response, vocal response, and the mind: what one sees appears to have a direct influence upon what one hears, and vice versa; all reflect the interpreter's state of mind. It seems, then, that expression of meaning is a fusion of three processes, involving mind, body, and voice. But these processes cannot be separated, for they happen at the same time and each is dependent upon the others. We explain them separately only for the sake of clarity. We offer some guides for possible improvement in visual expression in this chapter.

You should give attention to three aspects of your physical response: your established rapport with the audience by means of general poise, your use of audience contact, and your physical reaction to the meaning.

Poise

Poise is a synthesis of many things; it is acquired through good mental attitude, physical balance, and muscle tone.

Mental Attitude. What are you thinking as you face your class audience for the first time? The assignment should focus on sharing literary meanings and your study preparation should have generated a real desire to share your discoveries with your classmates. In this case, your attitude might be "Let's look at this selection together; then we can talk about its meanings." This way, no time is left for self-consciousness or worry about the hows of reading aloud.

Interest and enjoyment come from actively discovering literature more readily than from passively being entertained by it. If and when you read literature for an audience assembled to be entertained, you will be less tense if you think about them instead of yourself. A sincere interest in the audience, a pleasant expression, and an attitude of enjoying the selection with the audience can control your fears and convey a natural and friendly impression. But there are other things that you may find helpful. Attention to appropriate dress will make you feel at ease. Of course, nothing contributes more to inner calm than good preparation. Sometimes experience is all that is needed for building confidence. If you resist the impulse to express dissatisfaction with a performance, in the form of facial distortions or apologetic comments, you will gradually gain self-assurance. You will find that "nothing succeeds like success"; one successful performance and you are off with new confidence.

Exercises for freeing the body to respond to the text and for sharpening your awareness of the interplay between mind and body can be helpful in gaining poise and presence. A selection of such exercises is given at the end of this chapter.

Physical Balance. The right mental attitude can sometimes produce good posture with correct physical balance, but this is not always the case. Poor posture and other personal mannerisms often have to be brought under control by more direct means. A bad habit must first be recognized and then gradually eliminated through conscious attention in practice periods.

To speak of good posture means the body is in a state of balance, with head, shoulders, torso, legs, and feet in alignment, one over the other. There are no set rules; the best posture is that which does not draw attention and allows the body to respond easily to thought. The body should appear relaxed, but there should be enough muscle tension to give an impression and look of aliveness. Stand tall, to your full height, with your head up (not forward or back) and comfortably balanced. Do not pull the shoulders back; this makes the head come forward and the body tense. Keep the shoulders balanced and the spine straight. The weight of the body should be centered on the balls of the feet (weight on the heels gives the impression of withdrawal), or the weight may be put chiefly on the ball of the forward foot, with the other foot helping to maintain good balance. Find the position that is most comfortable for you, without being careless or too rigid. The feet should give secure support for your body weight.

The reading stand invites you to lean on it; don't. Use the stand lightly. If you stand too close to it, you give the impression of insecurity; if you stand too far away from it, with your hands behind your back, you give an audience the uncomfortable feeling that you may lose your place in the manuscript. When your hands rest lightly on the stand your body is in a balanced position that permits change, you and your audience will be much more comfortable. A reading stand is never a barrier if you use it correctly.

Muscle Tone. The body "talks" by slight changes in muscle tone: we can sense a person's anger or fear by the tension in his or her body; when a person is in a quiet, peaceful frame of mind, we can sense this by the muscular relaxation. Every change that takes place in the muscles is felt by the interpreter, and the feeling is projected to an audience. A vital, interested attitude of mind is the best means to bring about muscle tension that expresses the interpreter's aliveness and poise. Remember there is never a time for rest when you are thinking; your body, reflecting the continual activity of your mind, reveals the development of ideas.

Audience Contact

The oral interpreter must look at the script and still maintain eye contact with the audience. The solution to this is to be familiar with the material and to learn to read extended phrases at a glance, looking for the next phrase in the script while talking, instead of during a pause. In some cases, you may find it advantageous to have parts of the material memorized. However, if you do this, you should be careful not to lose contact with the script.

Open Stance. The eyes do more to establish communication with listeners than any other feature. Your eye focus varies according to the type of material you are reading and according to the role of the audience. Generally, when reading expository prose, you want to have direct eye contact with the members of the audience. You are talking to them, so you look at them. This is called the open stance.

Closed Stance. As the author's narrator, you let your eyes move naturally out and upward to an imagined area over the heads of your listeners. When you suggest characters engaged in a dialogue, you imagine the scene out front and withdraw from the audience completely. (See discussion of off-stage focus and Figures 14-1 and 14-2, Chapter 14.) This is the closed stance. The role assigned the people in the audience directs your relationship with them and determines your eye focus. The question of shifting eye focus becomes complicated in reading prose fiction, which may contain description, exposition, reflection, summary, and both direct and indirect address. This can best be explained through the illustrations to be found in Chapter 7.

Physical Responses to Literary Meanings

Overt Action. No manner of physical action is best for every occasion, for every audience, for every reader, every time. Each person has his or her own individual style. One interpreter may use broad gestures and somehow stay within the bounds of good taste, while another, using the same gestures, appears ridiculous. One person may use overt action and be effective; another may use no apparent action and be equally effective.

When we say that interpretive reading is a suggestive art, we do not mean that this eliminates movement and gestures. Physical response must be used by the interpreter with as much subtlety and variety as vocal response. But how does one suggest through overt action?

Reading imposes restrictions upon how much overt movement one can use, and a reading stand, with the script, also limits motion. Physical responses therefore differ from those used in acting. An actor lets us see an action in full; an interpreter only suggests the action by appropriate—but modified—gestures or other movements. Suppose a character in a play performs the actions of drinking a toast at a dinner party. The actor would perform the complete action with a real, filled glass. The interpreter would not have a glass, nor would you pantomime the full action of lifting, drinking from, and lowering the glass. How would you suggest the action? As you imagine the glass and the action of lifting it, you raise one hand slightly, perhaps no more than a few inches off the reading stand. With the hand in this position, you deliver the toast; then, with another slight upward movement of the hand, you pause, imagining the actual drinking action, and then lower your hand to the stand. With these small movements and the right facial responses, you enable the audience to join in envisioning the full action.

The language of the body is as expressive as that of speech. The face and eyes are perhaps most important for the interpreter, but the hands, fingers, shoulders, feet, in countless ways and combinations, are all capable of expressing the most subtle and varied meanings. But remember that only for laughs, as a clown, for example, would you use an energetic hand gesture while keeping other parts of the body immobile. The whole body must always be involved in a visual response.

Covert Action. Covert action is simply a change in the muscle tone of the body. We said earlier that the poised body should have the right degree of muscle tension to convey an impression of alertness. The interpreter finds that the material brings about changes in muscle tension; changes in attitude and emotions within a selection call for changes in body tensions. Anger tightens the muscles; love relaxes them. Covert action is of special value to the interpreter, because it is an effective means of outwardly suggesting the interior changes produced by the material.

Exercises for Gaining Poise

1   This exercise is for body relaxation and alignment. While standing, gradually tense the larger muscles of your body, and then, beginning with your head, relax each part of your upper body completely, until you feel limp, with the upper part of your body hanging over. Gradually come back to an upright position. Beginning at the base of your spine, try to feel your spine straightening, and as your upper body lifts, feel your shoulders resting easily and your head balancing comfortably on top of the spinal column.

2   This psychological exercise will help you keep good balance and the muscle tone, to suggest aliveness and presence.

Imagine vitality coming up from the earth into your feet. Feel the energy concentrated in the balls of your feet. Let this energy make you feel confident and in command. Now imagine this energy traveling up through your body, vitalizing your legs and uniting in your chest. Feel an expansion in your torso; feel this energy charge your body.

Exercises for Toneup

Next tone up the body with some movement exercises. These have been selected from warm-ups created by Nancy King, a teacher of theatre movement at the University of Delaware, who says:

> "The warm-ups . . . not only tone the body, but also stimulate creative movement, help establish good group rapport and facilitate proper working conditions for class, rehearsal, and performance."

1   *Stretching.*

> "Start out by stretching or extending your whole body in every direction, using your arms, head, legs, fingers and toes. Move around the room; do not confine yourself to one small area. . . . If you come into contact with someone who is stretching, try stretching to them without relaxing your energy. What kinds of stretch are possible when you work with a partner or two? How can you stretch when you do not use your arms? What kinds of feelings (if any) do you get when you stretch? . . . "

2   *Swinging.*

> "A swing is a loose, easy, relaxed movement that starts with energy, continues because of the momentum of the body, and ends with energy. A swing must have a free-flowing ease about it. . . . Try swinging various parts of your body separately: head, shoulders, arms, wrists, waist (upper body), and legs. Can you swing using your whole body? . . . Pay attention to your own rhythm. Is it full and expansive or is it tight and cramped? . . . "

3   *Striking.*

> "Striking movements use any part of the body and are short, sharp, clearly defined actions that are the opposite of stretching, languid movements. . . If you keep your breathing steady, you will find you are less likely to become tense. Remember to keep the movement short, sharp, and crisp. How does working with another person affect you?"

4   *Shaking.*

> "Shaking, or vibrating, movements are the hardest to do because they require the greatest muscle control. Shaking movements resemble shivering because they are tiny, quick, and constant. Try shaking in various positions, starting with isolated movements of the arm, leg, or face. . . "[1]

Exercises for Overt and Covert Actions

1   Recall an emotional experience and let your body muscles respond to it completely. Be sure that the mental response comes first, motivating the

---

[1] Lines from *Theatre Movement: The Actor and His Space* by Nancy King. Reprinted by permission of the author.

change in muscle tone. In each recall, concentrate on remembering the details and the atmosphere created by your experience.

Recall an experience that made you feel very angry, afraid, happy, elated, determined, or sympathetic.

2 Try to sense the difference between performing a specific action and suggesting it.

a As you say the italicized words, perform the action:

I am *turning around and around.*

I am *pulling you up from your seat.*

I am *trying to lift this table.*

I am *lifting this book.*

b Repeat the sentences, using only small gestures and covert action to suggest the actions.

3 Read the following passages aloud, responding to the imagery and emotions with varying degrees of covert and overt action.

a Respond to the exuberance of a young man who has suddenly discovered the meaning of life—his life:

> His heart trembled; his breath came faster and a wild spirit passed over his limbs as though he were soaring sunward. His heart trembled in an ecstasy of fear and his soul was in flight . . .
> . . . His throat ached with a desire to cry aloud, the cry of a hawk or eagle on high, to cry piercingly of his deliverance to the winds.[2]

b Respond to the varied images of "Circus at Dawn."

> . . . The great iron-grey horses, four and six to a team, would be plodding along the road of thick white dust to a rattling of chains and traces and the harsh cries of their drivers. The men would drive the animals to the river which flowed by beyond the tracks, and water them; and as first light came one could see the elephants wallowing in the familiar river and the big horses going slowly and carefully down to drink.
> Then, on the circus ground, the tents were going up already with the magic speed of dreams. All over the place (which was near the tracks and the only space of flat land in the town that was big enough to hold a circus) there would be this fierce, savagely hurried, and yet orderly confusion. Great flares of gaseous circus light would blaze down on the seared and battered faces of the circus toughs as, with the rhythmic precision of a single animal—a human riveting machine— they swung their sledges at the stakes, driving a stake into the earth with the incredible instancy of accelerated figures in a motion picture. And everywhere, as light came, and the sun appeared, there would be a scene of magic, order, and of violence.[3]

4 Read one of the following passages aloud, giving attention to appropriate overt gestures:

a The "Nose Speech" from *Cyrano de Bergerac* in Chapter 6.

b This passage from Act I, scene 2 of *The Merchant of Venice,* in which Portia is telling her waiting-woman, Nerissa, how she feels about each of her suitors:

---

[2] Lines from *A Portrait of the Artist as a Young Man* by James Joyce, copyright, 1944. Reprinted by permission of Viking Press.

[3] Lines from "Circus at Dawn" by Thomas Wolfe in *From Death to Morning,* copyright 1935. Reprinted by permission of Charles Scribner's Sons.

Nerissa. First, there is the Neapolitan prince.

Portia. Ay, that's a colt indeed, for he doth nothing but talk of his horse; and he makes it a great appropriation to his own good parts, that he can shoe him himself. I am much afeard my lady his mother played false with a smith.

Nerissa. Then is there the County Palatine.

Portia. He doth nothing but frown; as who should say, 'if you will not have me, choose:' he hears merry tales, and smiles not: I fear he will prove the weeping philosopher when he grows old, being so full of unmannerly sadness in his youth. I had rather be married to a death's-head with a bone in his mouth than to either of these. God defend me from these two!

. . .

Nerissa. What say you, then, to Falconbridge, the young baron of England?

Portia. . . . He is a proper man's picture; but, alas, who can converse with a dumb-show? How oddly he is suited! I think he bought his doublet in Italy, his round hose in France, his bonnet in Germany, and his behaviour everywhere.

5   Give the different kinds of response each stanza calls for:

Dream Variations[4]
Langston Hughes

To fling my arms wide
In some place of the sun,
To whirl and to dance
Till the white day is done.
Then rest at cool evening
Beneath a tall tree
While night comes on gently,
*   Dark like me—*
That is my dream!

To fling my arms wide
In the face of the sun,
Dance! Whirl! Whirl!
Till the quick day is done.
Rest at pale evening . . .
A tall, slim tree . . .
Night coming tenderly
Black like me.

6   Suggest the actions called for in these passages:

     a In Act IV, scene 3 of *Romeo and Juliet,* Juliet picks up the vial and dagger:

My dismal scene I needs must act alone.
Come, vial.

---

[4] Copyright 1926 by Alfred A. Knopf, Inc. and renewed 1954 by Langston Hughes. Reprinted from *Selected Poems,* by Langston Hughes, by permission of the publisher.

What if this mixture do not work at all?
Shall I be married then to-morrow morning?
No, no; this shall forbid it. Lie thou there.

b Othello takes Iago by the throat (*Othello*, Act III, scene 3):

Villain, be sure thou prove my love a whore;
[taking him by the throat]
Be sure of it; give me the ocular proof;
Or, by the worth of man's eternal soul,
Thou hadst been better have been born a dog
Than answer my wak'd wrath!

7   In two of the following passages, suggest each character by appropriate posture, movement, and gesture. Use a reading stand.

a In John Steinbeck's novel *Sweet Thursday*, a middle-aged woman gives advice to a younger girl:

If I was your age with your face and shape and what I know, there wouldn't be no man in the world could get away! I got the know-how—but that's all I got. Oh well! I'm going to tell you a few thousand things, Suzy, that if you would listen you'd get anything you want. But hell, you won't listen! Nobody listens, and when they learn the hard way it's too late. . . just remember a lot of things: first, you got to remember you're Suzy and you ain't nobody else but Suzy. Then you got to remember that Suzy is a good thing—a real valuable thing—and there ain't nothing like it in the world. It don't do no harm just to say that to yourself. Then, when you got that, remember that there's one hell of a lot Suzy don't know. Only way she can find out is if she sees it, or reads it, or asks it. Most people don't look at nothing but themselves, and that's a rat race.[5]

b Katharina in Act III, scene 2 of *The Taming of the Shrew* storms at Petruchio:

Nay, then,
Do what thou canst, I will not go to-day;
No, nor to-morrow, not till I please myself.
The door is open, sir; there lies your way.

c In Thomas Wolfe's novel *Of Time and the River* Uncle Bascom gives his view of woman's never-changing character:

He paused, stared deliberately across his hands, and in a moment repeated, slowly and distinctly: "The woman gave me of the tree and I did eat. Ah! that's it! There my boy, you have it! There, in a nutshell, you have the work for which they are best fitted." And he turned upon his nephew suddenly with a blaze of passion, his voice husky and tremulous from the stress of emotion. "The Tempter! The Bringer of Forbidden Fruit! The devil's ambassador! Since the beginning of time that has been their office—to madden the brain, to turn man's spirit from its highest purposes, to corrupt, to seduce, and to destroy! To creep and crawl, to intrude into the lonely places of man's heart and brain, to wind herself into the core of his most

---

[5] From *Sweet Thursday* by John Steinbeck. Copyright 1954 by John Steinbeck. Reprinted by permission of The Viking Press, Inc.

secret life as a worm eats its way into a healthy fruit—to do all this with the guile of a serpent, the cunning of a fox—that, my boy, is what she's here for . . . and she'll never change!" and, lowering his voice to an ominous and foreboding whisper, he said mysteriously, "Beware! Beware! Do not be deceived!"[6]

e In Eugene O'Neill's play *Long Day's Journey into Night,* Mary Tyrone, the wife and mother, is a drug addict. In this scene, she has been playing the piano; she examines her hands as she wanders in.

> I play so badly now. I'm all out of practice. Sister Theresa will give me a dreadful scolding. She'll tell me it isn't fair to my father when he spends so much money for extra lessons. She's quite right, it isn't fair, when he's so good and generous, and so proud of me. I'll practice every day from now on. But something horrible has happened to my hands. The fingers have gotten so stiff. The knuckles are all swollen. They're so ugly. . . . Let me see. What did I come here to find? . . . I'm always dreaming and forgetting.[7]

---

[6] Lines from *Of Time and the River* by Thomas Wolfe, copyright, 1963. Reprinted by permission of Charles Scribner's Sons.

[7] Reprinted by permission of Carlotta Monterey O'Neill and Yale University Press from *Long Day's Journey into Night,* by Eugene O'Neill. Copyright 1955 by Carlotta Monterey O'Neill.

Chapter 6

Guides for Vocal Communication

The voice mechanism has two separate functions: producing tone and producing words. The two functions are closely related and, at the same time, distinct. We use vocal tone instinctively. Speech is an acquired habit. The child cries instinctively, but he or she must learn certain movements of the tongue and lips before setting up the habits for producing words. Voice is the tone produced, which is dependent upon the vocal instrument the speaker was born with. This tone can be improved only to some extent by the use of good technique. The utterance of words, however, can be greatly altered by the knowledge and practice of correct speech sound production. Every voice is basically different from every other voice, but whole regional groups have certain identical speech habits. New habits (correct, or more pleasant, speech sounds) can replace old speech habits, but this takes interest and much time and effort on the learner's part. The professional actor is required to learn stage speech and to take every possible step toward perfecting the voice. These demands are not made in everyday life, but it is generally agreed that improvement of unpleasant voices and careless speech is an urgent need. Certainly, the sharing of literature for the pleasure of others demands a pleasing tone and clear, distinct speech.

To offer a complete program for voice and speech improvement is beyond the scope of this text. Our intention in this chapter is to lead you to a new awareness of voice and speech controls: to help you gain a feel for the proper use of the human voice mechanism, more clearly understand the techniques of projecting logical meaning, and to understand ways of controlling the variable attributes of voice—volume, pitch, quality, and timing.

Voice Production

There are three distinct factors that control voice production: the motor, the vibrator, and the resonator. A man-made instrument, such as the violin or trombone, may be compared to the human vocal instrument, since these same factors function in both.

The motor is the part of the instrument that supplies the force or energy that produces the tone. In the case of the violin, the motor is the arm movements of the violinist, which supply the energy; the trombone player supplies breath; the human voice uses the air exhaled from the lungs to initiate the sound. The exhaled air may leave the lungs as it entered them, as breath, or it may be vocalized in the larynx.

The vibrator is the part of the instrument to which this energy is transferred: the strings of the violin, the mouth plates of the trombone, or the vocal cords of a person. The vocal cords cause the exhaled air to be cut up into a series of waves which set up the fundamental tone and overtones. These sound waves are inherently weak and require additional means to build up the sound into full tones.

The resonator amplifies the fundamental tone and overtones: the wooden box beneath the strings of the violin; the pipe of the trombone; the mouth, the pharynx, and the nose cavities of human beings.

Control of Breathing

When words must be heard at a distance or when a long phrase is attempted in reading, more breath is needed than in normal conversation. The untrained speaker invariably obtains this additional breath incorrectly and is unable to control the outgoing breath effectively, with a consequent bad effect on tone quality. Practice procedures for correct breathing should focus on three objectives: relaxation, adequate breath supply, and good breath control.

Relaxation. Correct breathing can only be obtained in a well-poised body free of muscular tensions; no exercise can be helpful when the body is tense. First, relaxation of the large muscles controlling posture should be achieved, in order to bring about relaxation in the smaller muscles concerned with voice production. It is always wise to begin voice exercises with relaxation exercises.

Breath supply. In breathing for life, the cycle is a reflex consisting of a slow intake of breath and a quick release followed by a pause; for speech, this is reversed: the outgoing breath takes longer than the intake, and the pauses are long or short, according to the demands of the material being spoken. This means that through exercises you must become conscious of a change in the timing of your movements in breathing. First, it is important that the intake of breath, the supply, be sufficient. To insure this, you should become aware of proper control of the diaphragm and the abdominal muscles.

Breath control. The next step is toward developing control of the outgoing breath. Through exercises you learn how to quicken inhalation and slow exhalation.

Exercises for Breathing

1   For Relaxation

a Stretch and yawn. The stretching should be intense, but the yawning relaxed.

b Sit very erect and rigid. Tense your body and then, beginning with your head, relax each part of the body. Let your head fall forward and your arms dangle loosely.

c Stand and tense the muscles of your whole body; then, beginning with your head, relax each part of your body until you feel like a loose-jointed puppet.

d Apply tension followed by relaxation to your head, face, jaw, lips, tongue, palate, and throat.

2   For Inhalation

Place the fingers of each hand on your ribs, just in front of the armpits, with the thumbs pointing toward your spine. As air is drawn in, feel how your ribs move outwards. Start the movement at the back, where the thumbs are placed. Keep trying this until you sense this lateral movement of the ribs. The sensation should not be of ribs moving outward in front, but instead, that the back widens.

3   For Abdominal Breathing

Lie on the floor with a book on your abdomen. Breathe in and out, noticing the outward movement of your abdominal wall in front, on the sides, and in back, as you inhale. Watching the book rise and fall with the movement of your muscles will increase your awareness of abdominal breathing. Next, stand and take a deep breath, holding for a count of 3, feeling the tension of your muscles, then release it, vocalizing "ah."

4   For Controlling Exhalation

a Using abdominal breathing, sense your control of exhalation: take a deep breath, hold for a count of 3, then exhale, vocalizing "ah," forcing the air out gradually.

b Now, try to quicken inhalation and to slow exhalation. Gradually increase the exhalation count to 15.

in-2-3   hold-2-3   out-2-3

in-2-3   hold-2-3   out-2-3-4

in-2-3   hold-2-3   out-2-3-4-5

5   For Controlled Breathing in Reading

The transition from breathing as a technical exercise to using controlled breath in reading aloud should be made gradually. Consciously using lateral breathing and controlling the outgoing breath, test your control by breathing only where the marks // indicate:

> This is the house that Jack built //
> This is the malt that lay in the house that Jack built//
> This is the rat that ate the malt that lay in the house that Jack built//
> This is the cat that caught the rat that ate the malt that lay in the house
>   that Jack built//

*This is the dog that worried the cat that caught the rat that ate the malt
that lay in the house that Jack built //*
*This is the cow with the crumpled horn that tossed the dog that worried
the cat that caught the rat that ate the malt that lay in the house that
Jack built //*

Control of Phonation

When a person speaks, the pressure of the exhaled breath forces the vocal
cords in the larynx to vibrate, producing the fundamental sound. The
degree of tension in the vocal cords determines the rate of this vibrating
action and thus the pitch of the voice. A high degree of tension produces
rapid vibration and a high pitch; less tension produces slower vibration
and a lower pitch. The length and thickness of the vocal cords determine
the voice type; the vocal cords of men are generally longer and thicker than
those of women, which accounts for the difference between the voices of
men and women.

The vibrating action in the larynx is instinctive. When we desire to
speak or sing, the vocal cords come into the closed position. We should
make no attempt to feel the movements in the larynx; in fact, there is little
direct control we can or should exert over this part of the voice mechanism.
Nature has provided the vocal cords, and structural differences cannot be
changed. The best control that can be obtained is relaxation in the throat
area. Working for throat resonance is perhaps the best exercise for producing a clear, free fundamental tone.

Exercises for Control of Phonation

1   For Open Throat
       a Take the open, free position for the "ah": let your jaw drop and
open your teeth at least one inch apart, your tongue flat on the floor of the
mouth, with the tip touching the inner surface of your lower front teeth and
your soft palate raised. Start, but do not complete, a yawn. Repeat this until
you are able to feel the openness without the actual yawn. Memorize this
feeling. Practice until you can easily produce this open throat.
       b Maintaining this relaxation and openness,
           whisper HAH   HO   WHO, then vocalize
           whisper WHO   AM   I, then vocalize
Maintaining this relaxation and openness and directing the sounds forward to the lips, read aloud:

> Most men want poise.
> "God of our Fathers known of old."
> "Roll on, thou deep and dark blue ocean, roll."
> "Double, double toil and trouble;
> Fire burn and cauldron bubble."

Control of Resonance

The resonator consists of three principal cavities; the pharynx (throat), the
mouth, and the nose. These reinforce and amplify the fundamental tone

and the overtones produced in the larynx. The tone quality of a voice is at its best when each part of the resonator contributes more or less equally to produce the total effect of the general voice quality.

Exercises for Resonance

2   For Open Throat: Relax your head by rotating it; relax your throat by yawning; whisper HAH   HO   WHO, then vocalize. Sensing open throat and tone support, say:

> *Blow the man down, blow the man down,*
> *If he be white man, black man or brown,*
> *Weigh, heigh, blow the man down.*

3   For Nasal Resonance:
         a Inhale, and with your mouth closed, expel an [m] sound: hum. Think of your head as a dome and fill it with tone: Zoom, Zoom, Zoom, Boom, Boom.
         b Pause before the final nasal; gradually shorten the pause, making sure that no nasality is heard until the final nasal.

| ti . . . me | ti . . . me | time |
| ni . . . ne | ni . . . ne | nine |

Articulate the following with prolonged nasal resonance, but avoid nasalization of vowels and diphthongs:

> Ninety-nine times.
> Zoom went the sound.
> Advancing and prancing and glancing and dancing,
> Recoiling, turmoiling, and toiling, and boiling.
> The mountains were said to be in labor, and uttered most dreadful groans.
> People came together far and near to see what birth would be produced; and after they waited a considerable time in expectation out crept a mouse.
>
> (Aesop's Fables)

Word Production

The pronunciation of words varies in different localities, primarily because of differences in the habits of forming separate speech sounds and the connecting and combining of the sounds. This raises the question of standard pronunciation. What are the standards for speech utterance? Generally speaking, your standard should be the speech used by effective and cultured speakers in your own area. Each region in America has its own peculiar sound characteristics that give a natural flavor to each individual's speech, and when these characteristics do not call *undue* attention to themselves, they should be retained. If you keep the cultivated speech of your own locality as a standard, your speech will not draw attention to the speaking itself and it will be free of undue provincialism and carelessness.

Production of Speech Sounds

The different vowel sounds are determined principally by how the tongue changes the size and shape of the mouth resonator. For production of good, clear vowels, you need good breath support, your mouth and throat passages open and free of tension, flexible use of the articulators (primarily the tongue, lips, and jaw), and direction of the tone toward the front of the mouth.

When the outgoing breath stream is diverted, obstructed, or stopped in the mouth by the articulators, the resulting sound is a consonant. Vowels should be produced without muscular force or tension in the resonator; the clarity of consonants, on the other hand, depends upon how energetically the articulators move.

The exercises which follow serve as a check for a few troublesome vowel and diphthong sounds. You may wish to consult a voice and diction textbook for full coverage of sound production. Good references are listed in the Suggested Readings at the end of this chapter.

Exercises for Vowel and Diphthong Sounds

1 Vowels:

ĕ [ɛ] This vowel is heard in led, said, spread. Avoid substituting i for e, making get become git and pen become pin. Avoid prolonging the sound into a drawl, making fell become fe-uhl. Practice: end, enter, bury, ten, attention. Get the ten best-dressed men.

ă [æ] This vowel is heard in glad, add, sat. Avoid diphthongization or tension with nasality; keep the sound soft. Practice: man, land, campus, random. His mad fancy and random facts anger Ann.

ä [a] This vowel is heard in calm, farm, father. Don't be tense on this one; it is the most open of the sounds. Practice: artist, car, disarm. Don is fond of the college calm.

2 Diphthongs (compound vowel sounds; in producing, the voice glides from one vowel to another without a break in phonation, but the first of the two vowel components is always stressed.

ī [aɪ] This diphthong is heard in sky, buy, high. Don't nasalize it or fail to make it compound. Practice: time, lifelike, inviting, aisle. The wise use others' hindsight for their own foresight.

au [aʊ] Diphthong heard in cloud, now, about. Don't nasalize it or make it sound affected. Practice: county, owl, proud, bound. How now, brown cow?

er [ɛɚ] Diphthong heard in their, fair, pear. Sound the two elements. Practice: air, care, their, declare. Woman despair for the care of their hair.

Flow of Speech

In connected speech, speech sounds influence each other. Dropping or changing sounds in connected speech is not always careless speech; this may be an accepted pronunciation. Overprecise, pedantic speech interferes with smooth, varied, and natural speech. We will consider three ways to acquire a more natural conversational flow of speech: weak forms, assimilation, and clarity in a more rapid speech flow.

Weak Forms An outstanding characteristic of American speech is the general use of weak vowels in the unstressed syllables of polysyllabic words. For example, in the word "city" the *y* sound [i] is reduced to a weaker one, *ĭ* [ɪ]; in such words as "add*e*d," "nos*e*s," and "beautiful," *ĭ* [ɪ] replaces *ĕ* [ɛ] or *ē* [i] in the unstressed syllables. The neutral [ə] is, of course, the vowel most frequently used to replace another vowel in unstressed syllables. For example, "*to*day" becomes təday, "wom*a*n" becomes womən, "*co*nclude" becomes cənclude, and "pit*ifu*l" becomes pitifəl or pitəfəl.

Function words, i.e. articles, pronouns, prepositions, conjunctions, and auxiliaries, except when they are stressed for some special reason, generally use weak vowels in connected speech: "the" becomes [ðə] and "a" becomes [ə].

Assimilation *Assimilation* is the phonetic change of a sound by a neighboring sound. The most frequent such change is the omission of sound when two or more consonants are juxtaposed. Standard pronunciation of many words is different from the spelling. Thus, the italicized sounds are omitted from Chris*t*mas, han*d*kerchief, han*d*some, sof*t*en, of*t*en. In the pronunciation of "clothes," the *th* is dropped because it is too difficult to say [ð] before [z].

In conversation the flow of speech brings natural assimilative changes in phrases. We say "bread 'n' butter" and "cup 'n' saucer," and these simplifications are acceptable. Not all the assimilation that we hear is acceptable, however. There is a tendency for many people to nasalize a vowel before or after a nasal consonant and thus to nasalize the entire word: penny, nice, my, mountain, man, known. In careless speech we hear many omissions, substitutions, and additions which are not acceptable: "acts" becomes "axe," "fifths" becomes "fifs," "texts" becomes "teks," "hunting" becomes "huntin," "picture" becomes "pitcher," "length" and "strength" become "lenth" and "strenth," "I'll meet you" becomes "I'll meecha," "Would you mind?" becomes "Woojamine?"

Clarity in Rapid Speech Flow. A common handicap in interpretation is the inability of students to articulate sounds rapidly and still be understood. Listen to recordings by professional readers such as John Gielgud, Judith Anderson, and others, and note their ability to articulate distinctly and rapidly.

Exercises for Assimilation and Rapid Speech Flow

1   Pronounce words and phrases that point up use of weak forms and assimilation: president, Detroit, precedence, precedents, theatre, accident, civil, blossom, radiance, better, labor, murmur, ham and eggs, bread and butter, the girl and the boy, hot dog, red deer, black gloves, sit tight, glad day.

2   Stimulate movement of your lips and tongue:

| PPPPPP PAH | PPPPPP PAY | PPPPPP PEE |
| BBBBBB BAH | BBBBBB BAY | BBBBBB BEE |

TTTTT TAH   TTTTT TAY   TTTTT TEE
DDDDDD DAH   DDDDDD DAY   DDDDDD DEE

3   Exaggerating your lip movement, draw your lips back on the *ee* sound and, pushing your lips forward into a spout on the *oo* sound, whisper, then vocalize: *ee-oo-ee-oo.* Repeat (whispering, then vocalizing with the suggested articulation): *pe-pi-po-pum; te-ti-toe-tum; ve-vi-vo-vum; be-bi-bo-bum; de-di-do-dum; ze-zi-zo-zum.*

4   Now in some of Gilbert and Sullivan's songs and other rhythm verses, let the rhythm and swing voice the spirit of the verse. Keep your articulation crisp as you increase the pace:

> *Conceive me if you can,*
> *A crochety cracked young man,*
> *An ultra-poetical,*
> *Super-aesthetical,*
> *Out-of-the-way young man.*

> *You'd find the bread improved, I think,*
> *By getting better flour;*
> *And have you anything to drink*
> *That looks a little less like ink,*
> *And isn't quite so sour?*

> *To sit in solemn silence in a dull, dark dock*
> *In a pestilential prison, with a life-long lock,*
> *Awaiting the sensation of a short, sharp shock,*
> *From a cheap and chippy chopper on a big, black block.*

> *Beat! Beat! Beat! Beat!*
> *Beat the drum and march along*
> *To the thump of the drum and the toot of the fife*
> *To the thump thump thump of the drum and the toot toot toot of the fife*
> *To the thump-thumpety-thump of the big bass drum and the tootlety-*
>   *toot-toot of the fife.*[1]

> M   *Whistle, whistle, old wife, and you'll get a hen.*
> W   *I wouldn't whistle, said the wife, if you could give me ten!*
> M   *Whistle, whistle, old wife, and you'll get a cock.*
> W   *I wouldn't whistle, said the wife, if you gave me a flock!*
> M   *Whistle, whistle, old wife, and you'll get a coo.*
> W   *I wouldn't whistle, said the wife, if you could give me two!*
> M   *Whistle, whistle, old wife, and you'll get a gown.*
> W   *I wouldn't whistle, said the wife, for the best one in town!*
> M   *Whistle, whistle, old wife, and you'll get a man.*
> W   *Wheeple, whauple, said the wife, I'll whistle if I can!*

Vocal Techniques for Projecting Logical Meaning

To convey logical meaning when reading aloud, your mind perceives the writer's ideas in word groups as your voice phrases the words. At the same

---

[1] Martin Cobin. *Theory and Teaching of Interpretation.*

time, something else is going on; inflectional toning, emphasis, and subordination modify the meaning of thought groups. And all this appears to happen at the same time; these activities are fused into one.

What do we do in good conversational speech? We communicate ideas by blending words together into idea groups. We do not say She/is/coming/ today, but rather Sheiscomingtoday. In saying an idea group, we tend to blend one word into the next in a continuance of sound, and we pause at the end of each blended word group: Sheiscomingtoday/at noon. We use a falling or rising inflection at the end of these blended word groups to suggest a closed or continuing thought: She'scoming (falling); She'scoming (rising)/ifatallpossible (rising)/today (falling). We emphasize the words that carry the intended meaning, and we subordinate the others: She's coming*today* (today, not tomorrow); *She's*comingtoday (she, not he).

These observations point to three techniques we will consider in more detail: grouping, inflectional endings, and emphasis and subordination. The proper control of these three factors will result in a natural conversational pattern.

Grouping (Or Phrasing)

This technique is closely allied to analysis for understanding. People who understand the sense of what they are reading and who read ideas instead of words have no difficulty, but others must give special attention to the correct grouping of words before they can communicate ideas clearly.

Grouping is simply speech punctuation. In silent reading, punctuation marks help with understanding and are adequate guides to the intended meaning; in oral reading punctuation marks are helpful, but they are inadequate. The reader must supply additional speech punctuation. How do we group words? Are there any guides?

Words that make up a unit of thought should be grouped together. A good sentence is a complete thought, but within the sentence there may be smaller units—a clause, a phrase, or even a word. A pause between these idea or thought units serves to show relationships and to clarify meaning.

Guides for grouping. If you try to lift the thought of a sentence from the page and to say it as you would in conversation, you will find you have broken the sentence into word groups with pauses between the groups. We seem to do this automatically in conversational speech. Read "A Deep Sworn Vow" in two ways:

1   *Others because / you did not / keep*
       That / deep-sworn vow have been / friends of mine; /
       Yet always when I / look death / in the face, /
       When I clamber to / the heights of sleep, /
       Or when I grow / excited with wine,
       Suddenly / I meet your face. [2]

---

[2] Copyright 1919 by Macmillan Publishing Co., Inc., renewed 1947 by Bertha Georgie Yeats.

Because the pauses come in the wrong places, the word groups do not make sense. Now read the poem with these pauses:

> 2   *Others / because you did not keep*
> *That deep-sworn vow / have been friends of mine; /*
> *Yet always / when I look death in the face, /*
> *When I clamber to the heights of sleep, /*
> *Or when I grow excited with wine, /*
> *Suddenly / I meet your face.* [2]

This makes sense because each group is an idea unit that contributes to the whole meaning. Notice that the speech punctuation follows the written punctuation, except that there are additional pauses besides those indicated by the punctuation marks.

Read the second version aloud again, concentrating on the thoughts of the speaker. If you were thinking while you read, the pauses after "vow," "always," and "suddenly" were probably longer than the others. Timing, the use of pause and duration, plays an important part in conversational rhythm. This will be discussed in detail as it applies to vocal variety.

Exercise for Grouping

Use a slash mark (/) to indicate, according to your judgment, the idea groups that best project the logical meaning of the sentences. What do you learn about grouping in relation to punctuation?

> 1   The teacher says the student is a fool.
> 2   Jesus went up on the mountain and spoke.
> 3   And now there remain faith, hope, and love, these three; but the greatest of these is love. (Bible, I Corinthians xiii: 13)
> 4   She was, however, in the realization of what might happen, disturbed by his statement.
> 5   *There is so much good in the worst of us,*
> *And so much bad in the best of us,*
> *That it hardly becomes any of us*
> *To talk about the rest of us.*
>   *(Edward Wallis Hoch)*
> 6   If to do were as easy as to know what were good to do, chapels had been churches, and poor men's cottages princes' palaces.
>   (Shakespeare, *The Merchant of Venice*, Act I, scene 2)

Listen to a recording of Hamlet's "To Be, or Not to Be" soliloquy, as read by two British actors.*

Inflectional Toning

This technique relates to the pitch the voice takes at the end of idea groups. Some thought groups are complete, but others are part of a larger thought unit. In the poem "A Deep-Sworn Vow," the first complete thought ends

---

[2] Copyright 1919 by Macmillan Publishing Co., Inc., renewed 1947 by Bertha Georgie Yeats.

* Two good interpretations of this selection and other readings from *Hamlet* are those by John Gielgud (Victor L M 6007) and Maurice Evans (Columbia Masterworks Set M-340).

with "have been friends of mine," but there are three other idea groups contributing to the complete thought. When reading this aloud, if you ended each of these idea groups with a distinct falling vocal inflection, the sequence of the complete thought would probably escape the listener. Try it:

Others \
because you did not keep \
that deep-sworn vow \
have been friends of mine; \

It is difficult to make rules about anything as subtle as vocal inflection, but a few general statements can serve as guides. **When the word group expresses a complete thought or completes a series, the pitch drops. The vocal inflection suggests finality; the thought is complete, closed.**
When the idea group is only a part of a complete thought, the pitch rises, suggesting that there is something to follow. This is the open ending.
The open ending may be of two kinds: the open ending, which says through pause and upward inflection that more follows, or the carry-over ending, in which the vowel sound in the last word in a line of poetry is prolonged and carried over to the first word in the next line. More will be said about the carry-over ending in the chapter on poetry.
The rising inflection should be varied in pitch levels, stress, and duration. An insertion is an example of the stressed inflection:

We forgot, / and that is the real test, / who he was.

In a series of images the upward inflection need not be very strong, but it should be held long enough to give the listener time to see the images:

Here are workers, / loafers, / thinkers / and dreamers.

Exercise for Inflectional Endings
Read aloud:

1   He finds his house in ruins, his farm devastated, his slaves free, his stock killed, his barns empty, his trade destroyed, his money worthless; his social system, feudal in its magnificence, swept away; his people without law or legal status; his comrades slain, and the burdens of others heavy on his shoulders. Crushed by defeat, his very traditions gone: without money, credit, employment, material or training; and besides all this, confronted with the gravest problem that ever met human intelligence—the establishing of a status for the vast body of his liberated slaves.

(Henry W. Grady, "The New South")

2   *Whenas in silks my Julia goes,*
Then, then (methinks) how sweetly flows
That liquefaction of her clothes.

Next, when I cast mine eyes and see
That brave vibration each way free;
—O how that glittering taketh me!

(Robert Herrick, "Upon Julia's Clothes")

3   *If all be true that I do think,*
There are five reasons we should drink:
Good wine—a friend—or being dry—
Or lest we should be by and by—
Or any other reason why.

(Henry Aldrich, *"Causae Bibendi"*)

Emphasis and Subordination

Emphasis is regarded by many readers as the all important thing: but it is really the least important. Any untrained voice can emphasize. The difficult thing to do well is the opposite of emphasis—the slighting of certain subordinate parts of discourse.

(From *Aims of Literary Study* by Hiram Carson)

This is important, for the task of the oral interpreter is to find the words that carry the central thought of a passage or sentence, to emphasize these key words, and to learn to subordinate the others. Analysis of meaning and structure is the interpreter's guide for emphasis and subordination.

In regard to the selection as a whole, the highest point of interest (the climax) should be emphasized. The focal points within the parts should receive emphasis, with the degree determined by their relation to the climax. Naturally, low parts between focal points are subordinated.

In regard to sentences, emphasize words that point up the main idea of the sentence, that point up contrast, and that introduce new ideas. Words and parts of sentences frequently requiring subordination are articles, conjunctions, prepositions, and sometimes pronouns.

Emphasis and subordination. Don't expect to learn new ways to emphasize and subordinate by reading about how to do it; you can only learn through doing. Begin with a simple sentence: "She is coming today." If the idea you want to convey is that she, not he, is coming, you would say *She* iscomingtoday. What happened when you emphasized "she"? You probably said this word in a louder voice (more volume) and in a higher pitch, and you took longer to say it (more duration). If, on the other hand, you wanted to suggest that a man was involved and that she would not allow him to come, and instead was coming herself, "she" would be emphasized with a different quality of tone and perhaps with a suggestion of sarcasm. Remember that emphasis is achieved by changes in the manner of utterance, which have to do with the variable attributes of voice: pitch, quality, volume, and timing. A change in any one or any combination of these will emphasize some element of the sentence. The best way to correct overemphasis is to learn how to subordinate. Subordination in the sentence may be acquired in several ways:

"Throwing away" words and phrases by using weak forms,

By saying the words and phrases more rapidly,

By using an upward inflection before and at the end of the group of words,

Two women ⟋ (coming from opposite cultures) ⟋ faced each other.

By saying a difficult sentence as if you were saying it in conversation, and then trying to read it in the same way.

Exercise for Emphasis and Subordination

Read the following sentences aloud, emphasizing the key words and subordinating others. What vocal means will you use to emphasize or to subordinate?

1   Four of them were included; one of the four was a dancer.
2   Two of them were included; one was a dancer, the other a singer.
3   A house should be of the hill, not on the hill.
                                    (Frank Lloyd Wright, *An Autobiography*)
4   If you prick us, do we not bleed? if you tickle us, do we not laugh? if you poison us, do we not die? and if you wrong us, shall we not revenge?
                        (Shakespeare, *The Merchant of Venice*, Act III, scene I)
5   Good morrow, Kate; for that's your name, I hear.
                        (Shakespeare, *The Taming of the Shrew*, Act II, scene 1)
6   The thing that hath been, it is that which shall be; and that which is done is that which shall be done: and there is no new thing under the sun.
                                                (Bible: Ecclesiastes i: 9)
7   Four things on earth are small but they are exceeding wise: the ants are a people not strong, yet they provide their food in the summer; the badgers are a people not mighty, yet they make their homes in the rocks; the locusts have no king, yet all of them march in rank; the lizard you can take in your hands, yet it is in kings' palaces.
                                                (Bible: Proverbs 30: 24—28)
8   The grass withereth, the flower fadeth, because the spirit of the Lord bloweth upon it: surely the people is grass. The grass withereth, the flower fadeth: but the word of God shall stand forever.
                                                (Bible: Isaiah 40: 7—8)

As phrases are added to the sentence, try to subordinate smoothly:

9   A sense of timing is a determing factor in our lives.

A sense of timing, an element of luck, is a determining factor in our lives.

A sense of timing, an element of luck, affecting every successful person—artist or businessman, writer or politician—is a determining factor in our lives.

A sense of timing, an element of luck, but at the same time, the ability to sense and seize the right moment without faltering, affects every successful person—artist or businessman, writer or politician, who without this is likely to shine briefly and then fade from the scene.

The Variable Attributes of Voice and Vocal Variety

Because *volume, pitch, quality,* and *timing,* the variable attributes of voice, are dependent on each other, they can be combined in infinite variations to prevent vocal monotony and to express shades of meaning and feeling. Let us review their functions and our means of control.

Volume means loudness, which is controlled by our breathing—the supply of air and the force with which we exhale the breath. The pitch of the voice is its highness or lowness, as measured on the musical scale. Voice quality, or timbre, is the sum of characteristics that differentiate one voice from another. Pitch and quality are closely related: the pitch is determined by the original vibration of the vocal chords; the quality is determined by the amplification of this original sound in the resonator. Timing refers to the general rate of speaking and the use of pause and duration. Timing is largely determined by the personality and the meaning of what is being read, controlled by the mind.

Projection is another term that needs defining. Though often used interchangeably with volume or loudness, projection is a technique involving all our means of audible communication and, for that matter, visible as well. It is the technique of increasing loudness, resonance, rate, and of improving the articulation of speech sounds to reach, say, the deaf person in the last row. Projection of the voice toward a certain target is also largely controlled by the mind.

The variable attributes of the voice provide vocal variety, for more effective communication.

Variety in Volume

In addition to being sufficient for the speaker to be heard clearly, the volume should correspond with the feeling of the selection. The type of material and the ideas being expressed call for appropriate volume. Self-assurance, strength, or roughness may best be expressed by heavy volume or energy; conversational or straight expository material may best be projected with lighter volume.

Within each paragraph and each sentence there is need for variety in the volume. Certain words and phrases must be emphasized; in American speech, this is done most frequently by adding force or stress to the word or phrase. This clarifies meanings and, in some cases, distinguishes words. For example, the meaning of such words as "con'-duct" and "con-duct'" is determined only by the syllable stress. But while we recognize the importance of stress as a means of emphasis, we must recognize its dangers. As we pointed out in our discussion of emphasis, it is easy to emphasize a word by making it louder, and so the tendency is to overuse this, resulting in a monotonous stress pattern. Nothing is more disagreeable than too much punching of words.

One of the best ways to use volume variation is to apply loudness and softness to point up contrasts. Become conscious of levels of volume. A sudden change from loudness to softness, or vice versa, at an appropriate time, can enhance and help focus attention on meaning and emotion. Of course, all changes must be motivated by the context. But, in spite of the demands of the material, readers hesitate to use this kind of vocal variety. The exercises below should be done with exaggeration, with extreme contrasts in the use of loudness and softness.

Exercises for Variety of Volume

1   Do breathing exercises 1, 2, and 3 at the beginning of this chapter.
2   Count, maintaining your natural pitch level; start softly and

gradually increase the volume (keep your abdominal muscles in control of your breathing) until you are speaking as loudly as you can without straining your throat. Your purpose here is to increase the loudness while keeping the same pitch. Reverse the count from loud to soft.

3   Concentrating on correct breathing and placement of the tone in the front of the mouth, speak the following softly but with such sharp articulation that the words can be heard clearly in the back of the room:

> *In the silence of the night*
> *How we shiver with affright*
> *At the melancholy menace of their tone!*
>   *(Poe, "The Bells")*

> *The ferns and fondling grass said "Stay,"*
> *The dewberry dipped for to work delay,*
> *And the little reeds sighed "Abide, abide."*
> *(Sidney Lanier, "Song of the Chattahoochee")*

4   Vary the loudness and softness as indicated:

[softly] I hate you!
[louder] You're lying!
[softly] I don't believe a word you say!
[louder] You're a liar and a cheat!

[loudly, addressing an army]
Once more unto the breach, dear friends, once more;
Or close the wall up with our English dead.
[softer] In peace there's nothing so becomes a man
As modest stillness and humility:
[build to very loud]
But when the blast of war blows in our ears,
Then imitate the action of the tiger.
      (Shakespeare, Henry V, Act III, scene 1)

Variety in Pitch

In a general sense, intonation refers to the overall pattern of pitch. Some intonation pattern is inherent in almost all spoken languages. The Chinese use pitch to distinguish different meanings for what is otherwise the same word. Though pitch changes are not such a necessary part of the English language, they give emphasis and significance to words. Pitch changes can suggest the most subtle shades of meaning and emotion.

      Lack of range or of the ability to hear pitch variation can cause pitch monotony. Training in hearing differences is essential for any aspect of voice improvement, but nowhere is it more necessary than with pitch. Pitch monotony may be caused by a pattern—the repetition of an inflection or some other recurring sameness. These faults must be heard before they can be corrected. You should be aware of three ways to avoid pitch monotony: using different levels, from high to low; using steps, changes from one pitch to another; and using slides, inflections or movements of the voice up or down or up and down (rising, falling, and circumflex) within one phonation. We have already noted the role pitch plays in giving emphasis and in conveying the right meaning. Exercise to extend your range above and below the optimum pitch and practice exaggerated steps and slides can help you eliminate pitch monotony and increase your vocal flexibility and expressiveness.

Exercises for Pitch Variety

1   In the following sentences speak the first clause at your highest pitch and the second at your lowest, then reverse, from low to high:

> Don't come near me, or you'll be sorry!
> Get out of my way; you are crazy!
> How nice she is, but I distrust her.
> It's a beautiful day; let's go.

2   Practice for lively conversational steps and slides:

> *I said I had the tree. It wasn't true.*
> *The opposite was true. The tree had me.*
> *The minute it was left with me alone*
> *It caught me up as if I were the fish*
> *And it the fishpole. So I was translated*
> *To loud cries from my brother of "Let go!*
> *Don't you know anything, you girl? Let go!"*
> *(Robert Frost, "Wild Grapes")*[3]

> **Orlando. Did you ever cure any so?**
> **Rosalind. Yes, one, and in this manner. He was to imagine me his love, his mistress; and I set him every day to woo me: at which time would I, being but a moonish youth, grieve, be effeminate, changeable, longing and liking; proud, fantastical, apish, shallow, inconstant, full of tears, full of smiles; for every passion something and for no passion truly any thing. . . . And thus I cured him: and this way will I take upon me to wash your liver as clean as a sound sheep's heart, that there shall not be one spot of love in't.**
> **(Shakespeare, *As You Like It*, Act III, scene 2)**

3.   Suggest characters by pitch level and inflection:

> *"You are old, Father William," the young man said,*
>   *"And your hair has become very white,*
> *And yet you incessantly stand on your head—*
>   *Do you think, at your age, it is right?"*

> *"In my youth," Father William replied to his son,*
>   *"I feared it might injure the brain;*

---

[3] From *The Poetry of Robert Frost,* edited by Edward Connery Lathem. Copyright 1923, 1939, © 1967, 1969 by Holt, Rinehart and Winston. Copyright 1951 by Robert Frost. Reprinted by permission of Holt, Rinehart and Winston, Publishers.

But now that I'm perfectly sure that I have none,
  Why, I do it again and again."
                    (Lewis Carroll, Alice in Wonderland*)*

The Countess. Oh, I wish she hadn't brought up the Alps, Lucy. It always reminds me of that nasty moment I had the day Gustav made me climb to the top of one of them. . . . Anyhow, there we were. And suddenly it struck me that Gustav had pushed me. I slid halfway down the mountain before I realized that Gustav didn't love me any more. But love takes care of its own, Lucy. I slid right into the arms of my fourth husband, the Count.

(Clare Boothe Luce, *The Women***)**[4]

Variety in Quality

Since quality of tone is most closely associated with mood and feeling, it is a subjective voice element that is difficult to teach directly. An interpreter whose voice is normal and whose feelings are not overly restrained usually makes the appropriate quality change naturally and spontaneously.

Variety in quality is used to suggest emotional states, character, and age; each word is touched with the correct quality to suggest its emotional meaning. By the quality of tone used, you can make a word say just what you want it to say. If you touch a word with a soft mellow tone, it will mean one thing; a harsh tone will make it mean something else. Your ability to use variety in quality depends upon your sensitivity to the feelings evident in an author's tone and specific words and upon your control of resonance.

Exercises for Variety in Quality of Tone

1   Color these contrasting words with the appropriate tone quality to suggest their meanings:

sour–sweet	hard–soft	evil–good	hate–love
cold–warm	war–peace	sad–happy	revenge–forgiveness

2   Use a variety of qualities to suggest characters:
The pompous old time politician (too much mouth and throat resonance):

My friends, I come to you today to speak on a subject dear to the heart of every man, woman, and child in this great land.

The sickly, nagging woman (nasal, whiney quality):

I said to him, I says, Will, I'm a sick woman and one of these days you're going to be sorry.

---

[4] Lines from *The Women* by Clare Booth Luce, copyright, 1937. Reprinted by permission of Random House, Inc.

The giant calling (guttural, harsh quality):

Who's that tramping over my bridge?

A ghost (hollow quality):

I am the Ghost of Christmas Past. Rise and walk with me!

Bible narrator (rich, full quality):

And the earth was without form, and void; and darkness was upon the face of the deep.

3   Use varying qualities of tone to suggest feelings:

> **Cyrano de Bergerac. Ah, no young man, that is not enough! You might have
> said, dear me, there are a thousand things . . . varying the tone . . .
> For instance . . . here you are:—
> Aggressive: "I, monsieur, if I had such a nose, nothing would serve but I
> must cut it off!" . . .
> Inquisitive. "What may the office be of that oblong receptacle? Is it an
> inkhorn or a scissor-case?"
> Mincing. "Do you so dote on birds, you have, fond as a father, been at pains
> to fit the little darlings with a roost?"
> Blunt. "Tell me, monsieur, you, when you smoke, is it possible you blow the
> vapor through your nose without a neighbor crying 'the chimney
> is afire?" . . .
> Tender. "Have a little sun-shade made for it! It might get freckled!" . . .
> Dramatic. "It is the Red Sea when it bleeds!" . . .
> Rustic. "Hi, boys! Call that a nose? Ye don't gull me! It's either a prize carrot
> or else a stunted gourd!"
> Military. "Level against the cavalry!" . . .
> And finally in parody of weeping Pyramus: "Behold, behold the nose that
> traitorously destroyed the beauty of its master! and is blushing
> for the same!"—**

> **That, my dear sir, or something not unlike it, is what you would
> have said to me, had you the smallest leaven of letters or of wit. . . .
> (Edmond Rostand, *Cyrano de Bergerac*)**[5]

Variety in Timing

Timing involves duration and pause. The combination and variation of these two elements to form rhythm patterns and convey meaning keep the whole selection alive and interesting.

Duration of tone, also known as quantity, refers to the length of time individual speech sounds are held or prolonged. Prolongation of sounds within words and syllables is an effective way to bring out the lyrical qualities of the language. Elongating the sounds along with quality touch may also aid in suggesting emotional states. Too much long or short

---

[5] From *Cyrano de Bergerac* by Edmond Rostand, Mrs. Gertrude Hall Browell, trans. By permission of publisher, Doubleday and Co., Inc.

duration is monotonous; variety can be obtained by short duration, cutting a word off short, giving it a staccato effect.

The use of pauses in groupings and as a means of emphasis has already been explained. If too many words are emphasized this way, it becomes an obvious device. Various means, pause among them, could be used for emphasis. But certainly pause can be one of the most effective ways to point up emotional meanings, dramatic and comic. Listen to and notice how a comedian uses silences. A sudden pause may catch attention, highlight the humor, add suspense or dramatic intensity, but the pause should be motivated by the idea or emotion and never call attention to itself as a device.

The rate or tempo is dependent upon duration and pause. A person who reads too rapidly can correct this by increasing the duration of words and by using pauses. One who reads too slowly can concentrate on shortening the pauses and duration and avoid meaningless hesitation in speech.

The interpreter should be sensitive to the rate most appropriate for a character's utterance or for the dominant mood of a selection. A slow rate is associated with a heavy or melancholy mood; a rapid rate is generally more appropriate for a light or happy mood. But the general rate of speech must be varied with changes of mood within a selection. To meet these demands you should develop the ability to read at a variety of speeds, and especially to read rapidly with clear articulation.

Exercises for Variety in Timing

1   Read some of the exercises in this chapter aloud, comparing the appropriate rate for each to the rate for the others:
King Henry's speech from *Henry V*
Character lines (politician, nagging woman, and so forth)
The nose speech from *Cyrano de Bergerac*
Sakini's speech from *Teahouse of the August Moon*
2   Notice how the author controls timing in the following two stanzas. Read the first stanza to suggest the brook's rapid movement downhill; in the second stanza suggest the slowing of the water as it reaches the meadow:

> *Out of the hills of Habersham,*
> *Down the valleys of Hall,*
> *I hurry amain to reach the plain,*
> *Run the rapid and leap the fall. . . .*
>
> *The rushes cried "Abide, abide,"*
> *The willful waterweeds held me thrall,*
> *The loving laurel turned my tide,*
> *The fern and fondling grass said "Stay,"*
> *The dewberry dipped for to work delay,*
> *And the little reeds sighed "Abide, abide,". . .*
>   *(Sidney Lanier, "Song of the Chattahoochee")*

3   Practice this material for the pause:
Vary the reflection or thinking pauses as indicated:

Let me see now, // she was in my class. // I can remember her roommate / and where they lived. // Yes. // I can see their room. /// But what was her name?

Pause for suspense:

I was a low, / dull, / quick sound. /// I scarcely breathed.

Pause to point humor:

By the time you swear you're his /
Shivering and // sighing /
And he vows his passion is
Infinite // undying //
Lady, / make a note of this ///
One of you is lying.
     (Dorothy Parker, "Unfortunate Coincidence")[6]

Pause for transitions:

She was silent, but she knew the end had come.

* * * * *

A week or so later . . .

4   Practice this material for duration:
Read words in sentences staccato or with prolonged duration:

The sea is sad and calm; the stars are tarnished silver.
Get out of here and don't ever come back!
You're a different people—a whole different kind of people.
Excited? Who's excited?

5   Try to catch Sakini's inflectional pattern and staccato timing:

. . . Lovely ladies, kind gentlemen:
Please to introduce myself.
Sakini by name.
Interpreter by profession.
Education by ancient dictionary.
Okinawan by whim of gods.
History of Okinawa reveal distinguished record of conquerors.
We have honor to be subjugated in fourteenth century by Chinese pirates.
In sixteenth century by English missionaries.
In eighteenth century by Japanese war lords.
And in twentieth century by American Marines.
Okinawa very fortunate.
Culture brought to us. . . . Not have to leave home for it.

---

[6] From *The Portable Dorothy Parker*   Copyright 1926, renewed 1954 by Dorothy Parker. Reprinted by permission of The Viking Press.

Learn many things.
Most important that rest of world not like Okinawa.
World filled with delightful variation.
Illustration.
In Okinawa . . . no locks on doors.
Bad manners not to trust neighbors.
In America . . . lock and key big industry.
Conclusion?
Bad manners good business.
In Okinawa . . . wash self in public bath with nude lady quite proper.
Picture of nude lady in private home . . . quite improper.
In America . . . statue of nude lady in park win prize.
But nude lady in flesh in park win penalty.
Conclusion?
Pornography question of geography.
But Okinawans most eager to be educated by conquerors.
Deep desire to improve friction.
Not easy to learn.
Sometimes painful.
But pain makes man think.
Thought makes man wise.
Wisdom makes life endurable.
So . . .
We tell little story to demonstrate splendid example of benevolent assimilation of democracy of Okinawa.

(John Patrick, Teahouse of the August Moon)[7]

Suggested Readings

Anderson, Virgil. *Training the Speaking Voice.* London: Oxford University Press, 1977.

Black, John W., and Ruth B. Irwin. *Voice and Diction.* Columbus, Ohio: Charles E. Merrill Co., 1969.

Gamble, Teri and Michael. "Harnessing Resources," *Oral Interpretation: The Meaning of Self and Literature.* Skokie, Ill.: National Textbook Company, 1976.

Hagen, Uta. "Emotional Memory," *Respect for Acting.* New York: Macmillan, 1973.

————. "Sense Memory," *Respect for Acting.* New York: Macmillan, 1973.

King, Nancy. *Giving Form to Feeling.* New York: Drama Book Specialists Publishers, 1975.

Lee, Richard. "Behavioral Analysis in Oral Interpretation," *Southern Speech Communication Journal,* Summer 1974, pp. 379—390.

Mayer, Lyle. *Fundamentals of Voice and Diction.* Dubuque, Iowa: Wm. C. Brown Publishers, 1977.

---

[7] Reprinted by permission of G. P. Putnam's Sons from *Teahouse of the August Moon* by John Patrick   Copyright © by John Patrick.

Moore, Sonia. "The Method of Physical Actions," *Drama Review,* Summer 1965, pp. 91—94.

Salper, D. R. "The 'Sounding' of a Poem," *Quarterly Journal of Speech,* April 1971, pp. 129—133.

Schechner, Richard, and Cynthia Mintz. "Kinesics and Performance," *Drama Review,* September 1973, pp. 102—8.

Williams, David A., and Dennis Alexander. "Effects of Audience Responses on the Performances of Oral Interpreters," *Western Speech,* Fall 1973, pp. 273—281.

Part III

Application of Principles and Methods: Prose, Poetry, Drama

Chapter 7

Interpretive Reading of Prose

For the most part, this chapter focuses upon the interpretive reading of prose fiction. But first let us consider types of nonfiction prose which can be used for oral interpretation. These include letters, diaries, descriptions, biographies, speeches, and various types of essays. However, since some of these forms may be considered as elements implicit in the narrative, we will limit our discussion to a brief consideration of the speech and the essay.

Interpreting Expository Prose: Speech and Essay

The speech and the essay have much in common. They speak from the point of view of the author and address a general audience. They can both be classified as expository prose, which usually uses factual information, personal reflections, experience, light satire, or exaggerated humor to support the author's view. The writing may serve to stimulate, persuade, instruct, examine, amuse, or entertain the reader or audience.

Interpreter's Attitude

As we pointed out in Chapter 1, you approach the role of the public speaker when interpreting an address or an essay, because your audience contact is direct and your manner of delivery is personal. The difference lies in the fact that you are not the author of the words; you are trying to stimulate an appreciative response to someone else's ideas. You are not there either to take credit for the selection or, through your attitude, to criticize the author's ideas.

Focus for Analysis

The author's purpose should be clearly understood, and the tone of the writing carefully analyzed. Because the speech and the essay both deal with facts and ideas, you may fail to give enough attention to the emotional meanings. The emotional tone is revealed through a study of the particular facts and details included and by the way the writer has used words.

Examples: Three Short Speeches

Notice the sophisticated humor and the eloquent prose of Adlai Stevenson in this tribute he paid Eleanor Roosevelt at the time of her death.

> She has passed beyond these voices, but our memory and her meaning have not—Eleanor Roosevelt. She was a lady—a lady for all seasons. And, like her husband, she left "a name to shine on the entablatures of truth—forever." There is, I believe, a legend in the Talmud which tells us that in any period of man's history the heavens themselves are held in place by the virtue, love, and shining integrity of twelve just men. They are completely unaware of this function. They go about their daily work, their humble chores—doctors, teachers, workers, farmers (never, alas, lawyers, so I understand), just ordinary, devoted citizens—and meanwhile the rooftree of creation is supported by them alone. There are times when nations or movements or great political parties are similarly sustained in their purposes and being by the pervasive, unconscious influence of a few great men and women. Can we doubt that Eleanor Roosevelt had in some measure the keeping of the Party's conscience in her special care? . . . She thought of herself as an ugly duckling, but she walked in beauty in the ghettos of the world, bringing with her the reminder of her beloved St. Francis, "It is in the giving that we receive." And wherever she walked beauty was forever there.

Mr. Stevenson used a legend from the Talmud and polished, poetic phrases—"a lady—a lady for all seasons," "she walked in beauty in the ghettos of the world"—and other techniques to establish a reflective mood of dignity and warmth and a scholarly yet personal tone.

Here is one of the most inspirational addresses of our times. Young writers desperately in need of faith in themselves in the 1950s were renewed in spirit by Mr. Faulkner's words.

On Accepting the Nobel Prize for Literature[1]
William Faulkner

> I feel that this award was not made to me as a man, but to my work—a life's work in the agony and sweat of the human spirit, not for glory and least of all for profit, but to create out of the materials of the human spirit something which did not exist before. So this award is only mine in trust. It will not be difficult to find a dedication for the money part of it commensurate with the purpose and significance of its origin. But I would like to do the same with the acclaim too, by using this moment as a pinnacle from which I might be listened to by the young men and women already dedicated to the same anguish and travail, among whom is already that one who will some day stand here where I am standing.
>
> Our tragedy today is a general and universal physical fear so long sustained by now that we can even bear it. There are no longer problems of the spirit. There is only the question: When will I be blown up? Because of this, the young man or woman writing today has forgotten the problems of the human heart

---

[1] "Nobel Peace Prize Speech" by William Faulkner in *The Faulkner Reader.* Reprinted by permission of Random House.

in conflict with itself which alone can make good writing because only that is worth writing about, worth the agony and the sweat.

He must learn them again. He must teach himself that the basest of all things is to be afraid; and, teaching himself that, forget it forever, leaving no room in his workshop for anything but the old verities and truths of the heart, the old universal truths lacking which any story is ephemeral and doomed—love and honor and pity and pride and compassion and sacrifice. Until he does so, he labors under a curse. He writes not of love but of lust, of defeats in which nobody loses anything of value, of victories without hope and worst of all, without pity or compassion. His griefs grieve on no universal bones, leaving no scars. He writes not of the heart but of the glands.

Until he relearns these things, he will write as though he stood among and watched the end of man. I decline to accept the end of man. It is easy enough to say that man is immortal simply because he will endure; that when the last ding-dong of doom has clanged and faded from the last worthless rock hanging tideless in the last red and dying evening, that even then there will still be one more sound: that of his puny inexhaustible voice, still talking. I refuse to accept this. I believe that man will not merely endure: he will prevail. He is immortal, not because he alone among creatures has an inexhaustible voice, but because he has a soul, a spirit capable of compassion and sacrifice and endurance. The poet's, the writer's, duty is to write about these things. It is his privilege to help man endure by lifting his heart, by reminding him of the courage and honor and hope and pride and compassion and pity and sacrifice which have been the glory of his past. The poet's voice need not merely be the record of man: it can be one of the props, the pillars to help him endure and prevail.

Study Guides. What happened to you as you read this for the first time? When you read it again later? What three audiences does Faulkner address? Who does he say is the true recipient of the award? How does he define the true content of writing? Why are young writers in need of faith in themselves? Is Faulkner's style of writing here similar to his style in his stories and novels? How do you identify the tone? Does it change? What in essence is Faulkner saying?

This speech by the young playwright Lorraine Hansberry was addressed to fellow writers at a conference on "The Negro Writer and His Roots." This was in March 1959, just before her first play, *A Raisin in the Sun,* reached Broadway to be acclaimed the best play of the year by the New York Drama Critics Circle. Six years later, at the age of 34, Lorraine Hansberry was dead of cancer.

At the beginning of the speech, she explained that she had been taken aback by a young friend's severe view of life, because he could find no reason why man should want to survive in a world of corruption.

"I Wish to Live"[2]
Lorraine Hansberry

I answered him the only way I could: that man is unique in the universe, the only creature who has in fact the power to transform the universe. Therefore, it did not seem unthinkable to me that man might just do what the apes never will—*impose* a reason for life on life. That is what I said to my friend. I wish to live because life has within it that which is good, that which is beautiful, and that which is love. Therefore, since I have known all of these things, I have found them

---

[2] From the book *To Be Young, Gifted and Black: Lorraine Hansberry in Her Own Words* adapted by Robert Nemiroff. ©1969 by Robert Nemiroff and Robert Nemiroff as Executor of the Estate of Lorraine Hansberry.

to be reason enough and—I wish to live. Moreover, because this is so, I wish others to live for generations and generations and generations.

I was born on the Southside of Chicago. I was born black and a female. I was born in a depression after one world war, and came into my adolescence during another. While I was still in my teens, the first atom bombs were dropped on human beings at Nagasaki and Hiroshima, and by the time I was twenty-three years old my government and that of the Soviet Union had entered actively into the worst conflict of nerves in human history—the cold war.

I have lost friends and relatives through cancer, lynching, and war. I have been personally the victim of physical attack which was the offspring of racial and political hysteria. I have worked with the handicapped and seen the ravages of congenital diseases that we have not yet conquered because we spend our time and ingenuity in far less purposeful wars. I see daily on the streets of New York, street gangs and prostitutes and beggars; I know people afflicted with drug addiction and alcoholism and mental illness; I have like all of you on a thousand occasions seen indescribable displays of man's very real inhumanity to man; and I have come to maturity as we all must, knowing that greed and malice, indifference to human misery and, perhaps above all else, ignorance—the prime ancient and persistent enemy of man—abound in this world.

I say all of this to say that one cannot live with sighted eyes and feeling heart and not know and react to the miseries which afflict this world.

I have given you this account so that you know that what I write is not based on the assumption of idyllic possibilities or innocent assessments of the true nature of life—but, rather, my own personal view that, posing one against the other, I think that the human race does command its own destiny and that that destiny can eventually embrace the stars.

Study Guides. What happened to you as you read this speech for the first time? What reason does Lorraine Hansberry see for living? How would you identify her speech style? What qualities of character does she demonstrate? What does the speech tell you about her activities as a radical? What is the essence of her philosophy?

An Essay to Entertain

The following essay is taken from a little book that has known wide popularity since it was published in 1962. The book's cover explains: "Virginia Cary Hudson was a sprite of ten back in 1904 when she wrote the essays for a very understanding teacher in her Episcopal boarding school. Discovered in an attic trunk, the essays are even more entertaining today because of their distinct, early American flavor." Our selection combines the last two essays in the book, in which Virginia gives her sharp and honest impressions on religious matters.

From O Ye Jigs & Juleps![3]
Virginia Cary Hudson

In China there are two classes of people, the upper crust and the under crust, just like there is in Leesville. China has three religions stated by Mr. Confucius, Mr. Tao and Mr. Buddha. Leesville is ahead of China. Leesville has seven religions, Catholics, Episcopalians, Methodists, Baptists, Campbellites, Presbyterians, and Holy Rollers. I sure would love to see them roll, but my mother won't let me go. . .

---

[3]*O Ye Jigs & Juleps!* by Virginia Cary Hudson. Published by Macmillan. Reprinted by permission of Mrs. Martha C. Johnson.

My grandmother says people join different churches just like they buy different hats and umbrellas. My grandmother says the Catholics are just scared to death the old Priest will send them to Hell. I don't believe the one on our street would.... My grandmother says the Episcopalians are stuck up and some of them can strut sitting down. My grandmother says the Methodists are happy and sing loud and shout. Just plain noisy. My grandmother says the Baptists are narrow....

The Baptist Church is next door to our church. They sing as loud as they can all the time we are trying to pray. I bet the Lord can't hear one word we say. The Baptists sing about plunging sinners in a bloody fountain drawn from Emmanuel's vein. We sing about crown Him Lord of All. I think it is much more ladylike to crown the King than to be plunging around in a bloody fountain.... You sure hear plenty about Hell at the Baptist Church. When I go with Darthea, that preacher hollers himself red in the face about Hell.... If I have to go to Hell, I sure hope I go to the one for Episcopalians and don't, by mistake, get pushed in that hornpunching, and tailwagging, red-hot blazing one the Baptists are going to have....

My grandmother says the Presbyterians have blue stockings, but Miss Priscilla Ross never wears hers. She reads the Bible to children on Sunday afternoons.... My grandmother says she can't tell much about the Campbellites, but I can.... They asked me to their old church party and my mother made me go. And I wore my hat and it was summer, and Alice Coleman laughed because I had on my hat. I said to her, I said, "You shouldn't go in church without your hat." And she said, "You should too," and I said, "You shouldn't." And she said, "You should," and I said, "you shouldn't," then she said, "Who said so?" and I said, "St. Paul said so," and she said, "He didn't," and I said, "He did," and she said, "He didn't," and I said, "He did," and she said, "Fooie on St. Paul," and that is when I slapped her. Once for St. Paul, and I slapped her for the whole state of Christ's church universal and then I pinched her for myself. That slapping was righteous indignation, but that pinch was my own and the devil's idea.

She ran home from the church party screaming and yelling, but I stayed and ate my ice cream. And Miss Billie called my mother up. Miss Billie is Alice's mother. Whoever heard of a mother named Billie? My mother made me sit in my chair one whole hour and read St. Paul. She said that was a good day to read all St. Paul had to say. So I read about enduring all things and not to behave yourself unseemly. But I bet one thing. I bet St. Paul didn't know any Campbellites....

Next year Bishop Jordan is going to make me an Episcopalian. I hope I don't get stuck up, but if I do I guess the Good Lord will understand.... I hope I have not written too much. My mother says I talk too much.... It is now Thursday afternoon, fifteen minutes past two o'clock and the Lord have mercy upon us all.... Amen.

Study Guides. What happened to you as you read Virginia's essay? Can you relate anything in your own background to Virginia's experience? In what mood does she examine religious matters in Leesville? How do her moods change? Which dominates? How is she a product of her times? Does she give evidence of being one of the "upper crust" of Leesville? What would she be like at ten in the 1980s? What does Virginia say in essence?

Two Short Essays

Stereotypes: The Mother[4]
Mary Ann Ferguson

Images of women in literature have always been ambivalent; for every biological role there has been both a negative and a positive view. In the Biblical

---

[4] Mary Ann Ferguson. *Images of Women in Literature.* 2nd Edition Boston: Houghton Mifflin Company, 1977, p. 12.

creation myth, Eve, the mother of us all, is temptress who brought sin and death into the world. But the Virgin Mary, passively acted upon by the Holy Ghost, pondering in her heart the experience of her Son, is the Queen of Heaven, the Mother of God and, through Him, of us all. Eve could be tolerated as a necessary evil; Mary was worshipped as a model for all womankind. In Greek mythology, Pandora, sent to earth by the gods to marry and establish the human race, brings with her a magic box or vial; opening it, she releases not only all evil but the greatest gift man can have, hope. Both Eve and Pandora act in defiance of divine law. If they had passively obeyed (experienced the world vicariously, as Mary did), man would have been spared the particular kind of life known as human. In both myths, except for the action of a woman, mankind would have been godlike. Because of woman, man is condemned to be mortal; he must die. Yet every human being in his early years sees his mother as the bringer of life, the nurturer, the source of pleasure and comfort. He soon learns that she also takes away pleasure, she says no, and he blames her for denying satisfaction, no matter what her reasons may be. The role of mother is ambiguous. Myths about woman's dual nature are attempts to explain primordial reactions to her double role as the giver of life and death, of pleasure and pain.

The Stereotype[5]
Germaine Greer

Maybe I don't have a pretty smile, good teeth, long legs, a cheeky arse, a sexy voice. Maybe I don't know how to handle men and increase my market value, so that the rewards due to the feminine will accrue to me. Then, again, maybe I'm sick of the masquerade. I'm sick of belying my own intelligence, my own will, my own sex. I'm sick of peering at the world through false eyelashes, so everything I see is mixed with a shadow of bought hairs; I'm sick of weighting my head with a dead mane, unable to move my neck freely, terrified of rain, of wind, of dancing too vigorously in case I sweat into my lacquered curls. I'm sick of the Powder Room. I'm sick of pretending that some male's self-important pronouncements are the objects of my undivided attention. I'm sick of going to films and plays when someone else wants to, and sick of having no opinions of my own about either. I'm sick of being a transvestite, I refuse to be a female impersonator. I am a woman. . . .

Study Guides. What were your responses to these essays? Did you identify with both? With one more than the other? How do the authors' purposes compare? How do their attitudes compare? How does each support her central idea?

Guides for Speech and Essay

In this brief encounter with the speech and the essay, we have stressed three matters that need special attention when you are preparing to interpret this type of prose: the author's purpose, the author's organization and support of the central idea, and the writer's dominant mood and tone. We suggest you use an introduction to supply needed explanations and get the audience in the right frame of mind for listening.

We would remind you of three controls in the communicating act. Your stance should be open and your audience contact direct, though there

---

[5] From *The Female Eunuch* by Germaine Greer. Copyright © 1970, 1971 by Germaine Greer. Used with permission of McGraw-Hill Book Company.

may be times when indirect reflections or narrative elements call for modifying this directness. Take care that you do not overemphasize a point in an effort to make the ideas clear; instead, use subordination of phrases in a conversational flow and find ways to use the variable attributes of the voice to highlight the correct meaning. It is not necessary or desirable to assume the personality of the author; you remain yourself, projecting the author's thoughts and attitudes and trying to stimulate an appreciative response to the author's ideas.

Interpreting Narrative Prose: Short Story and Novel

Adapting to Meet Time Limits

You may lift out a section or scene from a story or novel. You select a chapter from a novel or the climactic portion of a short story that has special appeal for you and your audience. Be sure that your selection has structural completeness—beginning, middle, end. You may wish to introduce your reading with a summary of what preceded it, but sometimes a scene will stand alone without reference to the whole story.

It is possible to use more than one section from a novel or story and to tie these parts together with appropriate transitional narration. Each adaptation has its own unique problems, and you must find the most effective solutions.

You should be thoroughly familiar with the whole of a longer work before attempting to select a part. Your cutting should never distort the author's basic theme or purpose.

You may find material that can be used in its complete form with only minor cuts, or your lifted portion may need some deletions in order to meet time limits or to improve the reading. In either case you must consider ways of making minor cuts:

Cut directive tags such as "she said," "he said angrily," "they spoke rapidly," and the like, when you can identify the character and the response with voice and body suggestions.

Cut descriptions that do not directly affect the basic idea of the story. This is sometimes painful but necessary.

Cut subplots or inserted incidents from the past.

Minor characters may be cut, but it is sometimes possible to retain certain of their lines and assign them to another character.

Analyzing and Projecting Character

Many characters you encounter in fiction are realistic. Such a character may be engaged in a conflict with another character or with an opposing force of some kind, or the opposing force may be within the character's own personality. The character is a complex individual with an outer and inner personality and during the story usually undergoes some kind of change because of the circumstances in which he or she is placed. Though the narrator may tell some things about the character and other characters may give clues, the interpreter's discovery of a character's outer and inner personality should come chiefly through a study of what the character does, says, and thinks. Such a study should reveal the dominant motivation, the desire that stimulates the character's actions throughout the story; each want and each relationship is controlled by this basic desire. For instance, the motivating force of the character in the dramatic monologue "The Laboratory" is revenge; her immediate want is the poison, and this controls her relationship with the old man: she is willing to stoop and offer a kiss and to part with her jewels to obtain her immediate objective, the poison, which is the means by which she will satisfy her basic desire, revenge.

Your characterization of a central character should be guided by your knowledge of the character's outer and inner personality. For a time the interpreter should be concerned with the voice and body techniques that best represent the character's personality. It may be helpful to use a few direct means such as the play-acting exercise to help get the feel of a character's stance and movement, and you may give time to a consideration of the speech (diction and rhythm) most appropriate for the character. But as you proceed, these mechanical devices should be forgotten. The interpreter's control of characterization should be realized through concentration on the character's desires or wants while reading the lines. This kind of thinking discloses the inner motivations and gives undertone to each line the character speaks.

A minor character is flat or static and is usually typical of a certain social class or work group, rather than being developed as an individual. In preparing to suggest such a character you need to consider the dress, the speech, and the body mannerisms that belong to the particular group the character typifies. When the lines are read, the reader's stance, gestures, and vocal intonations should deepen the listener's awareness of the group the character represents.

Projecting the Situation and Its Movement

Transitions. Transitions need special attention when interpreting the story. Shifts in time and place can be clarified by emphasizing transitional words and phrases in the script, but when the transition is indicated only by a paragraph break, you must indicate the change with an extended pause and appropriate visible and audible responses. During a transitional silence, you should drop the thought and emotions just completed and take on the attitude of the next paragraph, remembering that the larger the transition, the longer the bridge of silence must be.

Climax. To handle a climax effectively, the oral interpreter must have a clear understanding of the way the author has built the intellectual and emotional intensity. Good control of both voice and body is needed in order to project this. The intensity may be built with an increase in vocal force, by a faster rate of speech, by raising the pitch, or by a combination of these. An intense build may be projected by muscle-tone change and controlled vocal intensity alone. The interpreter should take care not to build too soon or too quickly, or to use too much rise in pitch (strain), and should remember that a pause is useful before or after, or before *and* after, a climax.

Handling Dialogue

Differentiation. In projecting dialogue, you are often required to switch from one character to another quickly. One technical means that can be used to assist in differentiation of characters is the physical placement of the characters in an imagined scene out front, resulting in a change of eye focus for each character. Placement of characters, if not continued too long and if the eye focus changes within a narrow angle, can aid the audience in identifying the characters. But once the placement is suggested, it does not have to remain rigid.

Interplay. The interplay among characters in a scene is sometimes broken because of the interpreter's tendency to refer to the script between speeches, causing slight pauses in the dialogue. There is a simple way to correct this: you should finish one character's speech and immediately let the audience see the visible response of the next speaker; then, if necessary, you can look down (in character) and get the next words. You should look at the script during speeches or responses, not between them.

Now let us demonstrate how certain problems can be solved in a particular story.

Application of Short Story

First Confession[6]
Frank O'Connor

It was a Saturday afternoon in early spring. A small boy whose face looked as though it had been newly scrubbed was being led by the hand by his sister through a crowded street. The little boy showed a marked reluctance to proceed; he affected to be very interested in the shop-windows. Equally, his sister seemed to pay no attention to them. She tried to hurry him; he resisted. When she dragged him he began to bawl. The hatred with which she viewed him was almost diabolical, but when she spoke her words and tone were full of passionate sympathy.

"Ah, sha, God help us!" she intoned into his ear in a whine of commiseration.

"Leave me go!" he said, digging his heels into the pavement. "I don't want to go. I want to go home."

"But, sure, you can't go home, Jackie. You'll have to go. The parish priest will be up to the house with a stick."

"I don't care. I won't go."

"Oh, Sacred Heart, isn't it a terrible pity you weren't a good boy? Oh, Jackie, me heart bleeds for you! I don't know what they'll do to you at all, Jackie, me

---

poor child. And all the trouble you caused your poor old nanny, and the way you wouldn't eat in the same room with her, and the time you kicked her on the shins, and the time you went for me with the bread knife under the table. I don't know will he ever listen to you at all, Jackie. I think meself he might sind you to the bishop. Oh, Jackie, how will you think of all your sins?"

Half stupefied with terror, Jackie allowed himself to be led through the sunny streets to the very gates of the church. It was an old one with two grim iron gates and a long, low, shapeless stone front. At the gates he stuck, but it was already too late. She dragged him behind her across the yard, and the commiserating whine with which she had tried to madden him gave place to a yelp of triumph.

"Now you're caught! Now, you're caught. And I hope he'll give you the pinitintial psalms! That'll cure you, you suppurating little caffler!"

Jackie gave himself up for lost. Within the old church there was no stained glass; it was cold and dark and desolate, and in the silence, the trees in the yard knocked hollowly at the tall windows. He allowed himself to be led through the vaulted silence, the intense and magical silence which seemed to have frozen within the ancient walls, buttressing them and shouldering the high wooden roof. In the street outside, yet seeming a million miles away, a ballad singer was drawling a ballad.

Nora sat in front of him beside the confession box. There were a few old women before her, and later a thin, sad-looking man with long hair came and sat beside Jackie. In the intense silence of the church that seemed to grow deeper from the plaintive moaning of the ballad singer, he could hear the buzz-buzz-buzz of a woman's voice in the box, and then the husky ba-ba-ba of the priest's. Lastly the soft thud of something that signalled the end of the confession, and out came the woman, head lowered, hands joined, looking neither to right nor left, and tip-toed up to the altar to say her penance.

It seemed only a matter of seconds till Nora rose and with a whispered injunction disappeared from his sight. He was all alone. Alone and next to be heard and the fear of damnation in his soul. He looked at the sad-faced man. He was gazing at the roof, his hands joined in prayer. A woman in a red blouse and black shawl had taken her place below him. She uncovered her head, fluffed her hair out roughly with her hand, brushed it sharply back, then, bowing, caught it in a knot and pinned it on her neck. Nora emerged. Jackie rose and looked at her with a hatred which was inappropriate to the occasion and the place. Her hands were joined on her stomach, her eyes modestly lowered, and her face had an expression of the most rapt and tender recollection. With death in his heart he crept into the compartment she left open and drew the door shut behind him.

He was in pitch darkness. He could see no priest nor anything else. And anything he had heard of confession got all muddled up in his mind. He knelt to the right-hand wall and said: "Bless me, father, for I have sinned. This is my first confession." Nothing happened. He repeated it louder. Still it gave no answer. He turned to the opposite wall, genuflected first, then again went on his knees and repeated the charm. This time he was certain he would receive a reply, but none came. He repeated the process with the remaining wall without effect. He had the feeling of someone with an unfamiliar machine, of pressing buttons at random. And finally the thought struck him that God knew. God knew about the bad confession he intended to make and had made him deaf and blind so that he could neither hear nor see the priest.

Then as his eyes grew accustomed to the blackness, he perceived something he had not noticed previously: a sort of shelf at about the height of his head. The purpose of this eluded him for a moment. Then he understood. It was for kneeling on.

He had always prided himself upon his powers of climbing, but this took it out of him. There was no foothold. He slipped twice before he succeeded in getting his knee on it, and the strain of drawing the rest of his body up was almost more than he was capable of. However, he did at last get his two knees on it, there was just room for those, but his legs hung down uncomfortably and the edge of the shelf bruised his shins. He joined his hands and pressed the last remaining button. "Bless me, father, for I have sinned. This is my first confession."

At the same moment the slide was pushed back and a dim light streamed into the little box. There was an uncomfortable silence, and then an alarmed voice asked, "Who's there?" Jackie found it almost impossible to speak into the grille which was on a level with his knees, but he got a firm grip on the molding above it, bent his head down and sideways, and as though he were hanging by his feet like a monkey found himself looking almost upside down at the priest. But the priest was looking sideways at him, and Jackie, whose knees were being tortured by this new position, felt it was a queer way to hear confessions.

" 'Tis me, father," he piped, and then, running all his words together in excitement, he rattled off, "Bless me father, for I have sinned. This is my first confession."

"What?" exclaimed a deep and angry voice, and the sombre soutaned figure stood bolt upright, disappearing almost entirely from Jackie's view. "What does this mean? What are you doing there? Who are you?"

And with the shock Jackie felt his hands lose their grip and his legs their balance. He discovered himself tumbling into space, and, falling, he knocked his head against the door, which shot open and permitted him to thump right into the center of the aisle. Straight on this came a small dark-haired priest with a biretta well forward on his head. At the same time Nora came skeltering madly down the church.

"Lord God!" she cried. "The snivelling little caffler! I knew he'd do it! I knew he'd disgrace me!"

Jackie received a clout over the ear which reminded him that for some strange reason he had not yet begun to cry and that people might possibly think he wasn't hurt at all. Nora slapped him again.

"What's this? What's this?" cried the priest. "Don't attempt to beat the child, you little vixen!"

"I can't do me pinance with him," cried Nora shrilly, cocking a shocked eye on the priest. "He have me driven mad. Stop your crying, you dirty scut! Stop it now or I'll make you cry at the other side of your ugly puss!"

"Run away out of this, you little jade!" growled the priest. He suddenly began to laugh, took out a pocket handkerchief, and wiped Jackie's nose. "You're not hurt, sure you're not. Show us the ould head. . . . Ah, 'tis nothing. 'Twill be better before you're twice married. . . . So you were coming to confession?"

"I was, father."

"A big fellow like you should have terrible sins. Is it your first?"

" 'Tis, father."

"Oh, my, worse and worse! Here, sit down there and wait till I get rid of these ould ones and we'll have a long chat. Never mind that sister of yours."

With a feeling of importance that glowed through his tears Jackie waited. Nora stuck out her tongue at him, but he didn't even bother to reply. A great feeling of relief was welling up in him. The sense of oppression that had been weighing him down for a week, the knowledge that he was about to make a bad confession, disappeared. Bad confession, indeed! He had made friends, made friends with the priest, and the priest expected, even demanded terrible sins. Oh, women! Women! It was all women and girls and their silly talk. They had no real knowledge of the world!

And when the time came for him to make his confession he did not beat about the bush. He may have clenched his hands and lowered his eyes, but wouldn't anyone?

"Father," he said huskily, "I made it up to kill me grandmother."

There was a moment's pause. Jackie did not dare to look up, but he could feel the priest's eyes on him. The priest's voice also seemed a trifle husky.

"Your grandmother?" he asked, but he didn't after all sound very angry.

"Yes, father."

"Does she live with you?"

"She do, father."

"And why did you want to kill her?"

"Oh, God, father, she's a horrible woman!"

"Is she now? . . . What way is she horrible?"

Jackie paused to think. It was hard to explain.

"She takes snuff, father."

"Oh, my!"

"And she goes round in her bare feet, father."

"Tut-tut-tut!"

"She's a horrible woman, father," said Jackie with sudden earnestness. "She takes porter. And she ates the potatoes off the table with her hands. And me mother do be out working most days, and since that one came 'tis she gives us our dinner and I can't ate the dinner." He found himself sniffling. "And she gives pinnies to Nora and she doesn't give no pinnies to me because she knows I can't stand her. And me father sides with her, father, and he bates me, and me heart is broken and wan night in bed I made it up the way I'd kill her."

Jackie began to sob again, rubbing his nose with his sleeve, as he remembered his wrongs.

"And what way were you going to kill her?" asked the priest smoothly.

"With a hatchet, father."

"When she was in bed?"

"No, father."

"How, so?"

"When she ates the potatoes and drinks the porter she falls asleep, father."

"And you'd hit her then?"

"Yes, father."

"Wouldn't a knife be better?"

" 'Twould, father, only I'd be afraid of the blood."

"Oh, of course, I never thought of the blood."

"I'd be afraid of that, father. I was near hitting Nora with the bread knife one time she came after me under the table, only I was afraid."

"You're a terrible child," said the priest with awe.

"I am, father," said Jackie noncommittally, sniffling back his tears.

"And what would you do with the body?"

"How, father?"

"Wouldn't someone see her and tell?"

"I was going to cut her up with a knife and take away the pieces and bury them. I could get an orange box for three-pence and make a cart to take them away."

"My, my," said the priest. "You had it all well planned."

"Ah, I tried that," said Jackie with mounting confidence. "I borrowed a cart and practiced it meself one night after dark."

"And weren't you afraid?"

"Ah, no," said Jackie half-heartedly. "Only a bit."

"You have terrible courage," said the priest. "There's a lot of people I want to get rid of, but I'm not like you. I'd never have the courage. And hanging is an awful death."

"Is it?" asked Jackie, responding to the brightness of a new theme.

"Oh, an awful blooming death!"

"Did you ever see a fellow hanged?"

"Dozens of them, and they all died roaring."

"Jay!" said Jackie.

"They do be swinging out of them for hours and the poor fellows leaping and roaring, like bells in a belfry, and then they put lime on them to burn them up. Of course, they pretend they're dead but sure, they don't be dead at all."

"Jay!" said Jackie again.

"So if I were you I'd take my time and think about it. In my opinion 'tisn't worth it, not even to get rid of a grandmother. I asked dozens of fellows like you that killed their grandmothers about it, and they all said, no, 'twasn't worth it. . . . "

Nora was waiting in the yard. The sunlight struck down on her across the high wall and its brightness made his eyes dazzle. "Well," she asked. "What did he give you?"

"Three Hail Marys."

"You mustn't have told him anything."

"I told him everything," said Jackie confidently.

"What did you tell him?"

"Things you don't know."

"Bah! He gave you three Hail Marys because you were a cry baby!"

Jackie didn't mind. He felt the world was very good. He began to whistle as well as the hindrance in his jaw permitted.

"What are you sucking?"

"Bull's eyes."

"Was it he gave them to you?"

" 'Twas."

"Almighty God!" said Nora. "Some people have all the luck. I might as well be a sinner like you. There's no use in being good."

Literary Study

Initial Reading. You probably have mixed responses to this story, because of both the humor and the sadness of the situation. If you found this paradoxical, you might accept it as a challenge to discover more about the author's subtleties.

Analysis of Situation and Its Movement (Who, Where, When, How, and Why). The story is told in the past tense by a third-person narrator. At times, this storyteller is omniscient, knowing Jackie's inner thoughts and feelings, yet at other times the narrator almost drops from sight. Limiting the narrator's view increases the illusion of reality and our sense of immediate involvement in the action.

The three characters in the story are realistic; we see them vividly in our minds and feel we know them immediately. Nora appears to be a hypocrite, alternately sweet and sour, soft and shrill. Her dominant motivation seems to be to impress others with her goodness.

Jackie is an angry little boy, but we like him from the beginning. He is honest. He hates his sister most when he sees her come from the confessional with "her hands joined on her stomach, her eyes modestly lowered, and on her face an expression of the most rapt and tender recollection." His inward fears of damnation as he waits in the church, the "death in his heart" as he enters the confessional, and his feeling of panic inside are terribly and humorously clear. When Jackie confesses his terrible sin we understand what has been going on inside this little boy. His dominant motivation is to find love and understanding. Lack of love and attention has led him to want to rid himself of the family intruder, his grandmother; to bolster his deflated ego, he has made "courageous" plans for killing her and even doing away with the body. The priest, recognizing his very human need, gives him the respect and understanding that restores his confidence. We see Jackie change: at the church he expects only punishment and God's wrath, so he wants only to escape; when he finds that the priest offers a sympathetic ear, he wants to unburden his troubled heart. At the end he wants to impress Nora, but the hate is gone; he has something of his own.

The priest is a wonderful human being. We like him immediately because he is perceptive, because he is kind and compassionate, and because he laughs. He does not talk down to Jackie but shows respect for his courage, establishes a common ground and relieves the little boy of his terrible burden. He is not a soft, sentimental person. His voice is angry and authoritative at times. He seems able to view his own life and work with a sense of humor (he speaks lightly of the old ones he must get rid of. . .). Perhaps his dominant motivation is simply to treat the human condition—to condemn and to comfort as the need arises.

The setting is Ireland, and we are led to believe that it is a city, possibly Dublin. The journey to the church and the scene inside are created briefly and clearly. Jackie's first impression of the church establishes an atmosphere in close relation to his inner conflicts: "cold, dark and desolate," "grim iron gates," "intense and magical silence frozen within the ancient walls."

The story may be divided into three parts. The beginning or introduction includes the action before Jackie and Nora enter the church. The author provides exposition of place, time, and characters with economy and conciseness. The conflict between the boy and girl catches our attention at once. The girl's "Now you're caught!" is the high point of the introduction.

The body of the story is the action in the church. In the first scene, the tempo of the story is slowed and the atmosphere inside the church is created. In the next scene, the author introduces an obstacle—the confessional box. Jackie's trials within the box mount slowly and reach a high point when he tumbles into the church aisle. The sister, another obstacle, is taken care of by the priest. The exposition as Jackie waits his turn clarifies Jackie's changed state of mind: the priest is no longer a threat but a friend. This realization is the high point: "He had made friends, made friends with the priest, and the priest expected, even demanded, terrible sins." The final scene and the highest point in this part is the confession. Here we learn Jackie's sin: he has "made it up to kill me grandmother." The general mood is as Jackie tells his story quiet intensity with only light rises. Quietly the priest achieves his goal. His concluding speech: "I asked dozens of fellows like you that killed their grandmothers about it, and they all said, no 'twasn't worth it. . . . " is the master stroke of applied psychology.

The conclusion of the story is the last paragraph. The mood has changed: Jackie's eyes shine; he is a whistling, confident boy as he faces Nora.

The confession, beginning with "I made it up to kill me grandmother" and extending through the priest's last speech, may be considered the climax. Jackie changes as he answers the priest, and we know without being told that the priest's last speech has made a believer out of him. The climax seems attuned to the quiet atmosphere of the church. The author is more concerned with character than with rising peaks of action.

Style and Tone. The use of simple words, the Irish flavor of the dialogue, and understatement make "First Confession" a very warm and human story. The style is natural, economical, and satisfying. The dominant tone is humor, by which the author draws us sympathetically toward Jackie, "the sinner," and toward the priest who understands him.

Theme. The theme of the story is revealed through the dialogue. If there is a moral to be extracted, it is shadowed by subtle humor. Jackie's inner struggle with rejection, anger, revenge, and guilt might be anyone's, but this is so much for one small boy! The story's conflict takes place within Jackie.

Oral Interpretation

This story presents a question: how much of the story can be presented from Jackie's point of view? The illusion of Jackie as a real, live boy would be especially vivid and believable if he himself expressed his own attitude toward what happens. For instance, the description of the action in the confessional box might be very effective when read aloud if told by Jackie rather than by the third-person narrator.

When direct discourse (narrator reporting), indirect discourse (Jackie's thoughts), and dialogue are all used, you should practice until you can make the shifts with ease. Here, for instance, the narrator might say to the audience, "The knowledge that he was making a bad confession disappeared . . ." and Jackie's thoughts would follow immediately: "Bad confession indeed! He had made friends, made friends with the priest . . ."

There should be no difficulty in suggesting the three characters in this story, for they can be easily differentiated by the facial expression, body tone, and vocal characteristics suited to their ages. Nora's personality might be projected by a feeling of energy in the body, accompanied by a soft, overly sweet quality of tone and excessive steps and slides in pitch. Later, when she is alone with Jackie, her voice and body tone change in quality. One way to project the confusion and fear that Jackie is experiencing inside the confessional box could be to tense your muscles and use a breathy voice at a fast rate of delivery. But there may be no need for mechanical plans if the interpreter can control the characterization through concentration. With the dominant motivation of each character in mind, you can find a specific motivation for each speech or action. In the confession scene, the priest's words are motivated by his desire to understand and relieve Jackie's feelings; Jackie's lines are motivated by his desire to unburden his guilt. How could the interpreter use past observations and experiences to re-experience the emotion Jackie feels inside the confessional? You may remember a "terrible sin" from your own childhood and your dread of confessing it to someone. Perhaps you can recall some closed-in feeling or the fear of a great height, or any other terrible fear. Finding related experiences helps the reader believe the situations in the story. But even when using this approach, there may be times when technical plans are needed. For instance, the reader should be careful with Nora's speech that ends the story. This should not be too abrupt; the characterization should be held a moment, with appropriate thoughts directed toward Jackie. This will give the final artistic touch to the interpretation.

Narrative Prose Selections for Study and Performance

Two Short-Short Stories

The Bear Who Let It Alone[7]
James Thurber

In the woods of the Far West there once lived a brown bear who could take it or let it alone. He would go into a bar where they sold mead, a fermented drink made of honey, and he would have just two drinks. Then he would put some money on the bar and say, "See what the bears in the back room will have," and he would go home. But finally he took to drinking by himself most of the day. He would reel home at night, kick over the umbrella stand, knock down the bridge lamps, and ram his elbows through the windows. Then he would collapse on the floor and lie there until he went to sleep. His wife was greatly distressed and his children were very frightened.

At length the bear saw the error of his ways and began to reform. In the end he became a famous teetotaller and a persistent temperance lecturer. He would tell everybody that came to his house about the awful effects of drink, and he would boast about how well and strong he had become since he gave up touching the stuff. To demonstrate this, he would stand on his head and on his hands and he would turn cartwheels in the house, kicking over the umbrella stand, knocking down the bridge lamps, and ramming his elbows through the windows. Then he would lie down on the floor, tired by his healthful experience, and go to sleep. His wife was greatly distressed and his children were very frightened.

Moral: You might as well fall flat on your face as lean over too far backward.

A Box to Hide In[8]
James Thurber

I waited till the large woman with the awful hat took up her sack of groceries and went out, peering at the tomatoes and lettuce on her way. The clerk asked me what mine was.

"Have you got a box," I asked, "a large box? I want a box to hide in."

"You want a box?" he asked.

"I want a box to hide in," I said.

"Whatta you mean?" he said. "You mean a big box?"

I said I meant a box, big enough to hold me.

---

[7] Copr. © 1956 James Thurber. From *Further Fables for Our Time*, published by Simon & Schuster. Originally printed in *The New Yorker*.

[8] Copr. © 1935 James Thurber. Copr. © 1963 Helen W. Thurber and Rosemary Thurber Sauers. From *The Middle-Aged Man on the Flying Trapeze*, published by Harper & Row. Originally printed in *The New Yorker*.

"I haven't got any boxes," he said. "Only cartons that cans come in."

I tried several other groceries and none of them had a box big enough for me to hide in. There was nothing for it but to face life out. I didn't feel strong, and I'd had this overpowering desire to hide in a box for a long time.

"Whatta you mean you want to hide in this box?" one grocer asked me.

"It's a form of escape," I told him, "hiding in a box. It circumscribes your worries and the range of your anguish. You don't see people either."

"How in the hell do you eat when you're in this box?" asked the grocer. "How in the hell do you get anything to eat?" I said I had never been in a box and didn't know, but that that would take care of itself.

"Well," he said, finally, "I haven't got any boxes, only some pasteboard cartons that cans come in."

It was the same every place. I gave up when it got dark and groceries closed, and hid in my room again. I turned out the light and lay on the bed. You feel better when it gets dark, I suppose. I could have hid in a closet, I suppose, but people are always opening doors. Somebody would find you in a closet. They would be startled and you'd have to tell them why you were in the closet. Nobody pays any attention to a big box lying on the floor. You could stay in it for days and nobody'd think to look in it, not even the cleaning-woman.

My cleaning-woman came the next morning and woke me up. I was still feeling bad. I asked her if she knew where I could get a large box.

"How big a box you want?" she asked.

"I want a box big enough for me to get inside of," I said. She looked at me with big, dim eyes. There's something wrong with her glands. She's awful but she has a big heart, which makes it worse. She's unbearable, her husband is sick and her children are sick and she is sick too. I got to thinking how pleasant it would be if I were in a box now, and didn't have to see her. I would be in a box right there in the room and she wouldn't know. I wondered if you have a desire to bark or laugh when someone who doesn't know walks by the box you are in. Maybe she would have a spell with her heart, if I did that, and would die right there. The officers and the elevator man and Mr. Gramadge would find us. "Funny doggone thing happened at the building last night," the door-man would say to his wife. "I let in this woman to clean up 10-F and she never come out, see? She's never there more'n an hour, but she never come out, see? So when it got to be time for me to go off duty, why I says to Crennick, who was on the elevator, I says 'what the hell you suppose has happened to that woman cleans 10-F.' He says he didn't know; he says he never seen her after he took her up. So I spoke to Mr. Gramadge about it. 'I'm sorry to bother you, Mr. Gramadge,' I says, 'but there's something funny about that woman cleans 10-F.' So I told him. So he said we better have a look and we all three goes up and knocks on the door and rings the bell, see, and nobody answers so he said we'd have to walk in so Crennick opened the door and we walked in and here was this woman cleans the apartment dead as a herring on the floor and the gentleman that lives there was in a box." . . .

The cleaning-woman kept looking at me. It was hard to realize she wasn't dead. "It's a form of escape," I murmured. "What say?" she asked, dully.

"You don't know of any large packing boxes, do you?" I asked.

"No, I don't," she said.

I haven't found one yet, but I still have this overpowering urge to hide in a box. Maybe it will go away, maybe I'll be all right. Maybe it will get worse. It's hard to say.

Study Questions. Shortly after James Thurber's death, Mark Van Doren told of a conversation with him. Thurber said his greatest unhappiness was that he had always played up the bad in human nature, failing to bring out the good. Van Doren assured him that in writing as he had, he had reached man by pointing out weaknesses "funnily" and that this was a positive influence. After reading these stories, do you agree? Do you object to his view of the minor characters in "A Box to Hide In"? Is the narrator bordering on the psychotic or is he a sane person making fun of himself? What does he want?

What is satirized in each of the stories? How? What truth is Thurber pointing to in each of the stories? How would you characterize the two narrators vocally and physically? Were you surprised by the endings? How would you handle these vocally?

Scene Cutting From a Short Story

Everything That Rises Must Converge[9]
Flannery O'Connor

Julian's mother had to close her purse while she got down the bus step but as soon as her feet were on the ground, she opened it again and began to rummage inside. "I can't find but a penny," she whispered, "but it looks like a new one."

"Don't do it!" Julian said fiercely between his teeth. There was a street light on the corner and she hurried to get under it so that she could better see into her pocket-book. The woman was heading off rapidly down the street with the child still hanging backward on her hand.

"Oh, little boy!" Julian's mother called and took a few quick steps and caught up with them just beyond the lamppost. "Here's a bright new penny for you," and she held out the coin, which shone bronze in the dim light.

The huge woman turned and for a moment stood, her shoulders lifted and her face frozen with frustrated rage, and stared at Julian's mother. Then all at once she seemed to explode like a piece of machinery that had been given one ounce of pressure too much. Julian saw the black fist swing out with the red pocket-book. He shut his eyes and cringed as he heard the woman shout. "He don't take nobody's pennies!" When he opened his eyes, the woman was disappearing down the street with the little boy staring wide-eyed over her shoulder. Julian's mother was sitting on the sidewalk.

"I told you not to do that," Julian said angrily. "I told you not to do that!"

He stood over her for a minute, gritting his teeth. Her legs were stretched out in front of her and her hat was on her lap. He squatted down and looked her in the face. It was totally expressionless. "You got exactly what you deserved," he said. "Now get up."

He picked up her pocket-book and put what had fallen out back in it. He picked the hat up off her lap. The penny caught his eye on the sidewalk and he picked that up and let it drop before her eyes into the purse. Then he stood up and leaned over and held his hands out to pull her up. She remained immobile. He sighed. Rising above them on either side were black apartment buildings, marked with irregular rectangles of light. At the end of the block, a man came out of a door and walked off in the opposite direction. "All right," he said, "suppose somebody happens by and wants to know why you're sitting on the sidewalk?"

She took the hand and, breathing hard, pulled heavily up on it and then stood for a moment, swaying slightly as if the spots of light in the darkness were circling around her. Her eyes, shadowed and confused, finally settled on his face. He did not try to conceal his irritation. "I hope this teaches you a lesson," he said. She leaned forward and her eyes raked his face. She seemed trying to determine his identity. Then, as if she found nothing familiar about him, she started off with a headlong movement in the wrong direction.

[9] The concluding section of "Everything That Rises Must Converge" from *Everything That Rises Must Converge* by Flannery O'Connor. Copyright © 1961, 1965 by the Estate of Mary Flannery O'Connor. Reprinted with the permission of Farrar, Straus & Giroux, Inc.

"Aren't you going to the Y?" he asked.

"Home," she muttered.

"Well, are we walking?"

For answer she kept going. Julian followed along, his hands behind him. He saw no reason to let the lesson she had had go without backing it up with an explanation of its meaning. She might as well be made to understand what had happened to her. "Don't think that was just an uppity Negro woman," he said. "That was the whole colored race which will no longer take your condescending pennies. That was your black double. She can wear the same hat as you, and to be sure," he added gratuitously (because he thought it was funny), "it looked better on her than it did on you. What all this means," he said, "is that the old world is gone. The old manners are obsolete and your graciousness is not worth a damn." He thought bitterly of the house that had been lost for him. "You aren't who you think you are," he said.

She continued to plow ahead, paying no attention to him. Her hair had come undone on one side. She dropped her pocketbook and took no notice. He stooped and picked it up and handed it to her but she did not take it.

"You needn't act as if the world had come to an end," he said, "because it hasn't. From now on you're got to live in a new world and face a few realities for a change. Buck up," he said, "it won't kill you."

She was breathing fast.

"Let's wait on the bus," he said.

"Home," she said thickly.

"I hate to see you behave like this," he said. "Just like a child. I should be able to expect more of you." He decided to stop where he was and make her stop and wait for a bus. "I'm not going any farther," he said, stopping. "We're going on the bus."

She continued to go on as if she had not heard him. He took a few steps and caught her arm and stopped her. He looked into her face and caught his breath. He was looking into a face he had never seen before. "Tell Grandpa to come get me," she said.

He stared, stricken.

"Tell Caroline to come get me," she said.

Stunned, he let her go and she lurched forward again, walking as if one leg were shorter than the other. A tide of darkness seemed to be sweeping her from him. "Mother!" he cried. "Darling, sweetheart, wait!" Crumpling, she fell to the pavement.

Study Questions. What values are at issue in this cutting? Are you persuaded to accept the author's view, as projected by the narrator? Do you find the point of view simple or complex? What is Julian's attitude toward his mother and all she represents? Do you consider the cutting incomplete because of the way it ends? What is the significance of the last line? Would it be possible to project this? What does the story's title imply to you?

Short Story

The Chase[10]
Alberto Moravia

I have never been a sportsman—or, rather, I have been a sportsman only once, and that was the first and last time. I was a child, and one day, for some

[10] "The Chase" from *Command, and I Will Obey You* by Alberto Moravia, translated from the Italian by Angus Davidson. English translation Copyright© 1969 by Martin Secker & Warburg Limited. Reprinted with the permission of Farrar, Straus & Giroux, Inc.

reason or other, I found myself together with my father, who was holding a gun in his hand, behind a bush, watching a bird that had perched on a branch not very far away. It was a large, gray bird—or perhaps it was brown—with a long—or perhaps a short—beak; I don't remember. I only remember what I felt at that moment as I looked at it. It was like watching an animal whose vitality was rendered more intense by the very fact of my watching it and of the animal's not knowing that I was watching it.

At that moment, I say, the notion of wildness entered my mind, never again to leave it: everything is wild which is autonomous and unpredictable and does not depend upon us. Then all of a sudden there was an explosion; I could no longer see the bird and I thought it had flown away. But my father was leading the way, walking in front of me through the undergrowth. Finally he stooped down, picked up something and put it in my hand. I was aware of something warm and soft and I lowered my eyes: there was the bird in the palm of my hand, its dangling, shattered head crowned with a plume of already-thickening blood. I burst into tears and dropped the corpse on the ground, and that was the end of my shooting experience.

I thought again of this remote episode in my life this very day after watching my wife, for the first and also the last time, as she was walking through the streets of the city. But let us take things in order.

What had my wife been like; what was she like now? She once had been, to put it briefly, "wild"—that is, entirely autonomous and unpredictable; latterly she had become "tame"—that is, predictable and dependent. For a long time she had been like the bird that, on that far-off morning in ny childhood, I had seen perching on the bough; latterly, I am sorry to say, she had become like a hen about which one knows everything in advance—how it moves, how it eats, how it lays eggs, how it sleeps, and so on.

Nevertheless I would not wish anyone to think that my wife's wildness consisted of an uncouth, rough, rebellious character. Apart from being extremely beautiful, she is the gentlest, politest, most discreet person in the world. Rather her wildness consisted of the air of charming unpredictability, of independence in her way of living, with which during the first years of our marriage she acted in my presence, both at home and abroad. Wildness signified intimacy, privacy, secrecy. Yes, my wife as she sat in front of her dressing table, her eyes fixed on the looking glass, passing the hairbrush with a repeated motion over her long, loose hair, was just as wild as the solitary quail hopping forward along the sun-filled furrow or the furtive fox coming out into a clearing and stopping to look around before running on. She was wild because I, as I looked at her, could never manage to foresee when she would give a last stroke with the hairbrush and rise and come toward me; wild to such a degree that sometimes when I went into our bedroom the smell of her, floating in the air, would have something of the acrid quality of a wild beast's lair.

Gradually she became less wild, tamer. I had had a fox, a quail, in the house, as I have said; then one day I realized that I had a hen. What effect does a hen have on someone who watches it? It has the effect of being, so to speak, an automaton in the form of a bird; automatic are the brief, rapid steps with which it moves about; automatic its hard, terse pecking; automatic the glance of the round eyes in its head that nods and turns; automatic its ready crouching down under the cock; automatic the dropping of the egg wherever it may be and the cry with which it announces that the egg has been laid. Good-by to the fox; good-by to the quail. And her smell—this no longer brought to my mind, in any way, the innocent odor of a wild animal; rather I detected in it the chemical suavity of some ordinary French perfume.

Our flat is on the first floor of a big building in a modern quarter of the town; our windows look out on a square in which there is a small public garden, the haunt of nurses and children and dogs. One day I was standing at the window, looking in a melancholy way at the garden. My wife, shortly before, had dressed to go out; and once again, watching her, I had noticed the irrevocable and, so to speak, invisible character of her gestures and personality; something which gave one the feeling of a thing already seen and already done and which therefore evaded even the most determined observation. And now, as I stood looking at the garden and at the same time wondering why the adorable wildness of former times had so completely disappeared, suddenly my wife came into my range of vision as she walked quickly across the garden in the direction of the bus stop. I watched her and then I almost jumped for joy; in a movement she was making to pull down a fold of her narrow skirt and smooth it over her thigh with the tips of her long, sharp nails, in this movement I recognized the wildness that in the past had made me love her. It was only an instant, but in that instant I said to myself: She's become wild again because she's convinced that I am not there and am not watching her. Then I left the window and rushed out.

But I did not join her at the bus stop; I felt that I must not allow myself to be seen. Instead I hurried to my car, which was standing nearby, got in and waited. A bus came and she got in together with some other people; the bus started off again and I began following it. Then there came back to me the memory of that one shooting expedition in which I had taken part as a child, and I saw that the bus was the undergrowth with its bushes and trees, my wife the bird perching on the bough while I, unseen, watched it living before my eyes. And the whole town, during this pursuit, became, as though by magic, a fact of nature like the countryside: the houses were hills, the streets valleys, the vehicles hedges and woods, and even the passers-by on the pavements had something unpredictable and autonomous— that is, wild—about them. And in my mouth, behind my clenched teeth, there was the acrid, metallic taste of gunfire; and my eyes, usually listless and wandering, had become sharp, watchful attentive.

These eyes were fixed intently upon the exit door when the bus came to the end of its run. A number of people got out, and then I saw my wife getting out. Once again I recognized, in the manner in which she broke free of the crowd and started off toward a neighboring street, the wildness that pleased me so much. I jumped out of the car and started following her.

She was walking in front of me, ignorant of my presence, a tall woman with an elegant figure, long-legged, narrow-hipped, broad-backed, her brown hair falling on her shoulder.

Men turned around as she went past; perhaps they were aware of what I myself was now sensing with an intensity that quickened the beating of my heart and took my breath away: the unrestricted, steadily increasing, irresistible character of her mysterious wildness.

She walked hurriedly, having evidently some purpose in view, and even the fact that she had a purpose of which I was ignorant added to her wildness; I did not know where she was going, just as on that far-off morning I had not known what the bird perching on the bough was about to do. Moreover, I thought the gradual, steady increase in this quality of wildness came partly from the fact that as she drew nearer and nearer to the object of this mysterious walk there was an increase in her—how shall I express it?—of biological tension, of existential excitement, of vital effervescence. Then, unexpectedly, with the suddenness of a film, her purpose was revealed.

A fair-haired young man in a leather jacket and a pair of corduroy trousers was leaning against the wall of a house in that ancient, narrow street. He was idly smoking as he looked in front of him. But as my wife passed close to him, he threw away his cigarette with a decisive gesture, took a step forward and seized her arm. I was expecting her to rebuff him, to move away from him, but nothing happened: evidently obeying the rules of some kind of erotic ritual, she went on walking beside the young man. Then after a few steps, with a movement that confirmed her own complicity, she put her arm around her companion's waist and he put his around her.

I understood then that this unknown man who took such liberties with my wife was also attracted by wildness. And so, instead of making a conventional appointment with her, instead of meeting in a café with a handshake, a falsely friendly and respectful welcome, he had preferred, by agreement with her, to take

119

her by surprise—or, rather, to pretend to do so—while she was apparently taking a walk on her own account. All this I perceived by intuition, noticing that at the very moment when he stepped forward and took her arm her wildness had, so to speak, given an upward bound. It was years since I had seen my wife so alive, but alas, the source of this life could not be traced to me.

They walked on thus entwined and then, without any preliminaries, just like two wild animals, they did an unexpected thing: they went into one of the dark doorways in order to kiss. I stopped and watched them from a distance, peering into the darkness of the entrance. My wife was turned away from me and was bending back with the pressure of his body, her hair hanging free. I looked at that long, thick mane of brown hair, which as she leaned back fell free of her shoulders, and I felt that at that moment her vitality reached its diapason, just as happens with wild animals when they couple and their customary wildness is redoubled by the violence of love. I watched for a long time and then, since this kiss went on and on and in fact seemed to be prolonged beyond the limits of my power of endurance, I saw that I would have to intervene.

I would have to go forward, seize my wife by the arm—or actually by that hair, which hung down and conveyed so well the feeling of feminine passivity—then hurl myself with clenched fists upon the blond young man. After this encounter I would carry off my wife, weeping, mortified, ashamed, while I was raging and broken-hearted, upbraiding her and pouring scorn upon her.

But what else would this intervention amount to but the shot my father fired at that free, unknowing bird as it perched on the bough? The disorder and confusion, the mortification, the shame, that would follow would irreparably destroy the rare and precious moment of wildness that I was witnessing inside the dark doorway. It was true that this wildness was directed against me; but I had to remember that wildness, always and everywhere, is directed against everything and everybody. After the scene of my intervention it might be possible for me to regain control of my wife, but I should find her shattered and lifeless in my arms like the bird that my father had placed in my hand so that I might throw it into the shooting bag.

The kiss went on and on and on: well, it was a kiss of passion—that could not be denied. I waited until they finished, until they came out of the doorway, until they walked on again still linked together. Then I turned back.

Study Questions. How does the narrator's experience as a boy influence his behavior as a man? What is the source of the conflict in his relationship with his wife? How do you envision the wife? What does the narrator reveal about himself? Does he understand his own personality? Where does the tension reach its highest point? Are you prepared for the ending? How do you envision the relationship after the event?

Chapter 8

Interpretive Reading of Poetry

In What Ways Does Poetry Speak?

A poem often says one thing and means something else. It fools us. Robert Frost said about these lines,

> *He will not see me stopping here*
> *To watch his woods fill up with snow*[1]

"That's a poetry way of speaking. The woods are not going to fill up with snow. But if you don't like that way of fooling you won't ever like poetry."[2] How else does poetry speak? **Poetry says much in few words; it intensifies thought and feeling into a compressed, condensed form.**

In the following poem, Tennyson uses compression to express part of life's meaning:

Flower in the Crannied Wall
Alfred, Lord Tennyson

> *Flower in the crannied wall,*
> *I pluck you out of the crannies,*
> *I hold you here, root and all, in my hand,*
> *Little flower—but if I could understand*
> *What you are, root and all, and all in all,*
> *I should know what God and man is.*

---

[1] From *The Poetry of Robert Frost*, edited by Edward Connery Lathem. Copyright 1923, 1939, ©1967, 1969 by Holt, Rinehart and Winston. Copyright 1951 by Robert Frost. Reprinted by permission of Holt, Rinehart and Winston, Publishers.

[2] From Chester Morrison, "A Visit With Robert Frost." *Look Magazine*, March 31, 1959, p. 76. Reprinted by permission of the editors of *Look Magazine*, copyright 1959.

Could the mystery of Emily Dickinson's life be more intensely realized than through this brief portrait?

Emily Dickinson[3]
Linda Pastan

We think of her hidden in a white dress
among the folded linens and sachets
of well kept cupboards, or just out of sight
sending jellies and notes with no address
to all the wondering Amherst neighbors.
Eccentric as New England weather
the stiff wind of her mind, stinging or gentle
blew two half imagined lovers off.
Yet legend won't explain the sheer sanity
of vision, the serious mischief
of language, the economy of pain.

And how, could grief be more simply stated, yet more deeply sensed, than in these six brief lines?

Li-Fu-Jen[4]
Emperor Wu-Ti

The sound of her silk skirt has stopped.
On the marble pavement dust grows.
Her empty room is cold and still.
Fallen leaves are pitted against the doors.
  Longing for that lovely lady
How can I bring my aching heart to rest?

Poetry speaks in figures and symbols to say one thing and mean something else. In "Li-Fu-Jen," there are two images of sound, two of sight, one of feeling, then a question—and suddenly we know the speaker's grief, and more; we know our own. In the poem below, we find animation of abstractions, transfer of senses, juxtapositions—a variety of metaphorical dislocation, but the poet gives us clues to help us decode his meaning. Can you find them?

anyone lived in a pretty how town[5]
e. e. cummings

anyone lived in a pretty how town
(with up so floating many bells down)
spring summer autumn winter
he sang his didn't he danced his did.

---

[3] "Emily Dickinson" by Linda Pastan in *A Perfect Circle of Sun* published in Swallow Publishers, 1971. Reprinted by permission of the author.

[4] Copyright 1919 and renewed 1947 by Arthur Waley. Reprinted from *Translations from the Chinese,* translated by Arthur Waley, by permission of Alfred A. Knopf, Inc.

[5] Copyright 1940 by E. E. Cummings; renewed 1968 by Marion Morehouse Cummings. Reprinted from *Complete Poems 1913–1962* by E. E. Cummings by permission of Harcourt Brace Jovanovich, Inc.

Women and men(both little and small)
cared for anyone not at all
they sowed their isn't they reaped their same
sun moon stars rain

children guessed(but only a few
and down they forgot as up they grew
autumn winter spring summer)
that noone loved him more by more

when by now and tree by leaf
she laughed his joy she cried his grief
bird by snow and stir by still
anyone's any was all to her

someones married their everyones
laughed their cryings and did their dance
(sleep wake hope and then)they
said their nevers they slept their dream

stars rain sun moon
(and only the snow can begin to explain
how children are apt to forget to remember
with up so floating many bells down)

one day anyone died i guess
(and noone stooped to kiss his face)
busy folk buried them side by side
little by little and was by was

all by all and deep by deep
and more by more they dream their sleep
noone and anyone earth by april
wish by spirit and if by yes.

Women and men(both dong and ding)
summer autumn winter spring
reaped their sowing and went their came
sun moon stars rain

**Poetry speaks with musical accompaniment; the texture of sound
relationships color the thought and feeling and are part of the
poem's total meaning.**

We Real Cool[6]
Gwendolyn Brooks

> *The Pool Players*
> *Seven at the Golden Shovel*
We real cool. We
Left school. We

---

[6] "We Real Cool: The Pool Players. Seven at the Golden Shovel" from *The World of Gwendolyn Brooks* by Gwendolyn Brooks Copyright © 1959 by Gwendolyn Brooks By permission of Harper & Row, Publishers, Inc.

Lurk late. We
Strike straight. We

Sing sin. We
Thin gin. We

Jazz June. We
Die soon.

What Does Poetry Say?

The poem seldom presents a message; rather, it reveals a truth.
Archibald MacLeish has said that the poet presenting a work of art should

> present the poem not as a message in a bottle, and not as an object in an
> uninhabited landscape, but as an action in the world, an action in which we
> ourselves are actors and our lives are known.[7]

In What Ways Do Modern Poems Speak?

Consider the ways these modern poems speak to you.

Dreaming America[8]
Joyce Carol Oates

When the two-lane highway was widened
the animals retreated.
Skunks, racoons, rabbits—even their small corpses
disappeared from the road—transformed into rags
then into designs
then into stains
then nothing.

When the highway was linked to another
then to another
six lanes then nine then twelve rose
sweeping to the horizon
alone measured white lines.
The polled Herefords were sold.
When the cornfields were bulldozed
the farmhouses at their edges turned into shanties;
the outbuildings fell.

When the fields were paved over
Frisch's Big Boy rose seventy-five feet in the air.

---

[7] MacLeish. "Why Do We Teach Poetry?" *Atlantic Monthly*, April 1957.

[8] "Dreaming America" by Joyce Carol Oates. Reprinted by permission of author.

The Sunoco *and* Texaco *and* Gulf *signs competed*
on hundred-foot stilts
like eyeballs on stalks
white optic-nerves
miraculous.
Illuminated at night.

Where the useless stretch of trees lay
an orange sphere like a golf ball
announces the Shopping Mall, open
for Thursday evening shopping.
There, tonight, droves of teenagers hunt
one another, alert on the memorized pavement.

Where did the country go?—cry the travellers, soaring
past. Where did the country go?—ask the strangers.
The teenagers never ask.

Where horses grazed in a dream that had no history,
tonight a thirteen-year-old girl stands dreaming
into the window of Levitz's Record Shop.
We drive past, in a hurry. We disappear.
We return.

in Just-[9]
e. e. cummings

in Just-
spring   when the world is mud-
luscious the little
lame balloonman

whistles   far   and wee

and eddieandbill come
running from marbles and
piracies and it's
spring

when the world is puddle-wonderful

the queer
old balloonman whistles
far   and   wee
and bettyandisbel come dancing

from hop-scotch and jump-rope and

---

it's
spring
and
 the

  goat-footed

balloonMan   *whistles*
far
and
wee

Blue Girls[10]
John Crowe Ransom

Twirling your blue skirts, traveling the sward
Under the towers of your seminary,
Go listen to your teachers old and contrary
Without believing a word.

Tie the white fillets then about your lustrous hair
And think no more of what will come to pass
Than bluebirds that go walking on the grass
And chattering on the air.

Practice your beauty, blue girls, before it fail;
And I will cry with my loud lips and publish
Beauty which all our power shall never establish,
It is so frail.

For I could tell you a story which is true:
I know a lady with a terrible tongue,
Blear eyes fallen from blue,
All her perfections tarnished—and yet it is not long
Since she was lovelier than any of you.

Unknown Girl in the Maternity Ward[11]
Anne Sexton

Child, the current of your breath is six days long.
You lie, a small knuckle on my white bed;
lie, fisted like a snail, so small and strong
at my breast. Your lips are animals; you are fed
with love. At first hunger is not wrong.
The nurses nod their caps; you are shepherded
down starch halls with the other unnested throng

---

in wheeling baskets. You tip like a cup; your head
moving to my touch. You sense the way we belong.
But this is an institution bed.
You will not know me very long.

The doctors are enamel. they want to know
the facts. They guess about the man who left me,
some pendulum soul, going the way men go
and leave you full of child. But our case history
stays blank. All I did was let you grow.
Now we are here for all the ward to see.
They thought I was strange, although
I never spoke a word. I burst empty
of you, letting you learn how the air is so.
The doctors chart the riddle they ask of me
and I turn my head away. I do not know.

Yours is the only face I recognize.
Bone at my bone, you drink my answers in.
Six times a day I prize
your need, the animals of your lips, your skin
growing warm and plump. I see your eyes
lifting their tents. They are blue stones, they begin
to outgrow their moss. You blink in surprise
and I wonder what you can see, my funny kin,
as you trouble my silence. I am a shelter of lies.
Should I learn to speak again, or hopeless in
such sanity will I touch some face I recognize?

Down the hall the baskets start back. My arms
fit you like a sleeve, they hold
catkins of your willows, the wild bee farms
of your nerves, each muscle and fold
of your first days. Your old man's face disarms
the nurses. But the doctors return to scold
me. I speak. It is you my silence harms.
I should have known; I should have told
them something to write down. My voice alarms
my throat. "Name of father—none." I hold
you and name you bastard in my arms.

And now that's that. There is nothing more
that I can say or lose.
Others have traded life before
and could not speak. I tighten to refuse
your owling eyes, my fragile visitor.
I touch your cheeks, like flowers. You bruise
against me. We unlearn. I am a shore
rocking you off. You break from me. I choose
your only way, my small inheritor
and hand you off, trembling the selves we lose.
Go child, who is my sin and nothing more.

This is My Letter to the World[12]
Emily Dickinson

This is my letter to the world,
  That never wrote to me—
The simple news that Nature told,
  With tender majesty.

Her message is committed
  To hands I cannot see,
For love of her, sweet countrymen,
  Judge tenderly of me!

That Golden Afternoon[13]
Carol Gesner

But you sat there that golden afternoon
So stoically polite and courtly plain,
So full of "if per chance" and "rather"
—"But I really must explain"—
With sunlight on blue velvet:
                    books behind
All shelved by period and alphabet—
Brown, blue, and tannish yellow, several gray,
Some lavender, fine reds, a greeny-lime
Mysterious with gold trace down the spine
And motes of dust caught up as though a line
Of particles and atomies had danced
Quite off the sun—
Had coursed in perfect time
With all accounts celestial as they spun.

The laymen added sugar to their tea
And spoke of drying butterflies in glass
While all those sun motes settled on your cheek,
—"Derived from French through Arabic, not Greek"—
Drew up the ruddy traceries, the web
That nets about and wraps the you in you.
And then your eyes left studying the page
And lifted up to mine all amber-bold;
The throbbing web and sunlight burned to gold
And branded me forever: tagged and sold.

---

[12] Reprinted by permission of the publishers and the Trustees of Amherst College from *The Poems of Emily Dickinson*, edited by Thomas H. Johnson, Cambridge, Mass.: The Belknap Press of Harvard University Press, Copyright © 1951, 1955 by the President and Fellows of Harvard College.

[13] "That Golden Afternoon" by Carol Gesner. Reprinted by permission of the author.

come, gaze with me upon this dome[14]
e. e. cummings

come, gaze with me upon this dome
of many coloured glass, and see
his mother's pride, his father's joy,
unto whom duty whispers low

"thou must!" and who replies "I can!"
—yon clean upstanding well dressed boy
that with his peers full oft hath quaffed
the wine of life and found it sweet—

a tear within his stern blue eye,
upon his firm white lips a smile,
one thought alone: to do or die
for God for country and for Yale

above his blond determined head
the sacred flag of truth unfurled,
in the bright heyday of his youth
the upper class American

unsullied stands, before the world:
with manly heart and conscience free,
upon the front steps of her home
by the high minded pure young girl

much kissed, by loving relatives
well fed, and fully photographed
the son of man goes forth to war
with trumpets clap and syphilis

Wild Grapes[15]
Robert Frost

What tree may not the fig be gathered from?
The grape may not be gathered from the birch?
It's all you know the grape, or know the birch.
As a girl gathered from the birch myself
Equally with my weight in grapes, one autumn,
I ought to know what tree the grape is fruit of
I was born, I suppose, like anyone,
And grew to be a little boyish girl
My brother could not always leave at home.

---

[14] Copyright 1926 by Horace Liveright; renewed 1954 by E. E. Cummings. Reprinted from *Complete Poems 1913–1962* by E. E. Cummings by permission of Harcourt Brace Jovanovich, Inc.

[15] From *The Poetry of Robert Frost*, edited by Edward Connery Lathem. Copyright 1923, 1939, © 1967, 1969 by Holt, Rinehart and Winston. Copyright 1951 by Robert Frost. Reprinted by permission of Holt, Rinehart and Winston, Publishers.

But that beginning was wiped out in fear
The day I swung suspended with the grapes,
And was come after like Eurydice
And brought down safely from the upper regions;
And the life I live now's an extra life
I can waste as I please on whom I please.
So if you see me celebrate two birthdays,
And give myself out as two different ages,
One of them five years younger than I look—
One day my brother led me to a glade
Where a white birch he knew of stood alone,
Wearing a thin head-dress of pointed leaves,
And heavy on her heavy hair behind,
Against her neck, an ornament of grapes.
Grapes, I knew grapes from having seen them last year.
One bunch of them, and there began to be
Bunches all round me growing in white birches,
The way they grew round Leif the Lucky's German;
Mostly as much beyond my lifted hands, though,
As the moon used to seem when I was younger,
And only freely to be had for climbing.

My brother did the climbing; and at first
Threw me down grapes to miss and scatter
And have to hunt for in sweet fern and hardhack
Which gave him some time to himself to eat,
But not so much, perhaps, as a boy needed.
So then, to make me wholly self-supporting,
He climbed still higher and bent the tree to earth
And put it in my hands to pick my own grapes.
"Here, take a tree-top, I'll get down another.
Hold on with all your might when I let go."
I said I had the tree. It wasn't true.
The opposite was true. The tree had me.
The minute it was left with me alone
It caught me up as if I were the fish
And it the fishpole. So I was translated
To loud cries from my brother of "Let go!
Don't you know anything, you girl? Let go!"
But I, with something of the baby grip
Acquired ancestrally in just such trees
When wilder mothers than our wildest now
Hung babies out on branches by the hands
To dry or wash or tan, I don't know which,
(You'll have to ask an evolutionist)—
I held on uncomplainingly for life.
My brother tried to make me laugh to help me.
"What are you doing up there in those grapes?
Don't be afraid. A few of them won't hurt you.
I mean, they won't pick you if you don't them."
Much danger of my picking anything!
By that time I was pretty well reduced
To a philosophy of hang-and-let-hang.

"Now you know how it feels," my brother said,
"To be a bunch of fox-grapes, as they call them,
That when it thinks it has escaped the fox
By growing where it shouldn't—on a birch,
Where a fox wouldn't think to look for it—
And if he looked and found it, couldn't reach it—
Just then come you and I to gather it.
Only you have the advantage of the grapes
In one way: you have one more stem to cling by,
And promise more resistance to the picker."
One by one I lost off my hat and shoes,
And still I clung. I let my head fall back
And shut my eyes against the sun, my ears
Against my brother's nonsense; "Drop," he said,
"I'll catch you in my arms. It isn't far."
(Stated in lengths of him it might not be.)
"Drop or I'll shake the tree and shake you down."
Grim silence on my part as I sank lower,
My small wrists stretching till they showed the banjo strings,
"Why, if she isn't serious about it!
Hold tight awhile till I think what to do.
I'll bend the tree down and let you down by it."
I don't know much about the letting down;
But once I felt ground with my stocking feet
And the world came revolving back to me,
I know I looked long at my curled-up fingers,
Before I straightened them and brushed the bark off.
My brother said: "Don't you weigh anything?
Try to weigh something next time, so you won't
Be run off by birch trees into space."

It wasn't my not weighing anything
So much as my not knowing anything—
My brother had been nearer right before.
I had not taken the first step in knowledge;
I had not learned to let go with the hands,
As still I have not learned to with the heart,
And have no wish to with the heart—nor need,
That I can see. The mind—is not the heart.
I may yet live, as I know others live,
To wish in vain to let go with the mind—
Of cares, at night, to sleep; but nothing tells me
That I need to learn to let go with the heart.

You Are Odysseus[16]
Linda Pastan

You are Odysseus
returning home each evening

---

[16] "You Are Odysseus" is reprinted from *Aspects of Eve*, Poems by Linda Pastan, with the permission of W. W. Norton & Company, Inc. Copyright © 1970, 1971, 1972, 1973, 1974, 1975, by Linda Pastan.

tentative, a little angry.
And I who thought to be
one of the Sirens (cast up
on strewn sheets
at dawn)
hide my song
under my tongue—
merely Penelope after all.
Meanwhile, the old wars
go on, their dim music
can be heard even at night.
You leave each morning,
soon our son will follow.
Only my weaving
is real.

The River Merchant's Wife: A Letter[17]
Ezra Pound

While my hair was still cut straight across my forehead
I played about the front gate, pulling flowers.
You came by on bamboo stilts, playing horse,
You walked about my seat, playing with blue plums.
And we went on living in the village of Chokan:
Two small people, without dislike or suspicion.

At fourteen I married My Lord you.
I never laughed, being bashful.
Lowering my head, I looked at the wall,
Called to, a thousand times, I never looked back.

At fifteen I stopped scowling,
I desired my dust to be mingled with yours
Forever and forever and forever.
Why should I climb the look out?

At sixteen you departed.
You went into far Ku-to-Yen, by the river of swirling eddies,
And you have been gone five months.
The monkeys make sorrowful noise overhead.

You dragged your feet when you went out.
By the gate now, the moss is grown, the different mosses,
Too deep to clear them away!
The leaves fall early this autumn, in wind.
The paired butterflies are already yellow with August.
Over the grass in the West garden,
They hurt me. I grow older.

If you are coming down through the narrows of the river Kiang,
Please let me know beforehand,

And I will come out to meet you
As far as Cho-fu-sa.

On the Way Home[18]
Wallace Stevens

It was when I said,
"There is no such thing as the truth,"
That the grapes seemed fatter.
The fox ran out of his hole.

You . . . You said,
"There are many truths
But they are not parts of a truth."
Then the tree, at night, began to change,
Smoking through green and smoking blue.
We were two figures in a wood,
We said we stood alone.

It was when I said,
"Words are not forms of a single word,
In the sum of the parts, there are only the parts.
The world must be measured by eye";

It was when you said,
"The idols have seen lots of poverty,
Snakes and gold and lice,
But not the truth";

It was at that time, that the silence was largest
And longest, the night was roundest,
The fragrance of the autumn warmest,
Closest and strongest.

Problems in Communicating Poetry

Now let us consider some of the problems encountered in the oral interpretation of poetry.

Recognizing and Controlling Rhythmic Patterns

Unless there is a reason for using exaggerated effects, the poem's rhythm should remain a kind of underflow, with the meaning on top. But what are the patterns to be left as underflow? In patterned verse, we usually hear repetitions of sounds and of silence, breaks in the flow at approximately equal intervals, a pause at the end of one stanza and the beginning of another, and pauses at the ends of the lines.

---

[18] Copyright 1942 by Wallace Stevens and renewed 1970 by Holly Stevens. Reprinted from *The Collected Poems of Wallace Stevens*, by permission of Alfred A. Knopf, Inc.

Meter. We sometimes hear a recurrence of similar stresses or emphases within the verse line. In English there are four principal types of meter or beat (´ represents a stress; ˘ lack of stress):

1   *dă DÁ/ dă DÁ /dă DÁ/ dă DÁ /*
      I wán /dĕred lóne/ lў ás /ă clóud/
2   *DÁ dă/ DÁ dă / DÁ dă /DÁ dă/*
      Jén nў /kíss'd mĕ /whén wĕ/ mét- /
3   *dă dă DÁ / dă dă DÁ /dă dă DÁ /dă DÁ/*
      It wăs mán /ў ănd mán/ ў ă yéar / ă gó /
4   *DÁ dă dă /DÁ dă dă/ DÁ dă dă /*
      Thís ĭs thĕ /fórĕst prĭ /mé văl. Thĕ / . . .

Each interval marked off with a slash (/) is called a foot. The lines above are (1) iambic, (2) trochaic, (3) anapestic, and (4) dactylic meter. The feet that make up the lines are called (1) iambs, (2) trochees, (3) anapests, and (4) dactyls.

In patterned verse we hear a turning from and returning to one of these basic beats, or a related one. Poets depart from regular meter to prevent monotony, to draw attention to something, or to change a mood. Notice how in the first two lines of "A Deep-Sworn Vow," Yeats turns from his basic pattern of dă DÁ/ dă DÁ/ dă DÁ/ dă DÁ/ to draw attention to the words "others" and "deep-sworn vow":

ÓTHĕrs/ bĕCÁUSE/ yŏu DÍD/ nŏt KÉEP/
thăt DÉEP-/SWÓRN VÓW/ hăve bĕen FRÍENDS/ ŏf MÍNE/

A student who is sufficiently familiar with the four basic meters above can hear them and recognize each one of them in a line of poetry. If the beat is not immediately evident, certain clues can be of aid. Usually words of more than one syllable give a clue. But there are only two in the lines above, and they have different stresses: "OTHers" and "beCAUSE": DA da and da DA. Which of these stresses does the poet use more often? Read the line aloud. In this case, we hear the foot da DA more often than we hear DA da. This, then, is the basic beat, from which the poet occasionally deviates for emphasis and variety. To read a poem aloud, this is all we really need to know about meter.

Rhyme. We hear rhymed syllables in a regular order at the end of lines in some poetry.

> *The curfew tolls the knell of parting* day,   a
> *The lowing herd wind slowly o'er the* lea,   b
> *The ploughman homeward plods his weary* way,   a
> *And leaves the world to darkness and to* me.   b
> (*Thomas Gray, "Elegy Written in a Country Churchyard"*)

Of course, there are many varieties and uses of rhyme, but these need not concern us here. It is obvious that the rhymed syllables make the lines more evident to the listener when the poem is read aloud. Let us consider ways of handling these patterns.

First, there is the poetry line. You may pause at the end of every line, but when the sense of the line overflows into the next line, the pause sacrifices the meaning. On the other hand, instead of ignoring the line endings and muting the rhyme entirely, you should let timing play a part. In many cases the last word in a run-on line contains a long vowel sound that can be prolonged. You can substitute duration for the line-ending pause and thus preserve both the sense and the metrical line pause or its equivalent in time:

> On either side the river lie ——→
> Long fields of barley and of rye.
> (Tennyson, "The Lady of Shalott")

Here, the long *i* in "lie" is drawn out longer; an upward inflection is maintained and the long *i* sound flows into the word "long."

Next, how do we control meter in reading? We may turn away from the structural meter by adding internal pause in the line, by substituting duration (length) for the metrical stress (strength), and by reading short syllables and words faster to make the longer syllables stand out. Let us consider a specific poem, Blake's "The Tiger":

> Tí gĕr!/ Tí gĕr!/ búrn ˘ing/ bríght/
> In thĕ/ fór ĕsts/ óf thĕ/ níght/

These lines might be read with only two primary stresses:

> Tí ger! Tiger! burning bright
> In the fór ests of the night

This does not imply that no other syllables or words are stressed; it means that others are stressed in a different way. Duration is used instead of metrical stress. The poet's use of long sounds lets us lengthen the long *i* in the second "tiger," the first syllable of "burning," the long *i* in "bright" and "night." The reader also adds internal pauses in the line and hurries over the less important words "in the" and "of the." To represent this reading the lines are marked with an underscore to indicate duration stress and a slash to indicate pause:

> Tíger! Tiger!/ burning bright/
> In the forests/ of the night/

The strict line-end rhyme pattern in verse can be controlled in much the same way. The reader simply avoids emphasizing the rhyme, using duration instead of metrical stress, to give the word less prominence. You may divert attention to other words and phrases within the line by various vocal means, pitch inflection especially, to make the rhyme less noticeable. In the two lines from "The Tiger," the rhyme of "bright" and "night" is less evident with duration than with metrical stress.

Recognizing and Controlling Vocal Responses

Other vocal elements play a large part in making the reading of poetry effective. Clear articulation, pleasing vowel sounds, quality touch on words, and pitch variation are important.

John Ciardi, in reviewing albums of poets reading their own works, comments on the state of poetry reading in our time:

> There is a more or less standard way of reading in our time. That style may fairly be called "reticent," or "modest," or "hushed," or "choked back," or even—perhaps most accurately—"English department." Its premise seems to be that it is bad form to allow any voice coloration into the reading for fear that one may appear guilty of trying to persuade the reader to like the poem. It seems to be good form, on the other hand, to stand aloof from the poem, giving it the least possible *saying* at the same time that one's voice emerges in a reverent hush of dry precision. Such reading is more or less singsong, it tends to leave line-ends hanging in achingly understated suspension, it ticks along at an undeviating dead pace, and it is exactly calculated to make monotony the entire human condition. . . . The reticence of such readings may pass as honorable if one is ready to subscribe to the ideal of Puritan restraint, but let me argue that it is time to call down a damnation upon all such self-rapt primness. Gusto, too, is an honorable creed of life.[19]

Recognizing and Controlling Visual Responses

Read again the poem "Blue Girls," by John Crowe Ransom. You can increase your understanding and improve your communication by performing this one. As you read the poem aloud, you should feel the lively presence of the girls walking together under the towers of their seminary, chattering about their teachers and trivial matters. Catch in your own body their liveliness—a swaying of hips and tossing of hair as they move along. Begin to feel a tightening of muscles as you approach the warning tone of what is to follow. And when the statement of truth comes, state it directly, but with the vocal and bodily response to convey the emotional impact of the simple words. Perhaps you will find that vocal timing, pause and duration to correspond with your body response, will best project the emotional meaning. Work for this, then read again, concentrating only on the thought. You may want to reinforce your responses to the poem by acting it out with movement. Here we want to share a quotation from a poet highly qualified to instruct other poets. This is from *The Poet and the Poem*, by Judson Jerome.

> Actually, there is no language for describing this muscular response that poetry demands of the poet in composition and of the reader receiving the message. To speak of it is very much like trying to describe a painting or a symphony. . . .
> The practical consequences may seem a bit silly at first. That is, it helps to wave your arms when writing poetry. Get up from your machine or manuscript and walk around, assume postures, orate, act the poem—the whole thing line by

---

[19] John Ciardi, "Readings, Dronings, etc.," *Saturday Review*, January 15, 1966, p. 48. Reprinted by permission of John Ciardi.

line. . . . If you have a line for which you don't feel the inevitable gesture and tone, perhaps it is wrong and incomplete. It is better doing this acting privately as a composer working with his sheet beside the piano might play back for himself the themes or effects he has written. All this helps. Public performance (after the poem is finished) might intimidate you, but in your shyest littlest voice some shape of intention should come through.[20]

It's good to know that poets, too, engage in exercises to check or reinforce responses. Remember that you, as oral interpreter, both receive the gestures implicit in the poet's words and share them for an audience's empathetic response.

Recognizing and Controlling Types of Poetry

Further communication problems can best be considered in relation to three specific types of poetry: lyric, dramatic, and narrative. This division does not mean that there is no overlap of the lyrical, narrative, and dramatic qualities in poetry. Even the most subjective lyric may imply a narrative and a dramatic situation; a narrative or dramatic poem may have lyrical qualities. The classification merely emphasizes the point of view from which poetic experiences are told.

Lyric Poetry. The lyric expresses a poet's most subjective emotional reactions to experience, in a musical form. Emotion and song are at the heart of the lyric. We have already considered some lyric poems: "Blue Girls" is a reflective lyric; "in Just-" is a poet's response to spring. Here are two others, written in the 18th and 17th centuries. You may be surprised by their seemingly modern satirical tone:

Why So Pale and Wan?
Sir John Suckling

Why so pale and wan, fond lover?
  Prithee, why so pale?
Will, when looking well can't move her,
  Looking ill prevail?
  Prithee, why so pale?

Why so dull and mute, young sinner?
  Prithee, why so mute?
Will, when speaking well can't win her,
  Saying nothing do 't?
  Prithee, why so mute?

Quit, quit for shame! This will not move;
  This cannot take her.
If of herself she will not love,
  Nothing can make her:
  The devil take her!

---

[20] Judson Jerome. *The Poet and the Poem*, Revised Edition. Cincinnati: Writer's Digest, 1967.

Delight in Disorder
Robert Herrick

A sweet disorder in the dress
Kindles in clothes a wantonness:
A lawn about the shoulders thrown
Into a fine distraction,
An erring lace, which here and there
Enthralls the crimson stomacher,
A cuff neglectful, and thereby
Ribands to flow confusedly,
A winning wave, deserving note,
In the tempestuous petticoat,
A careless shoe-string, in whose tie
I see a wild civility,
Do more bewitch me than when art
Is too precise in every part.

In modern poetry, we often encounter strong feelings of anger directed toward the human condition or toward society. The projected attitudes and the forms in which they are written make their classification difficult. Are they lyric, dramatic, or narrative poems or are they really poetic prose? Perhaps a new category is in the making. In any case, emotional poems of a personal nature call for aesthetic distance on the part of the interpreter. You would probably not look directly at the audience or identify with the poet in any explicit physical sense; instead, the identification would be only in attitude. In some lyrics, the poet's thoughts and reflections are put directly into the mouths of characters. T. S. Eliot does this in "The Love Song of J. Alfred Prufrock." We would say that such lyrics approach the dramatic.

Dramatic Poetry. It is the immediacy of their events and relevations that place some poems in the dramatic mode. Thus we classify as dramatic only those poems in which the characters are immediately engaged in an action or receiving a revelation. Your attention has been called to the two types most often used by the interpreter—the dramatic monologue and the soliloquy.

In the *dramatic monologue,* a character addresses another character or characters imagined to be present. The action takes place in the present. "My Last Duchess' is a familiar dramatic monologue. Characterization is always the main thing, so the interpreter assumes a character role much like that of the actor.

The *soliloquy* differs from the monologue in that no other characters are present. The speaker is alone, reflecting. Your interpretation should be like that in the reflective lyric, with the difference that here yours is a character speaking in the present; the character's reflections are the result of involvement in an immediate situation. Browning's "Soliloquy of the Spanish Cloister" is a familiar example, and of course many are found in Shakespeare's plays.

Narrative Poetry. In narrative poetry, the chief interest is usually in the story, but the interest is sustained by the emotional and dramatic elements of the poem. Your analysis and oral reading of the narrative should emphasize the movement of the story and its build to climaxes. Character and character relationships must also be understood and projected through suggestion.

The narrative poem is told from the point of view of a more or less objective narrator who may or may not be the poet. If the story is told in the third person and in the past tense, rather than give the narrator any specific individuality, you merely represent an undefined storyteller. You look at the audience, bringing them in to share the changing scene. If the narrator speaks in the first person and participates in the story to some degree, you must use your own taste about characterization and eye-focus variation.

The *folk ballad* is a narrative with a strong story line which moves swiftly to a climax. Characteristics of the form are definite meter and rhyme pattern, repetitious refrains, and direct dialogue. You should interpret folk ballads simply and vividly. Here is one version of an old favorite:

Frankie and Johnny

Frankie and Johnny were lovers, O, how that couple could love.
Swore to be true to each other, true as the stars above.
He was her man, but he done her wrong

Frankie she was his woman, everybody knows.
She spent one hundred dollars for a suit of Johnny's clothes.
He was her man, but he done her wrong.

Frankie went down to Memphis. She went on the evening train.
She paid one hundred dollars for Johnny a watch and chain.
He was her man, but he done her wrong.

Frankie went down to the corner to buy her a bucket of beer.
She says to the fat bartender, "Has my lovingest man been here?
He is my man, but he's doing me wrong."

"Ain't going to tell you no story. Ain't going to tell you no lie.
I seen your man 'bout an hour ago with a girl named Alice Fry.
If he's your man, he's doing you wrong."

Frankie went back to the hotel; she didn't go there for fun.
Under her long red kimono she toted a forty-four gun.
He was her man, but he done her wrong.

Frankie went down to the hotel, looked in the window so high.
There she saw her loving Johnny a-loving up Alice Fry.
He was her man, but he done her wrong.

Frankie threw back her kimono; she took out her old forty-four.
Root-a-toot-toot three times she shot right through that hotel door.
She shot her man, 'cause he done her wrong.

Johnny grabbed off his Stetson. "O good Lord, Frankie, don't shoot!"
But Frankie put her finger on the trigger, and the gun went toot-a-toot-
toot.
He was her man, but she shot him down.

"Roll me over easy, roll me over slow.
Roll me over easy, boys, 'cause my wounds are hurting me so.
I was her man, but I done her wrong."

First time she shot him he staggered. Second time she shot him he fell.
Third time she shot him, O Lordy, there was a new man's face in hell.
He was her man, but he done her wrong.

"Oh, bring on your rubber-tired hearses, bring on your rubber-tired
hacks.
They're taking my Johnny to the burying ground, but they'll never bring
him back.
He was my man, but he done me wrong."

The judge said to the jury, "It's plain as plain can be.
This woman shot her man; it's murder in the second degree.
He was her man, but he done her wrong."

Now it was not murder in the second degree; it was not murder in the
third.
The woman simply dropped her man, like a hunter drops a bird.
He was her man, and he done her wrong.

"Oh, put me in that dungeon. Oh, put me in that cell.
Put me where the northeast wind blows from the northeast corner of hell.
I shot my man, 'cause he done me wrong."

Frankie walked up to the scaffold, as calm as a girl could be,
And turning her eyes to heaven she said, "Good Lord, I'm coming to Thee.
He was my man, and I done him wrong."

Now let us use Robert Frost's classic lyric to illustrate poetry analysis.

Application of Techniques

Stopping By Woods on a Snowy Evening[21]
Robert Frost

Whose woods these are I think I know.
His house is in the village though;

---

[21] From *The Poetry of Robert Frost*, edited by Edward Connery Lathem. Copyright 1923, 1939,
© 1967, 1969 by Holt, Rinehart and Winston. Copyright 1951 by Robert Frost. Reprinted by
permission of Holt, Rinehart and Winston, Publishers.

He will not see me stopping here
To watch his woods fill up with snow.

My little horse must think it queer
To stop without a farmhouse near
Between the woods and frozen lake
The darkest evening of the year.

He gives his harness bells a shake
To ask if there is some mistake.
The only other sound's the sweep
Of easy wind and downy flake.

The woods are lovely, dark and deep,
But I have promises to keep,
And miles to go before I sleep
And miles to go before I sleep.

Analysis

The Situation and Its Movement. The poem concerns a single incident. The narrator is driving through the countryside on a dark December evening. It is snowing. As he passes a patch of woods, he stops his horse to watch the snow falling into the deep, dark woods. He stays here for a time, reflecting on the scene, the owner of the woods, and his horse's reaction to the delay. Then he comes to a decision: he must be on his way.

The first stanza may be considered as the introduction, or Scene One. Here the narrator's relationship with the scene is established, but much is left unsaid. We are not told where he has been or where he is going on this winter night. We may wonder about the owner of these woods. Scene Two includes the next two stanzas. Here a conflict arises: the horse shakes his bells to urge the narrator along, but it is evident that he would like to stay. In the final scene, the last stanza, the narrator makes his decision. The poem is quiet, low in tension. Both the structural and the emotional climaxes come at the end with this decision.

Tone and Symbolic Meaning. The tone of the poem comes largely from its understatement. The poem seems to be about a simple incident, but something more is implied, and what is left unsaid is important. As the narrator stops for a private moment, viewing woods filling with snow, he is aware that the owner of the woods would think this is a strange thing to do. The owner is associated with the village, is more interested in village matters and in owning the woods than in viewing his property on a snowy evening. The horse shakes his bells; he, too, thinks it strange that the man should stop on the road on a snowy night. The horse and the owner of the woods symbolize the practical, utilitarian way of thinking and all that oppose or would be incapable of understanding a man's need for aesthetic moments such as this. At the end, the narrator accepts their view. His "promises"—values of duty, practical need, sound reasoning—win over his heart's need.

We may wonder about the repetition of the line, "And miles to go before I sleep." Is this a death wish? Frost always denied this meaning. Perhaps the poet didn't mean to have the poem suggest the death wish. Yet, there the suggestion is, along with the attitudes which place practical needs over aesthetic needs.

The tone is never bitter or heavy. The visual images set a pleasing tone: the dark, deep woods filling up with snow. We are aware of the silence and the sounds of "easy wind and downy flake" and of the harness bells breaking into this quiet. The repetition of sounds aids in conveying the quiet mood: the long *o* sound (know, though, snow, go), the *au* and long *e* sounds (out, house, sound, town; see, sleep, easy, sweep, keep) as in "sound's the sweep of easy wind and downy flake." The sounds make delicate music. There is an easy conversational flow to the lines, in spite of the fact that the poet adheres to strict pattern. Frost does not vary the regular four-stress iambic line, and except for the next to last line in the poem, the rhyme pattern is regular.

Theme. We can venture an opinion of what the poet is saying, but because the language is highly suggestive and deceptive in its simplicity, this poem will always have different meanings for different people and new meanings each time we read it.

The speaker's attitude seems to be acceptance of life's obligations without bitterness. Frost is not saying that the world is an ugly place from which to escape, nor is he preaching to make us remember our "promises." Perhaps he is showing us, through a simple incident, that we can find beauty by briefly separating ourselves from mankind. But, he seems to say, because of our duties and obligations, we cannot remain apart from mankind; the practical world exists, and it will continue to make its demands on us until we come to the end of life.

Aesthetic Effect. All the elements of structure—stanza form, meter, and rhyme—unify the poem. The simple incident and the simple words belong together. Even the larger implication at the end seems to have come about naturally, without plan.

Communicating Meaning

Let us consider the problem of handling the sound pattern. There is nothing in the mood or purpose of Frost's poem that demands a strong regularity of rhythm. So in this case, the interpreter should read the poem in a conversational style, preserving at the same time the beauty of the images and sounds. The poet makes this easy to do. In the lines which follow, the marks above the words represent the stresses. If the poem were read according to these marks, we would hear beats instead of sense. The slashes indicate the pauses between thought groups; the italics indicate the words emphasized by either volume stress or time duration. The words not italicized are subordinated, hurried along.

> *Whose* wóods *these áre* / *I* thínk *I* knów. //
> *His* hóuse / *is* iń *the* víllage thóugh; //

He wíll not sée *me* / stópping *hére*
To wátch *his wóods* / fill úp *with* snow. ///

My *líttle* hórse *must thiṅk it* qúeer
To stóp withóut a fármhouse *néar* /
Betwéen the wóods / *and* frózen láke /
The dárkest évening / *óf the yéar.* ///

He gíves *his* hárness bélls / *a* sháke
To ásk / *if thére is* sóme mistáke. /
The ónly óther *sóund's* / *the* swéep
Of éasy wínd / *and* dówny fláke. ///

The wóods *are* lóvely / dárk *and* déep, //
But Í have prómises / to kéep, //
And míles *to* gó *befóre I* sléep //
And míles *to* gó / *befóre I* sléep. ///[22]

The beauty of the language and the emotional meanings are
reinforced by giving the repeated long vowel sounds the proper duration.

Though the poem tells a story, it is predominately a reflective lyric.
The reader's contact with his audience should be indirect to a degree. You
should concentrate on the speaker's thoughts; the projection of the man's
attitude is important.

---

[22] Ibid.

Chapter 9

Interpretive Reading of Drama

Action is the essential element of drama. The play is not about characters in action; it *is* characters in action. The play and the novel tell a story, but their ways of telling it differ. In most short stories and novels, the story is told by a narrator who clarifies and amplifies the movement of a situation that has taken place in the past, while in most plays, the story is presented through dialogue and action taking place in the present.

For both the silent reader and the oral interpreter, the play demands that the characters be placed on an imaginary stage, the mind's eye. Obviously, the solo interpreter cannot perform the actions of a play or represent characters in action as the actor does. But through activating your own imagination, you can cause each listener to create the characters, scene, and action in the mind's eye. The interpretation of drama demands more preparation time than that of other literary forms.

Much of our previous discussion of the narrative is also applicable to the drama. In both forms, the emphasis is on plot and characters. The problems associated with the oral interpretation of narrative fiction are generally the same for the play, centering on the interplay of characters engaged in dialogue.

Scene Cuttings From Contemporary Plays

We will use scenes from two contemporary plays to demonstrate how to deal with specific problems in preparing and performing play cuttings. Seldom if ever can the solo interpreter use a full-length play in its entirety; time limits in the classroom and elsewhere make cutting a necessity. The first cutting given here is from a short play for two characters; the second is from a three-act play with four characters, but only three appear in our cutting. In this second example the text has been printed with all the usual stage directions; parts that would be cut are shown with a line drawn through them.

An Introduction and Cutting of "I'm Herbert"

This scene is from a play within a play. "I'm Herbert" appears as the third scene of *You Know I Can't Hear You When the Water's Running*, a popular comedy of the 1960s by Robert Anderson.

Picture with me a very old couple sitting in rocking chairs on a side porch. It is late spring. The couple, Herbert and Muriel, have summoned their fading energies to observe nature. Muriel, dressed with faded elegance, holds a rose in her hand.

HERBERT. Baltimore oriole (He shifts his glasses, scanning.) Bobolink. (Shifts again.) Rose-breasted grosbeak. (Shifts again and gets a little excited.) A black-billed cuckoo. (He speaks louder. . . .) Grace, I saw a black-billed cuckoo.

MURIEL. (Her eyes open.) My name is Muriel, foolish old man.

HERBERT. I know your name is Muriel. That's what I called you.

MURIEL. You called me Grace. Grace was your first wife.

HERBERT. I called you Muriel. You're just hard of hearing and won't admit it. . . . Grace . . . Grace . . . That's what I said!

MURIEL. There! You said it.

HERBERT. What?

MURIEL. Grace. . . . You called me Grace.

HERBERT. Silly old woman. You call me Harry. But I called you Grace.

MURIEL. Can't you hear yourself?

HERBERT. What?

MURIEL. I said can't you hear yourself?

HERBERT. Of course I can hear myself. It's you that can't hear. I say you call me Harry. Sometimes. Your second husband . . . and sometimes George . . . your first. . . .

MURIEL. A hearing aid's a cheap thing. . . .

HERBERT. See here, Grace. . . .

MURIEL. I'm Muriel.

HERBERT. You talk about me. . . . What about you? "Muriel. I'm Muriel."

MURIEL. Cuckoo!

HERBERT. (He takes up his binoculars.) Where? I wouldn't call you Grace. Grace was soft and gentle and kind.

MURIEL. Why'd you leave her then?

HERBERT. I didn't. She died.

MURIEL. Mary died. Your first wife. You got sick of Grace and left her and married me.

HERBERT. Left Grace for you?

MURIEL. Yes, you silly old man.

HERBERT. All wrong. Grace was my darling.

MURIEL. She drove you crazy.

HERBERT. My first love.

MURIEL. Mary.

HERBERT. Mary drove me crazy.

MURIEL. She was your first love. You've told me about it often enough. The two of you young colts prancing around in the nude.

HERBERT. Mary?

MURIEL. Yes.

HERBERT. I never saw Mary naked. That was her trouble. Cold woman.

MURIEL. That was Grace.

HERBERT. Grace I saw naked. Oh, how naked! There was never anyone nakeder.

MURIEL. You can only be naked. You can't be more or less naked.

HERBERT. You didn't know Grace.

MURIEL. Mary. I did know Grace.

HERBERT. Naked?

MURIEL. Keep a civil tongue in your head.

HERBERT. I never saw you naked.

MURIEL. No, and not likely to. What'd be the point? . . .

HERBERT. Old women forget . . . forget the joys of the flesh. Why is that?

MURIEL. I don't forget Bernie.

HERBERT. Who?

MURIEL. Bernie Walters.

HERBERT. Never heard of him.

MURIEL. My second husband. I was married to him when Harry came along. . . . But Harry went away and then you came along . . . a long time after. Platonic marriage. That's what we've had, you and I, George. But it's all right.

HERBERT. Platonic under the willow tree that June?

MURIEL. What willow tree?

HERBERT. Oh, I've been good to you, Mary, for all your carping and your falling off in your old age, because I remember that willow tree. Muriel never knew about it. We were wicked.

MURIEL. If I thought you knew what you were talking about, I'd get mad. But I know you're just babbling. Babbling Bernie. . . . That's you. Herbert used to say, "How can you listen to him babble?"

HERBERT. I'm Herbert.

MURIEL. If it makes you feel more secure. Go on. Keep reminding yourself.

HERBERT. You called me Bernie.

MURIEL. Oh, sure, sure. And you've never been to Chicago.

HERBERT. I have so. I went there when my daughter died.

MURIEL. Well, I'm glad you admit it.

HERBERT. Why shouldn't I admit it? It's so. You just try to confuse me . . . Bernie, Harry, George, Grace, Mary.

MURIEL. You started a long time ago, slipping. Only then you were more honest about it. Very touching. When we went to Florida and you gave me the tickets and said, "Grace, my mind's slipping, take care of the tickets."

HERBERT. Your name's Muriel.

MURIEL. Yes, yes, lovey. My name's Muriel.

HERBERT. You referred to yourself as "Grace."

MURIEL. (Sarcastic.) Oh, very likely. Very likely.

HERBERT. You said I gave you the tickets to Florida and said, "Grace, my mind's slipping."

MURIEL. Well, it was.

HERBERT. I've never been to Florida.

MURIEL. Ho-ho. Well, let's not go into it. The pongee suit.

HERBERT. I never owned a pongee suit.

MURIEL. You said it was the same suit you wore when you married Helen, and we had a long discussion about how ironic it was that you were wearing the same suit to run away with me.

HERBERT. Who's Helen?

MURIEL. You were married to her, silly.

HERBERT. I was running away to Florida with you and I was so old my mind was slipping and I couldn't remember the tickets?

MURIEL. Lovey, you're running a lot of things that happened at different times together now. Maybe you should just sit quietly for a while, Harry, till you get straightened out.

147

HERBERT. My name is Herbert.

MURIEL. That's right. We'll start from there. You're Herbert and I'm Grace.

HERBERT. You're Muriel.

MURIEL. That's right. Now let's just leave it at that now, or you won't sleep tonight.

HERBERT. I always sleep.

MURIEL. A fortune for sleeping pills.

HERBERT. I never had one in my life.

MURIEL. And you've never been to Chicago either, I suppose.

HERBERT. Never. Why should I have gone to Chicago?

MURIEL. Only because our daughter died there and we went to the funeral.

HERBERT. We had no children together.

MURIEL. I think we shouldn't talk any more now. You're getting confused.

HERBERT. You never let me near your lily-white body.

MURIEL. Ho-ho . . . and what about that afternoon under the willow tree? I think that's when we conceived Ralph.

HERBERT. Who is Ralph?

MURIEL. Ralph is your stepson. Good God!

HERBERT. I conceived my stepson under the willow tree?

MURIEL. I'd prefer it if we just remained quiet for a while. You can't follow a train of thought for more than a moment . . . and it's very tiring trying to jump back and forth with you. Just close your eyes and rest. . . . Are your eyes hurting you?

HERBERT. No.

MURIEL. That medicine must be very good then.

HERBERT. What medicine?

MURIEL. You see, that's what I mean.

HERBERT. I never had any medicine for my eyes.

MURIEL. Yes, all right. All right. Let's not argue, George.

HERBERT. I'm Harry.

MURIEL. Yes, yes. All right. We'll just hold hands here, and try to doze a little . . . and think of happier days. . . . (She takes his hand and they close their eyes and rock.)

HERBERT. (After a long moment.) Mmmmmm . . . Venice.

MURIEL. (Dreamy.) Yes. . . . Oh, yes. . . . Wasn't that lovely. . . . Oh, you were so gallant . . . if slightly shocking. . . . (She laughs, remembering.)

HERBERT. The beach. . . .

MURIEL. The willow tree. . . .

HERBERT. (Smiling.) You running around naked. . . . Oh, lovely . . . lovely . . .

MURIEL. Yes . . . lovely. . . . (They go on rocking and smiling, holding hands as the lights dim.)[1]

An Introduction and Cutting of *The Glass Menagerie*

Tennessee Williams's three-act play *The Glass Menagerie* tells the story of a family. Throughout the play, Amanda Wingfield, the mother, is battling life with great but confused vitality as she schemes and nags, trying to do the best for her children, Tom and Laura. Tom, the son, who dreams of being a poet, works, in a warehouse to support the family. Laura is the overly shy, slightly crippled daughter. Only one person outside this family group enters

---

[1] Reprinted by permission of International Creative Management © Copyright, as an unpublished work, 1966, by Robert Woodruff Anderson. © Copyright, 1967, by Robert Anderson.

the play—Jim O'Connor, a young man who works with Tom at the warehouse.

The action takes place in a drab flat in the tenement district of St. Louis in the Depression of the 1930s. We are given a view of a dimly lit living room with a dining area. Our attention is caught by a photograph on the wall. A handsome young man in a World War I doughboy's cap smiles out at us from his frame. This is the absent member of the family—the absent husband and father, who abandoned the others many years ago.

Our attention is also caught by two pieces of furniture, an ancient-looking victrola and an old-fashioned whatnot filled with tiny transparent glass animals. These two pieces are the beloved possessions of Laura. She escapes her world of reality by talking to the glass animals and playing old phonograph records that her father left behind.

This cutting is taken from Scene 7 of the play. This is the evening when they are entertaining a guest, a gentleman caller. Amanda, in an effort to find a secure place in life for Laura, has constantly nagged Tom to bring home a gentleman caller. The best Tom can do is Jim O'Connor. Amanda makes great preparations for what she considers the most important event in their lives. Dresses are made, a new rug and lamp purchased, her most tempting meal is prepared. Meanwhile, Laura discovers that the expected caller is the same Jim O'Connor she knew in her high school days, the most popular boy in the school and her one secret romance. Now she cannot face him. When he arrives, she is so overcome with shyness that she becomes ill and stays on the couch in the living room during dinner.

As we look in on the scene, Laura and Jim are alone in the living room. Amanda and Tom are offstage in the kitchen. All this has been carefully arranged and carried out by Amanda.

Jim, a very ordinary but nice young man, is sorry for Laura. Left alone with her, he gives her brotherly advice about overcoming her shyness and even manages to get her to try a dance with him. During the dance, he knocks against the whatnot and one of Laura's glass animals falls and breaks. It is her favorite, the unicorn.

JIM.   Aw, aw, aw. Is it broken?
LAURA.   Now it is just like all the other horses.
JIM.   It's lost its—
LAURA.   Horn!
         It doesn't matter. Maybe it's a blessing in disguise.
JIM.   You'll never forgive me. I bet that was your favorite piece of glass.
LAURA.   I don't have favorites much. It's no tragedy, Freckles. Glass breaks so easily. No matter how careful you are. The traffic jars the shelves and things fall off them.
JIM.   Still I'm awfully sorry that I was the cause.
LAURA.   (Smiling) I'll just imagine he had an operation. The horn was removed to make him feel less—freakish! (They both laugh.)
         Now he will feel more at home with the other horses, the ones that don't have horns. . . .
JIM.   Ha-ha, that's very funny! (Suddenly serious.)
         I'm glad to see that you have a sense of humor.
         You know—you're—well—very different!
         Surprisingly different from anyone else I know!

~~(His voice becomes soft and hesitant with a genuine feeling.)~~
Do you mind me telling you that?
~~(LAURA is abashed beyond speech.)~~
I mean it in a nice way . . .
~~(LAURA nods shyly, looking away.)~~
You make me feel sort of—I don't know how to put it!
I'm usually pretty good at expressing things, but—
This is something that I don't know how to say!
~~(LAURA touches her throat and clears it, turns the broken unicorn in her hands. Even softer.)~~
Has anyone ever told you that you were pretty?
~~(PAUSE: MUSIC. LAURA looks up slowly, with wonder, and shakes her head.)~~
Well, you are! In a very different way from anyone else.
And all the nicer because of the difference, too.
~~(His voice becomes low and husky. LAURA turns away, nearly faint with the novelty of her emotions.)~~
I wish that you were my sister. I'd teach you to have some confidence in yourself. The different people are not like other people, but being different is nothing to be ashamed of. Because other people are not such wonderful people. They're one hundred times one thousand. You're one times one! They walk all over the earth. You just stay here. They're common as—weeds, but—you—well, you're—Blue Roses!
~~(IMAGE ON SCREEN: BLUE ROSES, MUSIC CHANGES.)~~

LAURA.   But blue is wrong for—roses . . .
JIM.   It's right for you!—You're—pretty!
LAURA.   In what respect am I pretty?
JIM.   In all respects—believe me! Your eyes—your hair—are pretty!
         ~~(He catches hold of her hand.)~~
         You think I'm making this up because I'm invited to dinner and have to be nice. Oh, I could do that! I could put on an act for you, Laura, and say lots of things without being very sincere. But this time I am. I'm talking to you sincerely. I happened to notice you had this inferiority complex that keeps you from feeling comfortable with people. Somebody needs to build your confidence up and make you proud instead of shy and turning away and—blushing—
         Somebody—ought to—
         Ought to—kiss you, Laura!
         His hand slips slowly up her arm to her shoulder. ~~(MUSIC SWELLS TUMULTUOUSLY.)~~ He suddenly turns her about and kisses her on the lips. When he releases her, Laura sinks on the sofa with a bright, dazed look. Jim backs away and fishes in his pocket for a cigarette. ~~(LEGEND ON SCREEN: "SOUVENIR.")~~
         Stumble-john!
         ~~(He lights the cigarette, avoiding her look. There is a peal of girlish laughter from AMANDA in the kitchen. LAURA slowly raises and opens her hand. It still contains the little broken glass animal. She looks at it with a tender, bewildered expression.)~~
         Stumble-john!
         I shouldn't have done that—That was way off the beam.
         You don't smoke, do you?
         ~~(She looks up, smiling, not hearing the question. He sits beside her a little gingerly. She looks at him speechlessly, waiting. He coughs decorously and moves a little farther aside as he considers the situation and senses her feelings, dimly, with perturbation. Gently.)~~
         Would you—care for a—mint?

(She doesn't seem to hear him but her look grows brighter even.)
Peppermint—Life-Saver?
My pocket's a regular drug store—wherever I go . . .
(He pops a mint in his mouth. Then gulps and decides to make a clean breast of it. He speaks slowly and gingerly.)
Laura, you know, if I had a sister like you, I'd do the same thing as Tom. I'd bring out fellows and—introduce her to them. The right type of boys of a type to—appreciate her.
Only—well—he made a mistake about me.
Maybe I've got no call to be saying this. That may not have been the idea in having me over. But what if it was?
There's nothing wrong about that. The only trouble is that in my case—I'm not in a situation to—do the right thing.
I can't take down your number and say I'll phone.
I can't call up next week and—ask for a date.
I thought I had better explain the situation in case you—misunderstood it and—hurt your feelings . . .
(Pause. Slowly, very slowly, LAURA'S look changes, her eyes returning slowly from his to the ornament in her palm. AMANDA utters another gay laugh in the kitchen.)

LAURA. (Faintly.) You—won't—call again?
JIM. No, Laura, I can't. (He rises from the sofa.)
As I was just explaining, I've—got strings on me.
Laura, I've—been going steady!
I go out all of the time with a girl named Betty. She's a home-girl like you, and Catholic, and Irish, and in a great many ways we—get along fine.
I met her last summer on a moonlight boat trip up the river to Alton, on the *Majestic.*
Well—right away from the start it was—love!
(LEGEND: LOVE! LAURA sways slightly forward and grips the arm of the sofa. He fails to notice, now enrapt in his own comfortable being.)
Being in love has made a new man out of me!
(Leaning stiffly forward, clutching the arm of the sofa, LAURA struggles visibly with her storm. But JIM is oblivious; she is a long way off.)
The power of love is really pretty tremendous!
Love is something that—changes the whole world, Laura!
(The storm abates a little and LAURA leans back. He notices her again.)
It happened that Betty's aunt took sick; she got a wire and had to go to Centralia. So Tom—when he asked me to dinner—I naturally just accepted the invitation, not knowing that you—that he—that I—(He stops awkwardly)
Huh—I'm a stumble-john!
(He flops back on the sofa. The holy candles in the altar of LAURA'S face have been snuffed out. There is a look of almost infinite desolation. JIM glances at her uneasily.)
I wish that you would—say something.
(She bites her lip which was trembling and then bravely smiles. She opens her hand again on the broken glass ornament. Then she gently takes his hand and raises it level with her own. She carefully places the unicorn in the palm of his hand, then pushes his fingers closed upon it.) What are you—doing that for? You want me to have him?—Laura? (She nods.) What for?
LAURA. A—souvenir . . .
(She rises unsteadily and crouches beside the victrola to wind it up. LEGEND ON SCREEN: "THINGS HAVE A WAY OF TURNING

OUT SO BADLY!" OR IMAGE: "GENTLEMAN CALLER WAVING
GOOD BYE! GAILY.") At this moment AMANDA rushes brightly
back in the front room. She bears a pitcher of fruit punch in an
old-fashioned cut-glass pitcher and a plate of macaroons. (The
plate has a gold border and poppies painted on it.)

AMANDA. Well, well, well! Isn't the air delightful after the shower?
I've made you children a little liquid refreshment.
(Turns gaily to the gentleman caller.)
Jim, do you know that song about lemonade?
"Lemonade, lemonade
Made in the shade and stirred with a spade—
Good enough for an old maid!"

JIM.   (Uneasily) Ha-ha! No—I never heard it.

AMANDA. Why, Laura! You look so serious!

JIM.   We were having a serious conversation.

AMANDA. Good! Now you're better acquainted!

JIM.   (Uncertainly) Ha-ha! Yes.

AMANDA. You modern young people are much more serious-minded
than my generation. I was so gay as a girl!

JIM.   You haven't changed, Mrs. Wingfield.

AMANDA. Tonight I'm rejuvenated! The gaiety of the occasion, Mr.
O'Connor!
(She tosses her head with a peal of laughter. Spills lemonade.)
Oooo! I'm baptizing myself!

JIM.   Here—let me—

AMANDA. (Setting the pitcher down.) There now. I discovered we had
some maraschino cherries. I dumped them in, juice and all!

JIM.   You shouldn't have gone to that trouble, Mrs. Wingfield.

AMANDA. Trouble, trouble? Why it was loads of fun!
Didn't you hear me cutting up in the kitchen? I bet your ears were
burning! I told Tom how outdone with him I was for keeping you
to himself so long a time! He should have brought you over much,
much sooner! Well, now that you've found your way, I want you to
be a very frequent caller! Not just occasional but all the time.
Oh, we're going to have a lot of gay times together! I see them
coming!
Mmmm, just breathe that air! So fresh, and the moon's so pretty!
I'll skip back out—I know where my place is when young folks
are having a—serious conversation!

JIM.   Oh, don't go out, Mrs. Wingfield. The fact of the matter is I've got
to be going.

AMANDA. Going now? You're joking! Why, it's only the shank of the evening, Mr. O'Connor!

JIM.   Well, you know how it is.

AMANDA. You mean you're a young workingman and have to keep workingmen's hours. We'll let you off early tonight. But only on the
condition that next time you stay later.
What's the best night for you? Isn't Saturday night the best night
for you workingmen?

JIM.   I have a couple of time-clocks to punch, Mrs. Wingfield. One at
morning, another one at night!

AMANDA. My, but you *are* ambitious! You work at night, too?

JIM.   No, Ma'am, not work but—Betty!
(He crosses deliberately to pick up his hat. The band at the
Paradise Dance Hall goes into a tender waltz.)

AMANDA. Betty? Betty? Who's—Betty?
(There is an ominous cracking sound in the sky.)

JIM.   Oh, just a girl. The girl I go steady with!

AMANDA. (A long drawn exhalation.)
        Ohhh . . . Is it a serious romance, Mr. O'Connor?
JIM.   We're going to be married the second Sunday in June.
AMANDA. Ohhh—how nice!
        Tom didn't mention that you were engaged to be married.
JIM.   The cat's not out of the bag at the warehouse yet.
        You know how they are. They call you Romeo and stuff like that.
        (He stops at the oval mirror to put on his hat. He carefully shapes
        the brim and the crown to give a discreetly dashing effect.)
        It's been a wonderful evening, Mrs. Wingfield. I guess this is what
        they mean by Southern hospitality.
AMANDA. It really wasn't anything at all.
JIM.   I hope it don't seem like I'm rushing off. But I promised Betty I'd
        pick her up at the Wabash depot, an' by the time I get my jalopy
        down there her train'll be in. Some women are pretty upset if you
        keep 'em waiting.
AMANDA. Yes, I know—The tyranny of women! (Extends her hand.)
        Good-bye, Mr. O'Connor.
        I wish you luck—and happiness—and success! All three of them,
        and so does Laura!—Don't you, Laura?
LAURA. Yes!
JIM.   (Taking her hand.) Good-bye, Laura. I'm certainly going to trea-
        sure that souvenir. And don't you forget the good advice I gave
        you. (Raises his voice to a cheery shout.)
        So long, Shakespeare!
        Thanks again, ladies—Good night!
        (He grins and ducks jauntly out. Still bravely grimacing,
        AMANDA closes the door on the gentleman caller. Then she turns
        back to the room with a puzzled expression. She and LAURA
        don't dare to face each other. LAURA crouches beside the victrola
        to wind it.)[2]

Problems in Performing

Now let us consider some of the problems an interpreter might encounter
in these two play cuttings.

Preparing Listeners to Imagine Scene. The importance of an introduction to both cuttings is evident. Through explanation of what has led up to
the immediate situation and through describing the scene in introductory
remarks, the interpreter prepares an audience to envision the scene and to
follow the conflict to its outcome with interest.

Suggesting Character in The Glass Menagerie. All the visible manifes-
tations of each character must be based on the interpreter's understanding
of the mental and emotional characteristics of that character. In the last
cutting, Laura's shyness and sensitivity should be made evident by use of a
quiet, light voice and hesitant speech. The interpreter's body tempo should
be slow and appear awkward to suggest her insecurity and physical
handicap. When Laura makes light of Jim's breaking the unicorn by saying it has become "less freakish" and "more at home," we realize that this

---

[2] From *The Glass Menagerie*, by Tennessee Williams. Copyright 1945 by Tennessee Williams
and Edwina D. Williams. Reprinted by permission of Random House, Inc.

unicorn is a symbol of Laura and that she, too, might have been less freakish and more at home in the world. There is a moment when she almost believes that Jim is "that long delayed but always 'something' that we live for" that can become part of her life. At the end, her reaction to the lost dream is to seek escape (winding the victrola). We feel that she can find healing for the hurt in her world apart.

In contrast, Tom's tempo is quick and his vocal and body tones full of vitality, suggesting his outgoing personality and need for ego building. He is not overbearing; he is just an ordinary young man with ambition. He is trying to pull himself out of a dull warehouse job, to recover his old self-esteem of high school days. This encounter with Laura offers such an opportunity, so he is enjoying himself.

In this cutting, Amanda injects a bright, gay mood into a tense scene as she enters the living room. With a flexible voice touched with the warm tones of Southern speech, she plays the role of the charming (but much younger) Southern hostess. She is harboring high hopes in her heart that her scheme to find a husband for Laura is working. But her hopes are short lived; we see as well as hear her fear when Jim mentions a steady girl friend and when he announces "We're going to be married the second Sunday in June." However, Amanda manages to control her emotion during the mannered good-byes. It is only when the door closes on Jim that we see her (perhaps only for a moment) as lost and desolate. In her last line in the cutting (and certainly in her call, "Tom," which follows and could be added), we hear a note that tells us she will go on battling life in spite of the failures.

The interpreter should make no attempt to exactly represent men's and women's voices with pitch change, because this would sound false and draw attention to itself. A male interpreter might suggest the female characters by using his weaker vocal tones; a woman might suggest the men by using her stronger, deeper tones. The rhythms of the separate personalities and their responses to various moods in the scene should help to suggest the sex difference.

Suggesting Character in "I'm Herbert." The confused states of the old couple might be suggested by emphasizing the basic differences in their attitudes: Muriel is more sure of herself. She maintains a kind of aloofness, a belief in her own reality, which Herbert does not enjoy. He is easily riled by Muriel. His moods vary; his spurts of defiance build with all the physical energy he can muster. Their scene should be paced slowly and evenly to suggest their age. Since they are in rocking chairs, their age should be suggested by devitalized muscle tone; their movements should give the impression of diminished muscular activity, their shoulders slightly stooped and their heads held forward.

Suggesting Physical Actions. The scene from *The Glass Menagerie* presents some troublesome problems with props and physical contact. Because the stage directions are not read to the audience, the interpreter must suggest, through expression and small gestures, such actions as Jim's drawing articles from his pockets and Amanda's "baptizing" herself. The kiss is a key action in this scene, so it must be retained. Yet a kiss cannot be suggested without appearing ridiculous. As indicated in the script, the author's brief descriptive passage should be retained. This should be shared with the audience without breaking the mood of the scene.

The physical actions of the old couple in "I'm Herbert" are minimal. Herbert, in handling the binoculars, would hold them and put them down carefully, with a feeling of tension in the hands and with the least possible arm and shoulder movement.

Interplay and Placement of Characters. Perhaps the most difficult technique to master is that of suggesting, without the aid of the narrative voice, the interplay of several characters engaged in dialogue. The interpreter must not only suggest the personality of each individual in very short speeches, but show each character's responses to the other as well. For instance, when Amanda breaks in on a tense moment, we suggest that the author's narration be used for the transition. But then follows a scene where an interpreter must handle the split-second timing of the verbal and listening responses of three characters. It helps to place the characters in an imagined scene out front, above the heads of the audience. Amanda looks at both Jim and Laura, believing joyously that what she had hoped would happen has happened. Then she continues with her lemonade song. Jim's immediate uneasy response must be shown through facial expression, followed by his attempted laugh and verbal response. The tense scene continues in this way, with Laura's presence felt rather than heard, until the climax comes with Jim's line "We're going to be married the second Sunday in June," and Amanda's "sky falls."

The technique of envisioning the characters in a certain place in front of the interpreter can prove helpful in identifying characters, but the placements should not be made too broadly or remain static. You should remember that characters move about. Lines spoken to a character should be directed to the place where he or she is at the moment. For instance, Amanda should address Jim in different places as he prepares to leave, and her eyes follow his exit. Then her brave front—the tense body and forced smile—suddenly vanishes. We see her puzzled expression on her almost lifeless body before we hear her faintly uttered last line.

Thus, by applying the principles and techniques of oral interpretation to drama, the interpreter may transform a selection normally intended for several actors on the stage into a dramatic, compelling, and intelligible solo performance.

Chapter 10

Arranged Programs

The lecture recital and the reading hour are popular literary programs for public or class performance. Both may be arranged for a solo interpreter or for a group, and both illuminate and give focus to a theme. The difference between the two arranged programs lies in how the theme is developed.

The Lecture Recital

Defining the Term

The lecture recital develops a theme through commentary. Your purpose is to stimulate and affect an audience's attitude toward some aspect of your subject. Everything you select to read should focus and sharpen the theme. Much of the success of a lecture depends upon your ability to keep everything in your transitional commentary on theme.

An hour is a good length for a club lecture-recital program. Students in an oral interpretation class can usually be allowed no more than twenty minutes.

Discovering a Theme

A single selection may inspire your theme: you like what the piece has to say about communication, love, war, or nature, and this leads you on to a search for other writings on the same subject. You may wish to focus attention on a single novel, poem, or play; you may use several examples of one author's works; or you may develop the theme through the writings of many authors. There are countless methods as well as subjects to explore. You might wish to investigate some aspect of content, style, theme, characters, humor, philosophy, language, etc. of one of your favorite authors.

These modern authors are popular among students:

Robert Frost	Eudora Welty
e. e. cummings	Mark Twain
Emily Dickinson	James Thurber
T. S. Eliot	J. D. Salinger
Sylvia Plath	Katherine A. Porter
Anne Sexton	Ray Bradbury
Langston Hughes	D. H. Lawrence
Dylan Thomas	Ernest Hemingway
Wallace Stevens	William Faulkner
Carl Sandburg	Bertolt Brecht
Tennessee Williams	Neil Simon

These are just a few possible themes for the lecture recital:

Satires of Circumstance	Who Will Wash the Dishes?
The Creation in Literature	An Evening with Mark Twain
Lincoln the Man	Poets with a Cause
War Is Kind	Poetry and Laughter
Paranoia	Images of Women in Literature
I Wonder as I Wander	An Evening with Chekhov
Fathers	American Thoughts Reflected in
Swift's Masks	the Latest Pulitzer Prize Plays
The Liberated Woman	(Novels)
Unchauvinistic Shaw	Thomas Paine and American
A Portrait of the 60s (70s)	Independence
Americana Past and Present	Love Is Just a Four-Letter Word
Growing Up a Girl (Boy)	Earth's the Right Place for Love
The Greening of America	

Arranging Materials

If you properly develop one central idea, your lecture recital will have unity, but there are other points to remember if you want to give it variety, balance, and harmony:

The most dramatic selection should be used as the climax of the whole program. This should come somewhere near but not at the end.

The beginning selection should serve to establish a good relationship between the reader and the audience and to give them time to adjust to each other.

Although contrasts in mood within a program are good, it is usually wise to lead from one mood to another with material that shades rather than jumps into the next mood.

For a smoother flow, short selections can be grouped together; the audience should always be told of this beforehand.

The ending selection should be neither too short nor too long and should leave a sense of unity and harmony and give the impression of a satisfying finale.

The first part of Chapter 8 in this text is arranged like a lecture recital. We intended to illustrate in this way how poetry speaks and what it says in modern America.

Establishing Rapport

In the lecture recital, the interpreter's rapport with the listeners is important. The lecture should not be read; it should be talked. If the introduction, transitional comments, and conclusion are written out, they should be spoken directly to the audience and referred to no more than an effective speaker's notes are. Although some of the transitions between the readings may be short, these breaks should furnish a moment of relaxation and direct communication with the audience.

Examples

Here are three lecture recitals planned and given by students:
Robert Sherwood's Plays: Mirror to His Times (for a class audience)
1   Passage from *Robert E. Sherwood* by Robert Shuman
2   Passage from the preface to *Reunion in Vienna*
3   Character speech from *The Petrified Forest*
4   Character speech from *Idiot's Delight*
5   Scene cutting from *Abe Lincoln in Illinois*
6   Character speech from *There Shall Be No Night*
7   "A Colleague's Eulogy" by Maxwell Anderson
Authors on the Streets of Their Time (for a class audience)
1   London: Nineteenth Century
from *Sketches by Boz* by Charles Dickens
2   Wales: Twentieth Century
from *Quite Early One Morning* by Dylan Thomas
3   America: Twentieth Century
"The Square" and "You Musta Been Away" from *Look Homeward, Angel* by Thomas Wolfe
Women in Their Ebb and Flow of Life (for a women's club audience)
1   Passage from *The Diary of Adam and Eve* by Mark Twain
2   Poem Portraits: "Lucinda Matlock" by Edgar Lee Masters; "Mary Lou Wingate" and "Lucy Weatherby" from *John Brown's Body* by Stephen Vincent Benét; "Mother to Son" by Langston Hughes; "Aunt Jennifer's Tigers" by Adrienne Rich; "The Mountain Woman" by DuBose Heyward; "The White Magnolia Tree" by Helen Deutsch; "Little Old Lady in Lavender Silk" by Dorothy Parker
3   Portrait of Dolly Levi from *The Matchmaker* by Thornton Wilder
4   Two Modern Women View the Present Scene: Passages from "Gifts from the Sea Reopened" by Anne Morrow Lindbergh and "I Wish to Live" by Lorraine Hansberry

The Reading Hour

Focus

A reading program focuses on literary selections chosen to illuminate the theme and presented with little commentary. No attempt is made to evaluate any aspect of the literary selections. The interpreter's attitude is more or less "Here it is—enjoy it." Both the lecture recital and the reading hour elicit appreciation and enjoyment, but the listener should come away from a reading hour remembering the literature rather than what was said about it. The two differ in tightness of form. The lecture recital is highly structured, with much thought given to unity, balance, variety, progression; the reading hour is much more casual, with attention placed more on the literature and less on the structure of the program. By means of the commentary, the lecture recital evaluates particular aspects of the subject, which is not called for in a reading program.

Popular Types

The reading hour is a popular extension of the fine-arts program on various levels: Reading hours on college and university campuses offer traditional programs by single interpreters and experimental types by groups of interpreters. The Manhattan Theatre Club, like culturally directed groups in many other cities, sponsors a poetry series featuring contemporary writing. Groups from oral interpretation classes are transformed into performing ensembles, with interpretive reading programs and interpreters theatre productions for clubs and churches. Many such groups travel throughout their states with programs for elementary school children as well as adult groups.

Teachers of oral interpretation participating in festivals and summer workshops are being inspired by other teachers in the field. News of what is going on is now readily available through regional speech association bulletins and through The Institute for Readers Theatre, founded at San Diego State University in 1974 by Dr. William J. Adams.

Suggested Readings

Boleslavsky, Richard. *Acting: The First Six Lessons*. New York: Theatre Arts Books, 1949.

Campbell, Paul N. "Poetry, Non-Poetry, Prose, and Verse," *Western States Speech Journal*, Winter 1961, pp. 20–24.

Ferguson, Mary Anne, ed. *Images of Women in Literature*. Boston: Houghton Mifflin, 1973.

Gassner, John. *Form and Idea in Modern Theatre*. New York: Holt, Rinehart, and Winston, Inc., 1956.

Hansberry, Lorraine. *To Be Young, Gifted and Black*, Robert Nemiroff, ed. Englewood Cliffs, New Jersey: Prentice-Hall, 1969.

Heyen, William, ed. *American Poets in 1976*. Indianapolis: Bobbs-Merrill, 1976.

Jerome, Judson. *The Poet and the Poem*. Cincinnati: Writer's Digest, 1975.

Larrick, Nancy. "Pop/Rock Lyrics, Poetry and Reading," *Journal of Reading*, December 1971, pp. 184–190.

Lee, Charlotte, and Frank Galati. "The Interpretation of Drama" and "Building and Presenting a Program," in *Oral Interpretation*. Boston: Houghton Mifflin, 1977.

Maclay, Joanna, and Thomas O. Sloan. "Interpreting Nonfictional Prose," and "Interpreting Fiction," in *Interpretation: An Approach to the Study of Literature*. New York: Random House, 1972, pp. 13–127, 242–379.

McGaw, Charles. *Acting is Believing: A Basic Method for Beginners*. New York: Holt, Rinehart, and Winston, Inc., 1966.

Neihardt, John G. "The Interpretation of Poetry," *The Quarterly Journal of Speech*, February 1952, pp. 74–78.

Sloan, T. O. "The Persona as Rhetor: An Interpretation of Donne's 'Satyre III,'" *The Quarterly Journal of Speech*, February 1965, pp. 14–27.

Thomas, Wright, and Stuart Gerry Brown. *Reading Prose: An Introduction to Critical Study*. New York: Oxford University Press, 1952.

Thompson, Craig R., and John Hicks. *Thought and Experience in Prose*. New York: Oxford University Press, 1951

Thompson, David W., and Virginia Fredricks. *Oral Interpretation of Fiction: A Dramatistic Approach*. Minneapolis: Burgess Publishing Company, 1964.

Part IV

Group Interpretation:
Interpreters Theatre

Chapter 11

Introducing Interpreters Theatre

In the first three sections of this text, you were addressed as a solo interpreter; now, in Part Four, as a member of a group. The guides for interpreting and communicating literature alone apply as well to your study and performance with the group, but there is more. A member of a team deeply involved in planning and shaping the experience may sometimes be a performer, at other times an adaptor, designer, or director. This part of the book gives you an inside look at all that goes on in planning, directing, and performing in interpreters theatre.

Interpreters Theatre—What?

Interpreters theatre is group interpretation that puts the prime focus on literary texts. The term refers to a presentational style of theatre with four main features: it consists of a script created from a literary text or texts—prose, poetry, or drama; it calls attention to the literary text by using the narrative voice and techniques that give prominence to the story being told; it may be performed in almost any space without benefit of realistic scenery or theatrical effects; it invites, even solicits, the viewer's imagination.

As early as the 1930s, directors on university and college campuses were staging experimental play readings under various labels: concert theatre, staged readings, chamber theatre, platform theatre, readers theatre, interpreters theatre. Today the medium is generally called readers theatre. We have chosen to use the term interpreters theatre, in order to avoid the restriction of reading and to suggest a more open view in keeping with modern trends. Since quotations within this text may identify the medium as readers theatre, you should keep in mind that interpreters theatre and readers theatre are one and the same.

Interpreters theatre, the forms already mentioned, and Choric Theatre, Theatre of Fact, Story Theatre, etc. have much in common: all "serve . . . literature by providing insights into human experience through a creative appeal to the imagination of the audience." To further this, we propose to identify them collectively in this text as interpreters theatre, while recognizing the unique contributions of three—chamber theatre, theatre of fact, and choric theatre.

Interpreters Theatre—From Where?

Greek Origin

It can be said that drama, interpreters' theatre, and oral interpretation all have their origin in the ancient Greek chorus: when an actor stepped out from the Greek chorus and carried on a dialogue with the group, drama began; when dialogue was read by one actor (rhapsodes), interpretive reading began; when dialogue was read by two actors, interpreters theatre began.

Introduction in America

Interpreters theatre per se did not begin in America until the middle of the 20th century. It was introduced to the general public through two productions which toured America in the early 1950s. In the hands of professionals, these productions drew attention and acclaim to interpreters theatre as an exciting and seemingly new art form.

In 1951 *Don Juan in Hell,* produced as interpreters theatre, was hailed as "a new phenomenon" in theatre. The famous drama quartet of Charles Laughton, Charles Boyer, Sir Cedric Hardwicke, and Agnes Moorehead, seated on stools before music stands, spoke the lines of Shaw's four characters. This way of dramatizing literature became recognized as interpreters theatre's traditional method.

The adaptation of Stephen Vincent Benét's epic poem *John Brown's Body* was produced the next year, with Charles Laughton directing. Three performers, Dame Judith Anderson, Raymond Massey, and Tyrone Power, interpreted many roles. At the same time, a chorus of twenty helped carry the story forward and stir the audience with vocal sound effects. The three readers moved from lecterns to suggest various scenes—a battlefield, a ballroom, etc.—and lighting was used to help suggest various moods. Here already there was change: in material—an adaptation of a long narrative poem; in method—multiple casting and increased use of suggestive movement and lighting effects.

Both these productions appeared to bring this medium close to theatre but, at the same time, to create something new—a form demanding more creative audience participation.

Growth in Educational Theatre

Interpreters theatre gained its most enthusiastic following in educational theatre. College and university campuses provided a climate for experimentation, controversy, and growth during four decades (1930s–1960s) of change and development.

In the 1930s and 40s, the form usually remained a simple play reading. But following *Don Juan in Hell* and *John Brown's Body* in the 1950s, directors began staging interpreters theatre and experimenting with combinations of prose, poetry, and various literary forms. The simplicity of the staging and the use of scripts allowed a performance to be put together quickly. As a result, interpreters theatre became a popular vehicle for use in oral interpretation classes, for club entertainments, and as a training ground for fledgling actors in drama departments.

In the 1950s, articles appeared in speech and drama journals more and more frequently, attempting to define interpreters theatre and to challenge the traditional rules which had evolved through the years. Directors simply refused to be confined by the definitions; the rules were broken everywhere.

The 1960s brought more changes, more clearly defined practices, and recognition. Courses in interpreters theatre were added to speech and theatre curricula, and productions became more ambitious. Interpreters theatre was elevated to a new status on college and university campuses.

Evidence of Growth

The Interpretation Interest Group of the Speech Association of America noted the rising interest in interpreters theatre in the early 60s. The 1960–64 report listed twenty-one articles, dissertations, and theses written on the subject, and more than two hundred specific literary selections presented in interpreters theatre. Productions at conventions of the Speech Association in the 1960s were typical of material being adapted on campuses from coast to coast:

Book I of Benét's *John Brown's Body* was produced by Hunter College

An adaptation of Bradbury's novel *Dandelion Wine*, by Southwest Missouri State College

A compiled script *Battle of the Sexes*, by Central Michigan University

An adaptation of Camus's *The Stranger*, by University of Southern California

An adaptation of Fielding's *The Tragedy of Tragedies*, by Northwestern University

Readers Theatre for Children, by Southwest Missouri State College

A more recent bibliography reports activities on fifteen campuses in 1971. The report lists six articles, books, dissertations, and theses written during the year and more than seventy-five adaptations of prose, poetry, drama, and compiled scripts, featuring such contemporary subjects as women's rights, blacks, war, space, and ecology, presented in interpreters theatre. The report was an early indication of the compiled script's rise in popularity today.*

Research in the field has mirrored the increased interest in script construction. In addition to the interest shown by the traditional speech and theatre journals, William Forrest and Neil Novell published the first issue of *Oral English,* devoted exclusively to oral interpretation and featuring articles on interpreters theatre. In the winter of 1974 William Adams founded the Institute for Readers Theatre for the investigation of significant topics in interpreters theatre. Michigan State University's *Issues in Interpretation,* first published in the fall of 1975, addressed itself to problems in interpreters theatre and in other, related fields. With its publication of *Preview* in the spring of 1976, the American Writers Theatre Foundation stated that its emphasis would be on "theatrical works drawn from the wealth of prose and poetry not originally written for the stage."

Interpreters Theatre—To Where?

The old separations of interpretive forms are gone, and widely accepted generalizations set a new tone: a single performance of interpreters theatre may combine elements of chamber theatre, theatre of fact, and choric theatre; performances may even combine the media of dance, music, painting, photography, film and slides. And when a director mixes the combined forms well, using them to illuminate the meanings in the text, interpreters theatre may be greatly enriched.

Interpreters theatre today is a flexible, free form. "Flexible" is the key word. Although the old conventions are no longer binding rules, they have not been discarded. The traditional ground rules often serve certain texts and situations best.

Interpreters theatre initiated a way of sharing plays through group reading; today it is a hybrid form of theatre which allows all forms of literature to be presented in any manner that best features the text and gains involvement from the audience. It is clear that interest in interpreters theatre has grown steadily and remarkably as the medium has changed.

Interpreters Theatre—Why?

There are three main reasons why interpreters theatre is a popular way to perform literature.

First, it has dramatic appeal. The professional readings of drama

---

* Readers Theatre Bibliography Committee of the Speech Association of America, 1971. (Courtesy of the Chairman, Clark S. Marlor)

and poetry that inspired the form's rise to popularity in the middle of the 20th century gained an unusual and striking audience response. Critics immediately recognized a new kind of audience participation. As Robert Breen wrote, "Readers theatre asks us to go back to interaction with the audience. Readers theatre is interested in the relationship between the performer and the audience. There is now a new relationship: the audience is also on stage, participating."[1]

Second, interpreters theatre offers a broad scope of literary fare. All forms of literature can be adapted and used—prose and poetry, as well as drama. This extends its contribution to the sharing of literature for a variety of groups. Interpreters theatre adds to the cultural enrichment of all participants, performers and listeners alike.

Third, interpreters theatre has a practical appeal. The form can be presented anywhere—in classrooms, in living rooms, in student, community, or church centers, or in any other offstage space. These possibilities appeal not only to amateurs but to professionals as well.

In addition to this, interpreters theatre is recognized as a valuable educational tool on both the high school and the college levels. Preparation for and participation in interpreters theatre may enrich the student's background in literature through the variety of materials considered and studied. The student's deeper understanding of each particular piece of literature studied provides new insights into human relationships and into his or her own personality. The group nature of the activity may inspire the student's best efforts, which results in observable improvements in reading skills, in body control, in concentration, and in rapport with other members of the group as well. Individual contributions in building a script or in performing may awaken a real creative talent or motivate a desire for other creative efforts. Every teacher-director can give concrete examples of students whose participation in planning and performing interpreters theatre has brought about a heightened dedication to literature.

---

[1] Robert Breen. "Readers Theatre and the Audience," *Readers Theatre News,* Spring 1975, p. 6.

Chapter 12

Application of Forms, General Principles, and Methods

In this chapter we hope to clarify why certain principles, styles, methods, and techniques are applicable to interpreters theatre. Later we will deal more specifically with selecting, analyzing, and adapting materials and with staging and directing productions.

Use of Literary Forms

General Principles

All types of literature can be used in interpreters theatre, but some more readily than others.

Interpreters theatre calls attention to the literary text through narration and by utilizing methods and techniques that give prominence to the story being told.

In transferring literature to interpreters theatre, the adaptor may make cuts in the interest of necessary condensation, but should never distort the theme, tone, or the point of view of the original literary work.

Drama Adapted for Interpreters Theatre

Choice of Play. A play involving mainly mental rather than physical action is more easily used successfully in interpreters theatre. The wise director selects plays that deal with ideas, character, and character relationships.

The play is a natural choice for interpreters theatre because it is written in dialogue. However, plays with built-in narrators relieve the director of having to supply narration. Examples are Greek plays with a chorus, radio plays with unidentified narrators, and plays with character narrators, such as Tom in *The Glass Menagerie*.

Adapting the Play. In transferring most plays to interpreters theatre, an adaptor adds a narrator or narrators to the script, even though some narration may already be present. Narration helps the audience understand the plotline as the story unfolds. This fulfills the medium's basic intention of telling the story rather than acting it. Prose fiction, on the other hand, has a built-in narrator.

Prose Fiction Adapted

Interpreters theatre preserves the epic mode of fiction by retaining the storyteller; the perspective of the story is controlled by the author's appointed narrator, through whose eyes we see the action.

From our knowledge of literary fiction, we know that dramatic episodes, conveyed through dialogue and inner monologues, are frequently interrupted by narration. The narrator's voice may be present both on short "he said" tags and in explanations, descriptions, reflections, and summaries of what has happened so far.

Adapting. The adaptor's first concern is to identify the author's point of view. The storyteller's objectivity or subjectivity influences the participants' degree of involvement in the story. The objective view of external narrators speaking in the past tense tends to decrease emotional involvement; subjective, internal narrators speaking in the present tense promote immediacy and intimacy, increasing involvement. For instance, by changing the opening line of Ray Bradbury's novel *Dandelion Wine* from "It was a quiet morning" to "It is a quiet morning," the adaptor established a here-and-now view of events in which both the interpreters and their listeners could be closely involved.

The adaptor's analysis of the original material will help answer many questions about that work, which prepares the way for adaptation: "What actions and characters must be retained in the adaptation to keep the theme and tone intact?" "From whose view is the story told, and how can this be handled to best advantage in the adaptation?" "For this particular story, will the use of a single narrator, two narrators, a chorus, or a combination of these best represent the author's view?" The answers should be based on one's understanding of the material and on aesthetic principles. To illustrate this, we refer to a novel which has been adapted and performed successfully many times.

Example: Novel, *U.S.A.* In Dos Passos's novel trilogy *U.S.A.*, the episodes move through thirty years of American history, and the beginning and ending unify the whole: it begins with a description of an American youth in the early 1900s and ends with a description of an American youth in the 1930s. *U.S.A.* is a good vehicle for interpreters theatre because of its unique structure. Interwoven with the fictional plot are three other forms: biographies of well-known public figures; a "newsreel" containing snatches of songs, speeches, headlines, news items, etc.; and a "camera eye" representing the characters' memories. These devices furnish background and indicate the passage of and the changes wrought by time. The stories of the many characters take place in three periods of time: the early 1900s up to World War I, the war itself, and the years from World War I up to the 1930s.

It is evident that much cutting and rearranging were needed to adapt a novel of this length and complexity. The Paul Shyre-Dos Passos adaptation gives central place to the leading characters' stories, using only a few of the novel's biographies and camera eyes and tying the scenes together with selected lines from the news items and popular songs. The adaptors' use of the stories and devices emphasizes the novel's central theme and critical tone. The adaptation is faithful to the novel's various points of view: third-person narrators report on and judge the lives of both the fictional and real characters from the outside; the camera eyes presents a character's stream-of-consciousness point of view; and the news items and songs represent the popular public view at the moment.

This example indicates in general how to alter original material while keeping the theme, tone, and point of view intact. In addition to large cuts, other changes may be necessary: cutting the directive "he said" tags to help dialogue flow more smoothly or allowing a character to summarize some omitted parts.

On the other hand, there are short short stories, such as the fable, which require no changes at all. Thurber's fable "The Moth and the Star," for example, can best be told by the characters themselves.

MOTHER MOTH. He told his mother about this and she counseled him to set his heart on a bridge lamp instead. "Stars aren't the thing to hang around," she said; "Lamps are the thing to hang around."
FATHER MOTH. "You get somewhere that way," said the moth's father. "You don't get anywhere chasing stars."
YOUNG MOTH. But the moth would not heed the words of either parent.
(from *Fables for Our Time*, by James Thurber)

The narrative, with its obvious moral, can be told from the points of view of its three character narrators. The humor is highlighted by using the characters as objective narrators.

Each literary text, then, presents its own unique adaptation problems. The manner in which an adaptor uses prose fiction or any other literary form always depends upon the particular material. However, there is a related form, designed especially to present narrative fiction as it is written. Chamber theatre may be considered as distinct from interpreters theatre. As interpreters theatre has undergone changes, using all types of material, staging techniques, and shifts in focus, the differences between the two forms have become less. However, there are still specific differences in use of material and in performance, and these will be pointed out.

Prose Fiction Adapted for Chamber Theatre

Chamber theatre uses fiction in a manner that gives emphasis to the author's point of view, while allowing the dialogue to be staged

more dramatically with onstage focus and pantomime than in traditional interpreters theatre.

An adaptor of chamber theatre assigns lines flexibly in order to give emphasis to the narrator's view and to preserve the piece as it was written.

Assigning Lines. You may cut a long text to the desired length, but you do not otherwise change the text. You use the narrative form as it is written, seeking to control the shifting perspective by how you assign the lines. For instance, the line "He said that it was much too early for everyone to go" would be spoken as written, as indirect discourse (reported rather than spoken directly). But who would say the line, the narrator or the character to whom the line refers? Obviously, it might be assigned to either one. You must proceed with care when handling indirect discourse, making decisions as to who is saying what. Certainly, the narrator would rarely speak all the indirect discourse, for the arranger would miss dramatic opportunity to emphasize subtleties in the script. For example, consider the interpretations of the line "He said that it was much too early for everyone to go." Should it be assigned to an omniscient narrator or to an unsympathetic character who considered the comment an insult? Indirect discourse or even narration is not automatically assigned to the narrator just because it is not dialogue easily attributed to a character. States of mind, disposition, and character relationships are sometimes best clarified in narration spoken by a character who reveals private thoughts rather than by a narrator who comments upon them. On the other hand, if the above line appeared in direct discourse, as " 'It is much too early for everyone to go,' he said with some force," you would assign the direct quote to the character; the description tag might be assigned to the narrator or the character.

Handling Narrative Tags. This raises another question concerning chamber theatre's use of the narrative form exactly as it is written. Does this mean that all the "he said" tags must be retained in a performing script? No. The rule needs to be tempered with aesthetic judgment. We should remember that the frequent "he saids" are needed in the initial written form of the story, to help the reader understand the changes of character. This is not usually necessary in chamber theatre, for we have different characters, who are visible to the audience, saying those lines. So the adaptor is expected to retain some of the tags to preserve the narrative effect, but good theatrical judgment eliminates some tags, lest their continual use bore the audience.

Choice of Material to Emphasize Point of View. Stories and novels in which a close relationship between the narrator and the other characters exists are best suited to chamber theatre. The action of the narrator who is also a character in the story is naturally integrated with the action of the story. Examples are the boy in Truman Capote's "A Christmas Memory" and Sister in Eudora Welty's "Why I Live at the P.O." Playing a dual role, such a character moves easily in and out of the story's action both as character and as narrator. A physical reality for the unidentified narrator who is outside the story should be found and developed. A story in which interaction between narrator and characters is not feasible is not a good choice for chamber theatre.

Use of Other Prose Types

Essays, letters, diaries, and documentary materials may also be adapted for interpreters theatre.

The essay usually requires the addition of dialogue when transferred to interpreters theatre. Letters and diaries lend themselves well to adaptation: Jerome Kilty's *Dear Liar* is a pleasant comedy of letters, and Mark Twain's *The Dairy of Adam and Eve* is delightfully entertaining. Since the 1960s, documentary material has become a most popular form. In 1963, when this new type of play appeared, with the off-Broadway production of *In White America*, a reviewer for *The New York Times* wrote,

> ". . . I don't see how anything could have made the story of the American Negro more theatrical or moving than this chronological arrangement of actual documents and excerpts from documents. . . . "

Poetry Adapted for Interpreters Theatre

Narrative poems which contain dialogue are well suited for interpreters theatre. The problems in adapting the long narrative poem are essentially the same as those for drama and narrative fiction: the narrative tells the story by the poet's narrator. As in other adaptations, the adaptor keeps the poet's point of view, central theme, and tone. Long narrative poems, such as Benét's *John Brown's Body* or Milton's *Samson Agonistes,* are comparable to the novel and require many cuts. A poem like Frost's "The Death of the Hired Man" is comparable to the short story and is easier to adapt.

A lyric poem may be arranged for a choral group, but the lyric and other types of short poems are used most often in compiled scripts.

Compiled Scripts

A composite may be one of three types: excerpts from a literary work which features only a part of the whole; a script composed of selections tied together around a theme; a script featuring documentary materials.

Use of excerpts. The intent behind an adaptation is to present the literary selection as a work of art, on its own terms, as a whole, but the intention of a composite is to feature only a part of the whole—an attitude, a single character's story, or a relationship.

Use of miscellaneous materials. The material selected may be intended to tell something about the author and the author's works (*Thurber Carnival, An Evening's Frost*) or the material may consist of works by many authors. An example of this second type is "Images in Black and White," a script compiled and produced as an oral interpretation class project. The materials used included both literary works and documentary excerpts: the Bible, the slave episode from Benét's *John Brown's Body*; J. W. Johnson's poems "Mask" and "Creation"; Langston Hughes's poems "Merry-Go-Round" and "Necessity"; an excerpt from Langston Hughes's prose "J. B. Simple"; James Baldwin's "A Letter": from *The Fire Next Time;* excerpt from *A Raisin in the Sun* by Lorraine Hansberry; Don L. Lee's poem

"But He Was Cool: or He Even Stopped for Green Lights"; and Nikki Giovanni's poem "Status"; Petition to Congress 1970; Supreme Court Decision 1954; excerpt from "Long Shadow of Little Rock"; short excerpts from speeches by black and white leaders; news items and headlines from 1918 to 1976; and a short statement from a speech by a Klansman. These materials were arranged in chronological order; the news items and music tied the parts together. The compilation told the dramatic story of the black man's struggle in a white man's world, ending with a hopeful but realistic view of the struggle ahead.

Theatre of Fact

A form or extension of interpreters theatre which draws its materials from documents or other factual materials is called theatre of fact.
What is it? A theatre of fact script is more than a series of reports. Meticulous care must be given to selecting data that will present the facts and at the same time be emotionally engaging. It seeks some universal truth, a reality which the heart and mind can discern. As author of the compiled script *Lest We Forget: Kent State,* Professor Robinette tried to present a "macroscopic world view" of a factual happening.

> It is only by accident that the scene is Kent State; it could be any campus or town throughout the U.S. and it is only by accident that the actors are students and guardsmen; they could have been from any vocation. For the play is about the enigma of symbols, using people only as its manifestation. Thus, the people make the play specific, thereby enabling an audience to identify easily with the characters; the incident is also specific—an event known to most Americans; however, the truth is universal.

How is it used? Successful on- and off-Broadway, television, and college and univeristy campus productions attest that theatre of fact is an effective type of interpreters theatre. Those on the educational scene have employed actual documents and excerpts from documents, speeches, journals, official records, interviews, and conversations to depict such subjects as the assassination of John F. Kennedy, the life of Patton, the life of Harry S Truman, the career of the Beatles, the plight of the red man, women's liberation, ecology, and many others.

Use of Casting Principles

General Methods

Casting methods for interpreters theatre are varied and flexible and are chosen by the adaptor-director to illuminate the meaning of the particular text.
   Multiple casting promotes the alienation that an interpreters theatre production may ultimately depend upon.
Flexibility in assigning roles. As we have said, the narration in a script

may be assigned to a single narrator or to a group of narrators. Likewise, the method of assigning character roles is flexible: each character role may be assigned to one actor, one role may be assigned to more than one actor, or several roles may be assigned to one actor.

Multiple Casting. In the Shyre-Dos Passos adaptation of *U.S.A.,* all the lines are assigned to six actors; each interprets both character and narrator roles and serves as a voice in the chorus. This multiple casting adds an alienation effect to the whole, allows many groups (labor, big business, politics, etc.) to be presented as fragments of reality, and stresses how the news media interpret events and change.

Sometimes new insights into complex characters, such as split personalities, for example, can be gained by assigning a single role to more than one interpreter. When a character tells his or her own story, a director may find that double casting (giving one actor both a narrative role and a experiencing role) not only allows the shifts to flow more smoothly, but also brings out subtle psychological differences between the views.

Typecasting. Typecasting is usually less evident in interpreters theatre than in conventional theatre, because the characters are shown rather than created realistically. This gives a director the freedom to place less importance on a character's visual requirements and to generalize character roles by using multiple casting, without regard to sex or other physical considerations. The audience generally accepts such breaks with standard casting if the method is made clear early and is consistently used in the production.

Use of Staging and Performing Principles

Foundation Principles

Conventions are generally accepted ground rules that define the relationship between the audience and the performers.

Interpreters theatre conventions are that the actors maintain some direct contact with the audience, the actors suggest or show characters and actions rather than performing them realistically, the staging remains symbolic and suggestive rather than realistic, and the listeners become imaginatively involved in a recreated literary experience.

Through a careful analysis of a chosen literary work, an adaptor-director builds an adaptation that is faithful to the author's intent. This analysis is the foundation for both the staging and the performing plans. The best manner of expressing the meaning of a particular script should emerge through the director's analysis, making for a harmony of styles in the production.

Staging Principle

The staging and performing of interpreters theatre reflect the way the director interprets the text; the cues for scene placement, set,

and movement and the use of properties, scripts, costume, lighting, and music come from the specific text with which the director is working.

Style. Based on the medium's conventions, the general style of interpreters theatre is presentational or nonillusionistic. However, within this frame a production may have its own particular style, based upon the director's interpretation of the literary work in question and on the director's own creativity. Style is achieved mainly by the choice of values—plot, character, theme, and qualities of mood—within the text that are emphasized, and by the choice of certain methods and techniques to use in accomplishing this. For instance, the director may choose a simple set or one comparable to that of an elaborate theatrical production, offstage focus or offstage combined with onstage focus, scripts or no scripts, much movement or no movement.

Determining style. Today, symbolic theatrical effects are readily accepted, even expected. How does a director go about choosing effects that will be in harmony with the spirit of the material? The director's imagination determines this. For instance, the director of *Royal Gambit*, envisioning Henry VIII's first entrance, realized the need for an elevated level from which Henry can dominate. Focusing on Henry with each of his wives in other important moments gave the director clues for the entire set: various stage areas to suggest many "places" and different levels with a platform and steps to allow the interpreters to take varied positions. Moments in the "out-of-time" scenes suggested stylized movement and special lighting effects. Using the imagination in this way, the director was creatively unifying the subject matter and its expression.

One danger to be considered is that a director's theatrical effects may become excessive and, as a result, distract from rather than aid the interpretation of the author's meaning. The overall effect of the staging for interpreters theatre should be more simple than elaborate; utilitarian in its use of space, providing a comfortable environment for performers; and symbolic.

Alienation Principle

In interpreters theatre, the narrative interpolations create an alienation effect for both the interpreter and the listener.

The actor-interpreter, making no pretense of being a character, shows the character through suggestion while maintaining his or her own identity. This establishes aesthetic distance from the character and gives the interpreter the freedom to judge the character's actions. The listener, aware of both the character and the interpreter at the same time, has no illusions and knows that this is make-believe. This establishes aesthetic distance from the characters, allowing the audience the freedom to judge the characters' actions and the author's meaning.

Interplay: Ensemble Playing

Interpreters theatre demands a high degree of interplay, or ensemble playing. When the full cast remains on stage throughout a production, each interpreter must stay visually in tone with the others; movement from nonscene to action scene and the use of offstage focus require considerable control of physical interplay. The use of a speaking chorus forces each reader to depend upon every other reader to come in on cue. The use of stylized movement demands precision in ensemble work and, when it is used as an accompaniment to spoken words, great care in coordinating action with words.

A successful performance of chamber theatre demands good ensemble playing. To coordinate words, pantomimed action, and narrative interpolations in chamber theatre, interpreters must depend upon each other and work as a team. Many hours of practice are required to perfect the difficult timing, yet the actual performance must be unhurried and seemingly spontaneous.

Chapter 13

Building Scripts:
Selecting, Analyzing, Adapting

Rather than use an already published adaptation, a director may prefer to build an adaptation of the chosen literary work. So scripts for interpreters theatre are often written as they are needed.

Success in building a script depends upon good judgment in selecting the literary text, in analyzing the original text, and in using adaptation techniques. In this chapter, these matters will be related to a particular text, the three-act play *Royal Gambit.** In learning to adapt literary works by following our suggested process, you should read both the original play and our adaptation in Chapter 16.

Selecting Original Text

The choice of a literary text is influenced by your particular situation and by literary criteria. You would find *Royal Gambit* a good choice if your situation calls for a simple set and a small cast. The play can be cut to your required time without distorting the author's purpose or theme. You would also need to decide whether your particular audience would find *Royal Gambit* interesting, suitable, and understandable. But let us tell you why we selected it for demonstrating adaptation.

We recognized that many characteristics of interpreters theatre are built into the play (characters become narrators who speak directly to the audience, etc.), but this was not the main reason we selected it. We recognized that its unusual form, its distortion of time, and its language make the play strikingly individual, in a way that calls for imaginative

---

* Arrangements should be made to purchase individual copies for the class or to have copies placed in the library. *Royal Gambit* is published by Samuel French.

staging. We also considered the theme timely, one that concerns modern man. And we found still another reason: the play's central theme can be more clearly revealed by adding two narrators rather than relying on narration through dialogue, which the original play requires. We wanted to demonstrate for students how the addition of narrators, representing the playwright's omniscient voice, can give emphasis to the theme (in this case, a buried one). We believe *Royal Gambit* can be an even more effective play when adapted for interpreters theatre and that it is a good choice for a full evening's performance.

Analyzing the Text

Analysis of the original material is the foundation for building and staging a script and for directing and performing it. You must depend upon your understanding of theme, point of view, structure, characters, and tone throughout the process of planning the production and directing the performance.

Theme

We believe the playwright is saying that the humanistic philosophy realized by Henry VIII brought progress without thought for the human condition, that people became victims of the new knowledge and laws which he himself set in action. Extending the consequences of this philosophy into the future, the play suggests that these destructive forces reach their zenith in the 20th century and that any return to a sane existence depends upon first a returning to God's moral laws.

Structure: Movement of the Action

In his use of timing, Hermann Gressieker employs a free form which makes *Royal Gambit* different from the conventional play. There are flashbacks and extensions of the action into the future; soliloquies and direct address are injected into the dialogue, rather than kept distinct from it. The play begins with an overview "beyond time" and ends "out of time," with the six wives accepting Henry's heritage.

The main action of the play concerns Henry's acquisition and disposal of his wives. The pattern begins with the dissolution of his marriage to Katarina of Aragon, and proceeds through his alliances with Anne Boleyn, Jane Seymour, Anna of Cleves, Kathryn Howard, and Kate Parr. Each episode furnishes a complication, foreshadows another, and climaxes in the wife's dismissal or death. Although the play is divided into acts, the form is episodic and the plot is merely a thread tying the episodes together to bring out the theme. Henry's destructive wielding of power and his complete self-righteousness create an expectation of downfall, which comes at the end, but is not a very dramatic fall. He dies of a heart attack, knowing that he leaves a troubled world, still believing that he is indispensable and that the world is the worse for his passing. The play emphasizes _theme_ and _character_ rather than plot.

Point of View

In the original play, the author's view is revealed through the dialogue alone. In the adaptation, the playwright's omniscient point of view is made evident through the dialogue and given emphasis by the narrators. The characters have the power to see into the future, to comment, and to judge. Katarina of Aragon seems to be the chief exponent of the author's view.

Analysis of Character

Henry Tudor, King of England, the epitome of the Renaissance man, becomes the embodiment of contemporary liberal thought. He defies the church and the world, makes his own rules, and justifies his every act as a call of conscience. Anne Boleyn says of him: "Good is what pleases you; wicked, what proves troublesome." His queens recognize him as pompous, lustful, calculating, and destructive, and yet they are drawn to the man. His power and judgments are feared, but the man is loved. His basic motivation is preservation of his ego; he must justify his every act. This sustains him, while it causes him to appear more and more ridiculous in our eyes.

Katarina of Aragon, in the beginning, is a queen fighting for her rights. After her dismissal and imprisonment, she is seen as a happier and wiser woman. Separated from the anxieties of the age, living the simple life, she holds fast to her strong religious beliefs and finds great peace of mind. She emerges as the true queen, the one Henry wants by his side at the end. Her basic motivation is to live, and to help others to live, according to God's laws.

Anne Boleyn is a beautiful, haughty, quick-witted young woman with modern views. Her basic motivation is to satisfy her own ego. She is pleased to have Henry turn Europe upside down for her, and at the end she is confident of her own worth, never doubting that she will remain the one great passion of Henry's life.

Jane Seymour, though of royal blood, is shown as a simple soul, fearful of court life and caught in its intrigues. She wants only a simple life, a home in the country with an earl and children; instead, she dies producing a son for Henry.

Anna of Cleves, the fourth bride, becomes Henry's wife in name only and is then quickly set aside with the title "Sister of the King." She is physically unattractive to Henry, but he likes her. She is blunt and straightforward, and she possesses a fine sense of humor which Henry enjoys. She says to Henry, "You have a damned sly way of shaping life to suit you." He calls her ". . . the only woman I've ever been able to talk with, and you have such a nose. I could almost overlook it." Anna wants to make the best of what she has, to partake of life, to enjoy its physical pleasures and its material possessions. Anna is like Henry in her calculating ways and her love of gold. In the end, she says that she and Henry might have had a lot of fun together, and we believe this.

Kathryn Howard Henry sees in his declining years as one who combines all the youth and beauty of England. In truth, she is a troubled young woman, a victim of Henry's liberal ideas. Her childhood indiscretions are well known and, as queen, she becomes the victim of blackmailers. Hoping for mercy, she confesses everything to Henry and is condemned to die. Her basic drive is to escape her predicament, to find something to hold on to.

Kate Parr, the last wife, is an intelligent, quick-witted woman who views the man and his philosophy with a sense of humor. Her primary motivation is to stimulate Henry's mind and jar his ego, to make him squirm as well as laugh. She nurses Henry in his old age, a role given her by circumstances; her great pleasure comes in arguing with Henry about the accomplishments of his modern world.

Analysis of Tone

Gressieker's emphasis on theme, which probes into good and evil and raises challenging questions concerning the modern age, gives a strong warning with religious overtones, relieved, however, by humor. The dialogue is vivid and evocative; the playwright has a poet's feeling for language, and he lightens the play with wit.

The timing devices allow the characters to make humorous comments as well as introspective analyses of their situations. Henry, with his great zest for life, likes to laugh (a woman is more attractive to him if she is capable of the witty retort and the clever barb). The playwright calls the play "an erotic moral tragicomedy." He sees Henry as a lustful man whose "justified" destructive acts are moral tragedies; but he also sees Henry, stalking through life with his pompous flare and his calls of conscience, as a kind of comic.

Adapting Original Text

In converting a literary text into a performing script for interpreters theatre, a director-adaptor is translating the literary work, changing it and adding something to it by way of aural and visual effects. The literary analysis of the work is the foundation, but the adaptor should also have some definite ideas about the staging, about what the eye is to see. It would be wrong to discuss the adapting techniques without thought for the staging, for the two processes are so closely bound that they merge in actual operation. We consider them separately here only to simplify and make matters less confusing.

Adapting Techniques

The procedures given here for cutting, rearranging, and molding the original work into a new form proceed in logical order from the general to the specific. The plan is an aid in adapting the novel or any other long work, such as *Royal Gambit.*

Assigning the Cast of Characters. An adaptor must consider how narration is to be handled and what characters must be retained to preserve the author's purpose. In the case of *Royal Gambit,* we decided early that the addition of the narrative voice not only would be feasible but would also help clarify the play's theme. We thought that a chorus of two might be best suited to the play's style and that the cast of the adaptation would have to include all those of the original play, since to cut any character would distort the play's theme. The main problem concerned the narration—whether to create it or to find it within the play's dialogue.

As we considered the lines that might be assigned to the narrators, we began to see the two narrators performing somewhat different functions. We decided, where possible, to assign the lines that tie the scenes together, move the action, and summarize omitted actions to Narrator One. Narrator Two's lines comment on the man and the age. Doing so gave each narrator a personality.

Building General Content. The question of what scenes from the chosen literary work should be retained directs attention to the whole play or novel. Guided by the analysis of the text's theme and tone, the adaptor builds content by cutting in (marking parts to be retained) large segments. Among the cut-outs are brief segments and lines to be considered later. These possible cut-ins are marked in a special way so they can be located easily.

In the cast of *Royal Gambit,* the adaptors cut in segments and lines throughout the play that give emphasis to the theme and pervading tone; these lines were often assigned to the narrators. This resulted in retaining portions of many scenes, with both large and small segments cut out.

Adjusting and Building In. After reviewing the large cut-ins, the adaptor must direct attention to the second cutting. At this time, character and narrative lines may be assigned and a place found for the marked segments in the omitted parts. These are inserted into the adaptation. Care should be taken to select key lines that move the story forward or give emphasis to character motivation.

In adjusting the general content of *Royal Gambit,* the narrators got many of the character lines from the omitted sections. Henry's death scene was cut and key lines from this were transferred to other scenes. In the adaptation, Henry dies offstage, which avoids complicated staging. All lines assigned the two narrators were taken directly from the play, limiting the narrators' roles. Another adaptor might have extended the roles by writing some of the narration.

Molding a New Form. As the retained parts are adjusted, a new form emerges. Having abandoned the author's divisions (chapters in a novel, acts in a play), the adaptor structures the retained parts into scenes or episodes, then builds the narrative bridges needed to tie the segments together. At this point, it is important to make an outline of scenes and bridges.

In the adaptation of *Royal Gambit,* the action and narration were

185

divided into eleven scenes. An outline titled the scenes and indicated the bridges, which were constructed from lines in the play. Identifying the mood of each scene provided a means of checking the variety and overall tone. The script in Chapter 16 demonstrates the allocation of lines in the final adapted form. The playing time was reduced from two and a half to approximately one and a half hours.

Evaluating Adaptation

In evaluating the performing script, an adaptor must consider certain questions. Has the author's point of view been retained? Does the adaptation tell a story that moves forward to a climax? Has variety been achieved by contrasting scenes? Have sufficient narration and description been retained or added? Has the author's tone been retained, or have omissions changed the tone? Does the retained content accurately project the theme?

After this study, the adaptor may decide to make adjustments, adding, subtracting, or reassigning certain lines. Building a script is a cumulative and continuing process; changes in the script will no doubt be made during rehearsals.

Finally, the adapter should be aware of the importance of permissions. When a literary selection is presented as interpreters theatre in a public performance, the producer must secure permissions and pay the royalty fee specified by the author's publisher or agent. Interpreters theatre productions often do not require the royalty fee necessary for staged plays. But no copyrighted work should be adapted or produced without written permission from the agent or publisher.

Chapter 14

Staging Interpreters Theatre

Visual Elements for Staging

Staging interpreters theatre involves careful planning of how the visual elements of the production are to be used. They include the focus, set, transitions, movement, scripts, lighting, sound effects, music, and costumes. Your use of these elements is influenced by the conventions of the medium, by your interpretation of the original literary material, and by your own creativity. The staging, representing your interpretation of the script, rests on values in the text that you wish to emphasize.

The visual elements are interdependent: the use of focus will influence the plans for set and movement; the shape of the playing area will influence the grouping and movement; the set and the available lighting will influence how one scene flows into the next.

Before demonstrating the staging of *Royal Gambit,* we want to clarify these visual elements and the uses a designer-director makes of them.

Use of Focus: Scene Placement

The focus means where each scene is placed and where, to whom, and how the lines are directed.

Offstage Focus. As a solo interpreter, you are already familiar with the principle of offstage focus: passages within a text, such as descriptions, explanations, summaries, etc., that generalize are shared directly with the audience (open stance); passages of dialogue and, to some extent, inner reflections intended to be overheard by the audience, are removed from the audience (closed stance) and by imagining the scene taking place in a visual field not on the stage, but out front, on a level with the interpreter's eyes. When interpreting dialogue between two or more characters, the interpreter places the characters in the imaginary scene out front, moves the eyes slightly to the right when addressing one character and to the left for the other (See Figure 14–1).

Borrowing this oral interpretation principle, interpreters theatre uses both types of offstage focus: two or more interpreters share literary passages directly with the audience, and in dialogue scenes their eyes move as they address characters in the envisioned scene out front (See Figure 14–2).

The audience as well as the interpreters must see with the mind's eye, imagining the scene, the characters, and the action. For the most part, the action in interpreters theatre does not occur onstage, but is experienced through the interpreters' and the audience's imagination. Thus, interpreters theatre is often called theatre of the mind.

Though offstage focus remains the distinguishing principle of interpreters theatre, directors are no longer confined to its use alone. Onstage and offstage focus may be combined (See Figure 14–3).

Onstage Focus. Directors find that a change from offstage to onstage focus is a means of giving emphasis to a scene or a dramatic moment. Marion and Marvin Kleninau report this example:

> In a readers theatre version of *Dark of the Moon* produced at the University of Wisconsin, Dr. Jean Scharfenberg used focus to isolate and reinforce one of the main dramatic climaxes of the play. Throughout the production, the lines were directed forward toward the audience, but at the climactic moment in

Fig. 14–1 Offstage Focus: Solo Reader

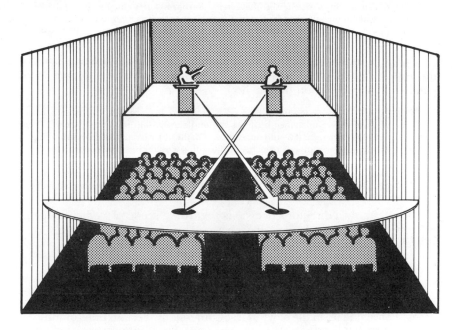

Fig. 14–2 Offstage Focus: Two Readers

Fig. 14–3 Onstage Focus: Two Actors

189

question, the two leading characters, Barbara and John, turned and looked directly at one another for the first time. It was a moment of awareness and the director used the technique of focus in a way to make that moment unique.[1]

It is important to base shifts in focus on a clear understanding of the author's intentions. Dr. Wallace Bacon cites the way two scenes were handled in a production of Othello:

> The action when Iago stabs Roderigo was presented onstage, because without seeing this stage business the audience would miss the intended effect (words referring to it would not suffice). On the other hand, Othello's strangling of Desdemona was placed offstage, because this would give Shakespeare's intended emphasis—the effect of the deed on the character of Othello rather than on the deed itself. Both characters, facing front, suggested the agonies of the scene, giving dramatic focus to the effect of the deed on Othello—as Shakespeare intended.[2]

Usually a director's decisions regarding scene placement depend on study of the aim and mood of each scene in relation to the whole. These decisions greatly affect the staging of other visual elements.

Special Use of Focus

Interpreters theatre also uses focus to stress subtle meanings within passages. For instance, in the story "First Confession," certain lines of indirect discourse technically belong to the narrator, but really more closely represent the boy's thoughts, and so we assigned them to that character. Note in this passage how the lines in italics are spoken in an imagined scene out front as the boy's reflective thoughts would gain emphasis from the focus change:

> . . . The sense of oppression that had been weighing him down for a week, the knowledge that he was about to make a bad confession, disappeared. *Bad confession indeed! He had made friends, made friends with the priest. And the priest expected, even demanded terrible sins. Oh Women! Women! It was all women and girls and their silly talk. They had no real knowledge of the world.*

In other instances, a director may find that subtle humor or philosophical musings, which are usually focused as reflective thoughts, can be sharpened when the lines are shared directly with the audience.

Change in focus, then, can give emphasis to dramatic moments, to certain scenes, and to particular lines.

Use of Set

Placement of Playing Areas. As director, you must plan a way to use space and the cast's arrangement on the set so that scenes can flow

---

[1] Marion and Marvin Kleninau "Scene Location in Readers Theatre: Static or Dynamic," *The Speech Teacher,* September 1965

[2] Wallace Bacon. *The Art of Interpretation.* New York: Holt, Rinehart and Winston, Inc., 1972.

smoothly and quickly. You also need to plan for both direct and dramatic presentations: the narration shared directly with the audience from elevated levels or the forestage and the reading or acting of dialogue scenes, interpreted in designed stage areas or in static groupings.

Interpreters theatre may be staged almost anywhere—in any open area of space, in an arena, or on a thrust or a proscenium stage—either with a minimum of set pieces or with an elaborate arrangement of platforms, step units, and ramps.

Set Pieces. Small platforms, chairs, stools, one or more lecterns, ladders, benches or a combination of such pieces may be used in the playing space. These are good choices because of their flexibility and because they allow an audience to make imaginative extensions of the set.

The playing area can be planned to represent outdoor or indoor places, and the repeated use of the area establishes the suggestion in the minds of the audience; the addition or removal of a chair, a bench, a richly colored cloth, a guitar, or some other appropriate prop can change the suggested scene. Even the actors themselves may become parts of the set. For example, in a production of Lanford Wilson's *The Rimers of Eldritch,* all the actors remained on stage. During the outdoor scenes between Eva and Robert, the actors turned their backs to the audience, resting their hands on their hips or folding their arms to suggest trees. Effective and suggestive lighting confirmed the illusion. With the aid of music and light change, a basic set can be adapted to suggest many places.

Props. A production may use literal or imagined properties. Generally, hand props in interpreters theatre are only suggested, but when actual props serve a particular purpose in telling the story, then they are literalized. A prop may be needed to establish a certain stage area as a place in the story. In a production of "Why I Live at the P.O.," many hand props, such as dishes, food, cards, etc., were merely suggested, but, because of their particular significance, the suitcase and the rocking chair that replaced the story's hammock were real.

Handling Transitions

As a general rule, all members of an interpreters theatre cast enter and exit at the same time and remain clearly visible through the performance. This presents unique problems for the director. There are three aspects of transitional change you must carefully consider: the entrance and exit of the full cast, the shifts between scenes, and the entrances and exits of characters in each scene.

Entrance and Exit of Cast. As we have said, a production may be staged on a stage or other area, with darkness serving as a substitute for a front curtain. When the performance is ready to begin, a signal is given and the lights are lowered for a few seconds, during which the members of the cast enter and take their positions; the lights are then brought up and the performance begins. The ending is handled in the same way. There is no real need to lower the lights, however. The cast may walk on while the stage is lighted and, at the end, hold their positions for a moment and then simply walk off. The audience will accept this as appropriate for a presentational type of performance.

Also, you can emphasize a scene or create a mood even before the performance begins. In a production of T. S. Eliot's *Murder in the Cathedral,* the audience entered a dimly lit three-quarter-round auditorium to see a simple altar illuminated by the projection of a stained glass window. When the audience was seated, organ music began. Choir boys entered, and the lights grew brighter as they lighted candles; the cast entered in a procession comparable to a procession before a mass and took their positions. The ending was the reverse of this: the music began, and the cast moved off; the choir boys put out the candles, and the altar again reflected the colors of the stained glass window. In this manner, the entrance and exit of the characters became an integral part of the performance.

Certain adaptations call for another kind of opening and closing: a narrator, a character, or a property person may come on alone, explain something about the story to be told (in some instances, summarizing what has gone before) and introduce the characters as they enter. Modern playwrights sometimes employ these built-in narrators, but, when they are not already written into the material, the adaptor may add lines for such a scene-setter.

Shifts in Scene. A narrator used at the beginning, as just described, may continue as scene-shifter, coming out between scenes to explain and perhaps to make slight changes in the set. But more often, interpreters theatre has many short scenes that need to flow quickly, almost to blend into each other. To provide a short transitional pause between scenes, a director may use two simple techniques: the shift may be suggested simply by an attitude change projected by the cast's body tone change, or the cast may change positions for the next scene.

However, light and music changes are the most effective means of creating smooth-flowing transitions: the lights dim or even black out entirely, the music for the scene just finished changes to introduce a different mood, and the lights come up on the next scene.

Entrances and Exits into Scene. As a general rule, characters in interpreters theatre do not move in and out of the scene as actors do in a play. Changes in position, evocative movements, or some other means must indicate the scene entrances and exits. A director may have an interpreter who is visible but does not take part in the scene turn slightly away to suggest removal from the scene in progress. On the other hand, the director may have such a character stay involved. An excellent example is Gerald Friedman's masterful staging of Eudora Welty's *The Robber-Bridegroom.* To emphasize the storytelling nature of the production, the actors not involved in the scene would simply sit in groups listening intently and enjoying the production as part of the audience, rising and again becoming characters or parts of the set as the script demanded.

The interpreter entering a scene may turn and speak, rise and speak, or move to a lectern or playing area and speak. Having exited, the interpreter quickly assumes the offstage attitude. In some cases, the freezing device can be used to suggest an exit or the passage of time. In a freeze, all action stops abruptly and the interpreters hold their positions. But in other situations, a change of lighting may indicate the exit, or a spot illuminating a character may indicate the entrance.

Use of Movement

Creating Distance. In its use of space, interpreters theatre has advantages over the conventionally staged play: the proscenium frame of the stage confines the actor's movements. Interpreters theatre, using the proscenium frame or the open platform, extends the stage into the audience, both through addressing characters in an imagined area in front of the stage and through sometimes having the cast move forward toward the audience. For instance, in staging the story "First Confession" for interpreters theatre, the interpreters can create the illusion of a walk on a crowded street by imagining that the events are taking place out front and by taking small, slow-motion forward steps. Characteristic body tensions aid the illusion. Such movement and placement of scene allow an audience to complete the illusion by using their imagination.

Expressing Style. Movement should help express the style and tone of a text. For instance, in directing *Royal Gambit,* you want to express the cultural tone of the Renaissance both in the characters' movements and in the groupings, or stage pictures. Sometimes, however, the movement is directly functional, a means of getting a character or group into a position to be seen and heard, to receive the audience's attention.

Focusing Attention. Like any theatre director, a director of interpreters theatre can give prominence to a character by having the interpreter stand, step out from a group, come forward toward the audience, or move to a higher level on the stage. A character can also be given space and contrast by moving the others.

Movement can also emphasize relationships. Although usually given a designated area to move from and return to, the narrator is not always so confined. It is usually possible—and often helpful—in emphasizing relationships for the narrator to move close to the characters while describing and commenting on them.

Creating Special Effects. Stylized movements, dance, or other unusual effects can emphasize the humorous, bizarre, or striking quality of a scene. In a production of *Dandelion Wine,* a chorus performed weightless, dreamlike movements that built up tension to make the "fever dream" scene more striking. In an adaptation of "The Secret Life of Walter Mitty," students formed the revolving door for Walter Mitty to enter. Thurber's stories and fables lend themselves to playful effects. When a script features such subjective factors as memories, inner life, etc., stylized movement may express the abstract nature of the action. It is important to remember that use of these techniques depends upon the nature of the material being performed.

Use of Scripts

The use of scripts is not mandatory in interpreters theatre, for there are more ways to emphasize the text than by simply putting scripts in the hands of the performers. However, should you choose to use scripts, you should do so not for the sake of tradition but rather to create an effect that will emphasize meanings within the text.

Creating an Alienation Effect. The visible script implies an aesthetic distance appropriate to interpreters theatre. As we explained in our overview of principles, this gives the audience a double view: realizing the simultaneous presence of the interpreter and the character, listeners are inclined to focus on the author's ideas and meanings.

Symbolizing Meanings. A director may use the script as a means of emphasizing character and character attitudes: a book may be bound in a color that symbolizes the character's personality or be chosen to suggest the character's function, such as a script resembling a Bible for the character of a minister. An interpreter may use the book so as to suggest a character's attitude and change in attitude, suggesting dependence or restraint when using the book and a release from the restraint or dependence when discarding it. When scripts are used by a chorus of voices, there usually should be uniformity in the size and color of the books and in how they are used.

The script may be used as a symbol; in a sense, it suggests the presence of the author. In a production of *John Brown's Body,* the script, a large, impressive-looking volume, was placed, with considerable ceremony, in a raised central position, where it remained throughout—unused. The script represented a presence and performed an aesthetic function in harmony with this particular production.

Use of Lighting

Bridging and Creating Effects. In interpreters theatre, a medium devoted to suggestion, effective lighting becomes one of the director's most valuable aids. The examples cited in this chapter have pointed out its usefulness in beginning and ending a production, in bridging scenes, and in bringing characters on and off the stage. Light changes direct the viewer's focus of attention; lighting is also a means of controlling the emotions of the audience. Special effects can be created in order to reveal subtle meanings and suggest contrasting moods.

Special effects include the projection of images on a background: slides of newspaper clippings are suggested for *Lest We Forget: Kent State;* a stained glass window effect serves as a religious symbol for *Royal Gambit;* over head lighting in *The Rimers of Eldritch* created a ghostly effect, while soft yellow lighting with subtle shadows created the illusion of trees and buildings.

Lighting the House. The amount of light in the theatre during a performance can vary. Though we have long become accustomed to "overhearing" actors while we are sitting in a dark theatre, we are adjusting to new roles and conditions in modern theatre. When members of the audience are asked to be active participants, the lighting may be the same for audience and interpreters. When the members of the audience become participants, the lights on them may be lowered slightly; when the audience is emotionally involved, the house may be in darkness. More light in the theatre encourages interaction between audience and characters.

Use of Music and Sound Effects

Setting Tone. Music is used to enrich a production, serving as a bridge to emphasize the impact of the last episode and to create the proper mood for the next. The repetition of a musical theme can provide the right tone and give unity to a production. Everyone who has seen the film *Lilies of the Field* remembers how well the repetition and the rhythmic lilt of the song "Amen" caught the spirit of the film. The music can be modified in various ways for certain effects, too. In a production of *Dandelion Wine,* the director chose "In the Good Old Summertime" as the transitional music. The familiar, nostalgic words and melody supported the idyllic mood of the piece perfectly. However, as Douglas Spaulding's world slowly disintegrated because of his inability to accept change, the music reflected this; the recordings had been altered substantially by the introduction of dissonant chords, which became increasingly dissonant as the production progressed. Thus the music was an excellent complement to the mood.

Visible Effects. Live sound effects are often used. The production of *John Brown's Body* directed by Charles Laughton featured a chorus of twenty, singing Civil War songs and suggesting battle sounds with their voices and marching with the rhythmic tapping of their feet. In a production of *Under Milk Wood*, bells, a money till, two pieces of wood to suggest slamming doors, and other sound props were used in full view of the audience.

Use of Costumes

Uniformity. Usually, some degree of uniformity in dress is a good idea. For a casual look, the men could wear dark pants and turtleneck sweaters, and the women, skirts and blouses; if the production requires a formal appearance, the men could wear tuxedos, and the women, long, dark dresses. Color can accentuate a character's personality or the tone of the whole production: bright colors for humor, pastels for fantasy, dark for tragedy, and so on. But unobtrusive, even neutral clothes usually seem to be the best choice. This is certainly true for multiple casting.

Suggestion. Sometimes costume props, such as hats or scarfs, are added to the basic dress to suggest character. In the Broadway production of *Spoon River Anthology,* the women interpreters imaginatively used scarfs and shawls to change their appearance as they changed roles. Costumes for suggesting character change often remain visible and the actual changing of the costume is done before the audience, becoming an integral part of the performance. Ocasionally a production calls for literalized costumes (See *Royal Gambit*).

The Book of Job, a religious choric drama arranged and staged by Orlin and Irene Corey, furnishes an impressive example of this use of visual elements. The exalted spiritual tone of the material, an arrangement of the King James Version, is given austere yet striking staging through its setting, costumes, and makeup. Ten figures with masklike painted faces move in stylized patterns, clothed in robes of rich red and gold, blue and purple. Both the costumes and the makeup suggest the mosaic patterns of stained glass windows. The interpreters perform in a natural amphitheatre under the stars. A sheer rock cliff forms the backdrop, and where the orchestra pit would normally be in a theatre, there is a man-made reflecting pool. Hearing the ancient poetry spoken and chanted in chorus, with living mosaic figures reflected in the crystal-clear pool, can be a deeply moving experience.

So far in this chapter, we have discussed the physical or visual elements employed in interpreters theatre. Now let us see these elements working together in the staging of *Royal Gambit*.

Production Notes for Royal Gambit

What values within this play help shape the director's production concept?

Guides for Production Concept

In *Royal Gambit* the playwright mixes history and fantasy. It is his intention for an audience to see Henry both as a man and as a symbol of modern humanity. This suggests that the staging should be a synthesis of realism and fantasy: scenes which focus on Henry's actual life could be literalized through onstage focus, period costuming, etc.; the out-of-time scenes could be staged abstractly through offstage focus, stylized movement, imaginative lighting effects, and so forth.

Perhaps the most important factor in the staging is the script's distortion of time. In addition to the out-of-time scenes at the beginning and end of the play, the playwright gives his characters the power to look into the future and see Henry's humanistic philosophy at work in the 20th century. These projections, however, are few and occur only in the dialogue. Unless certain lines are effectively emphasized, the play loses its central meaning and becomes confusing for the audience. However, in the adaptation for interpreters theatre, this problem is somewhat alleviated: two narrators share many of the prediction lines directly with the audience. Through focus, the narrators aid in emphasizing this submerged theme.

The tone of the play is a mixture of the tragic and comic, with religious overtones. The playwright says that man's loss of moral values results in tragedy and chaos, but he says this within the frame of comedy, as Henry's great pomposity and repeated attempts to justify his actions become ludicrous. Yet the play, dealing as it does with tragic deaths and moral values, might become too heavy. To counteract this, the director needs to make the most of the lighter tones in the author's characterizations and use of language.

How can a director use visual and aural elements to highlight these values through the staging?

Highlighting With Focus

In the literal, onstage focus part of the production, Henry and his six wives enter and make their exits as in a conventional play. They speak their lines from memory and move about freely, suggesting the cultural attitudes of the place and time. In contrast, the out-of-time scenes should be played with offstage focus, and the psychological distortions of these scenes should be further highlighted through stylized patterns of movement. The two narrators, using scripts and offstage focus, should speak directly to the audience, either from basic step positions or from the forestage. A director might have the narrators remain onstage to watch the scenes in progress, adding to the alienation effect.

Selecting Set

A director could consider three types of staging: arena, thrust, or proscenium.

Arena (Figure 14–4). The four corner entrances could be enhanced by arches. Abstract blocks which are a part of the set should be moved as needed.

Thrust or Three-Quarter Round (Figure 14–5).

Proscenium (Figure 14–6). The Xs on the platform steps suggest the narrators' basic positions.

In any of these types of staging, the playing areas could be used to suggest various places: rooms within the King's palace, a chapel, a room in

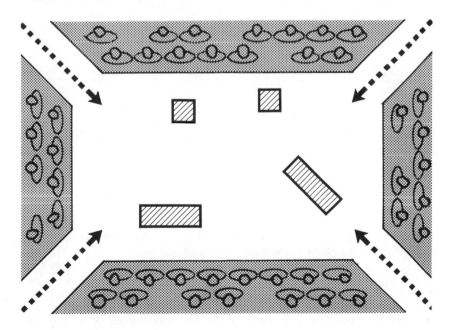

Fig. 14–4   Arena Staging

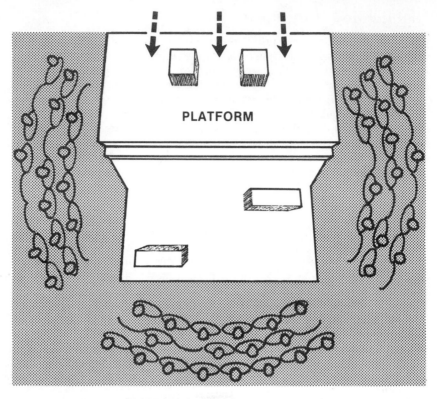

Fig. 14–5   Thrust or Three-Quarter Round Staging

the Tower. Benches and throne-like chairs to suggest both the Renaissance and the modern styles might be designed.

Handling Transitions

For smooth flow of the many scenes, the transitions should be controlled with light and music, sometimes fadeouts extended with music, sometimes blackouts with the next scene picked up by the lighting.

Music and Sound

To underscore changes in mood, three types of music are needed: organ ✔ music; some bright, happy tunes; and music to suggest a royal fanfare. The only other sound effect is the tolling of bells.

Lighting

In addition to providing general area light and controlling scene changes, the lighting must give emphasis to the prediction lines: Katarina and

198

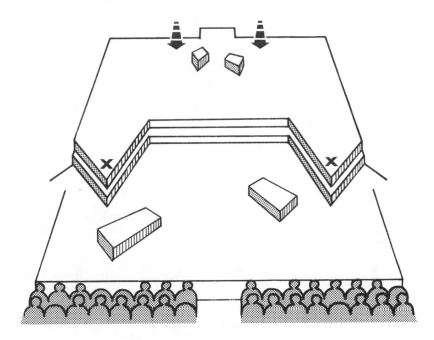

Fig. 14–6   Proscenium Staging

narrators in Scene 3 and Henry's prayer in Scene 9. The center top step of the platform could be used as the focal point of several special lighting effects. In addition, two manually operated lights for the narrators are needed. If it is used, the projected light on the stained glass window effect should remain dim throughout.

Costumes

Costumes of the period serve to make the scenes seem real and to particularize the characters, to give them separate identities. It is suggested that the narrators be costumed in black tights and tunics, which blend with the other costumes.

Hand props should only be suggested in pantomime, but costume props should be used. Rapid scene changes require props that can be changed quickly: a headdress, a ruff, an overskirt, or a cape. Stylized movements of the Queens' head veils in the first and last scenes suggest both the abstract quality of the scenes and the group's meaning.

Henry - Red   Anna of Cl - Blue
Katl - Black & Red
Anne B. Gold

199

Chapter 15

Directing the Production

In this chapter, we address you as a student-director of interpreters theatre. We offer guides for conducting rehearsals, coordinating a production, and leading others in a creative group experience.

If your group has had a hand in initiating the production, building the script, and planning the production, so much the better, for this is the kind of teamwork that molds a group into an ensemble. But let us suppose that this is not the case. Instead, you have been given the assignment of planning and directing *Royal Gambit*. Let us assume, also, that your production concept is similar to that explained in the last chapter. How do you put these plans into operation?

Casting

At some point in your prerehearsal planning, you considered the best casting method to use; whether to cast on a one-to-one basis or to use multiple casting, and how to assign the narration. In *Royal Gambit*, you are casting seven character roles on a one-to-one basis, and you are casting two people as narrators.

Tryouts

You should be well prepared for tryouts. Your evaluation of each person who tries out is based on what you need to hear and see: the voice's resonant quality, flexibility, and clarity of diction; the body's general responsiveness and flexibility; the mobility of facial expression for suggesting states of emotion and thought; evidence of the performer's sensitivity and imagination and of a cooperative spirit and reliability. If a chorus of voices is to carry the narration, you should test the contrast and blending of voices in groups. And if multiple casting is used, you must check each individual's ability to make sharp distinctions between character roles. Don't be authoritative; let the group see your interest in and your enthusiasm for the project ahead.

Rehearsals

The director of interpreters theatre conducts rehearsals in much the same way as any stage director, dividing the process into a series of logical steps: read-through and discussion, blocking the basic positions and general movement, rehearsing details, and rehearsing the whole production for unity and polish. The first and second steps might take from one to four rehearsals each; the third step would probably require three-fourths of the rehearsal time, and, for a full evening's production, at least six rehearsals should be reserved for the fourth step. The time for the complete schedule varies according to the length and nature of the script and experience of the cast. *Royal Gambit* would probably require thirty two-hour rehearsals. On the other hand, a traditionally staged short scene might require no more than four one-hour rehearsals.

Rehearsal for Read-Through and Discussion

You should ask your cast ahead of time to read the full script and come to this rehearsal prepared to share their responses to and questions about the play. You should also ask them for their ideas about the rehearsal schedule so that the rehearsal plan and the means of controlling it can represent a group agreement. Try from the start to foster a feeling of working together as a group. In order for each cast member to feel deeply about what he or she is giving to the performance, everyone must have a part in shaping the production from the beginning.

The purpose of this rehearsal is to have the cast gain an understanding of the story they are preparing to tell, so the read-through, taking no more than half of the rehearsal time (two rehearsal periods), is followed by a discussion of the script's meaning. Questions from all members of the group will lead to a lively exchange of ideas concerning the theme and the characters and narrators in relation to the movement of the situation, the changing needs, and the pervading tone.

Share your production concept with the group, but explain its flexibility. With the group, you will be testing this concept as you work together in rehearsals. Costume sketches and a model of the set might be shown at this time, so that the interpreters have a broad idea of the total concept of the performance—from the script, the director, the designers, and each other.

Rehearsal for Blocking: Assigning General Movement

When interpreters theatre is staged simply, the blocking rehearsal is little more than another read-through. On the other hand, a blocking rehearsal for a completely staged performance can be comparable to that for a staged play. Since *Royal Gambit* is in this category, we will concentrate on the more elaborate type of production.

Blocking Process. Blocking is a slow and tedious process at best, but it becomes less mechanical if the director takes time to explain the quality and tone of each scene and the motivation for every movement. Only after general movement is tentatively set, though still subject to change as necessary, can the cast begin to concentrate on interpretation.

Blocking *Royal Gambit*. You should explain the first out-of-time scene and the stylized pattern of movement the interpreters use for it. Then you place Henry up center (UC), the six wives kneeling in the center area, and the narrators in stop positions. On cue, each wife removes her veil; on cue, each stands and speaks; on cue, the narrators move into their areas and speak; and on cue, the director calls, "Blackout." The characters are then asked to move offstage or to take positions for the next scene, before "lights up." The scene is then repeated with movement and light calls until each cast member understands and has the appropriate cue lines underlined and movements indicated in his script. The blocking of the entire script continues in this way.

Rehearsals for Detailed work

These require the greater part of the rehearsal period; they get to the heart of problems and stimulate growth. Now is when your production concept is being tested and each interpreter's performance is pulled apart and put together again. For amateurs this often requires a great deal of guidance and stimulation.

Director's Preparation. In order to prepare yourself for guiding line interpretations and character motivations, you should break the scenes into small units and examine each. Your divisions may be made according to changes in relationships or intentions. These divisions are called motivational units, or beats. A beat may cover only a few lines, or it may extend for a full scene before the relationship is changed. You will find it helpful to mark the line in the script where each new beat begins and to write down its meaning or objective. For instance, a new beat begins at the end of Scene 2 in *Royal Gambit*. After a light, teasing scene showing Henry's pursuit of Anne Boleyn, Henry turns to her (new beat, foreshadowing world-shaking change):

> HENRY. By all the saints, Anne, tell me how I may win you at last.
> ANNE. You could if you were to belong to me, were mine—in all your splendor, mine alone!
> HENRY. I knew you would demand it. I could not expect less.

In this short beat, Henry's serious demand and Anne's answer release a new complication. As a result of Anne's demand, Henry, and hence England, will break with the Roman Catholic church. This is a brief moment of tension with overtones of great significance. When you are fully aware of each change in relationship and mood, you will be better prepared to direct the interpreters who will show the changes.

Directing Detailed Work. In rehearsals, as you work on details of characterization, vocalization, line readings, body expression, and movement, you will use both the direct technical approach and the psychological approach (Chapters 4, 5, and 6). We suggest that during this period you arrange private work sessions with individuals and small groups and encourage each interpreter to have a time to practice alone every day as well.

But both in rehearsals and in private work, it is most important that you encourage each interpreter to find his or her own ways that feel best.

We suggest that you begin each rehearsal with a group activity—warm-up exercises. The warm-ups may consist of a few select voice and body exercises from this text. They may also be used during rehearsals: when voices become tense or listless, stop the rehearsal for a ten-minute break for warm-ups.

Directing Interplay. Interpreters theatre requires that directors give attention to both vocal and physical interplay. Offstage focus scenes require the interpreters to pick up cues quickly and maintain physical focus on imaginary characters in a rather vague area out front. To make this area less vague, ask members of the cast who are not in the scene being rehearsed to stand in the center of the audience area, to represent the characters being addressed. After directing dialogue to actual people in rehearsal, an interpreter's interplay with imagined characters is more easily projected.

One of the most important techniques to learn is the rapid pickup of cues, so that lines almost overlap, like real speech. Inexperienced performers must be shown how to do this, since an accelerated tempo is more effectively accomplished by picking up cues than through rapid reading.

The immediacy and spontaneity of a chamber theatre-style production, as well as the use of a chorus, demonstrate the need for good ensemble work in interpreters theatre. Let us add something more regarding chorus work.

Directing the Chorus. Interpreters theatre borrows from the ancient Greek chorus and its modern descendants—choral speaking, choric theatre, and symphonic drama. The Corey production of *The Book of Job,* for example, is choric theatre. The dialogue is biblical prose, and the overall emphasis is on choric interpretation rather than delineated characters. In interpreters theatre, choric interpretation plays a supportive role, but character delineation is the main thing. The author of *Slatefall* calls it a play for voices. Though it uses music and choral response, the primary focus is on the characters, reacting to a tragic event.

Plays chosen for interpreters theatre may have special parts for choral speaking; these include all Greek drama, as well as modern works such as T. S. Eliot's *Murder in the Cathedral*. However, as we said earlier, the director may add a chorus to handle the narrative and descriptive portions of a literary work, especially if the original uses highly poetic language. The director's goal in doing this is to mold the voices of the chorus into a symphony that will enhance the emotional tone of the literary text. Words often become important because of the way they sound and are paced: a voice announces "The hero is here!" and voices in the chorus ask with increased intensity, "Where?" "Where?" "Where?" Voices may blend in unison or in sequence, bringing out all the beauty of the vowel sounds, and then suddenly break out with sharp consonant sounds, suggesting a contrasting mood. Even when the interpreters speak in sequence without special effects, each reader must depend upon every other reader to come in at just the right moment, with just the right tone and emphasis. When stylized movement accompanies the spoken words, a great deal of precision drill is needed to coordinate the movement with the words.

A director using a chorus should be realistic and either keep the chorus work uncomplicated or include in the schedule the necessary time to accomplish a more ambitious goal. There are choruses that work together over a long period of time with outstanding results. Wallace Bacon describes a performance of such a group, a modern Greek chorus performing Euripides' *Hercules Furens* at a summer festival. This example demonstrates the ultimate in timing for ensemble playing:

> ... the choir not only spoke but moved and half chanted. Tall staves in the hands of the members of the chorus were used to punctuate the measured tread of the speakers' feet; they fell as one upon the earth, absolutely coordinated in time. While the voices differed in quality and pitch, they were as one in attacking and sustaining words and phrases. The effect was electric. The listener felt at once the strange position of the chorus in the play: actor and yet not actor; part of the action and yet not part of the action; human and yet not human being but a force. This was orchestration in the fullest sense.[1]

Whether two or twenty in number, the chorus in interpreters theatre is a unit.

Good ensemble work is perhaps the director's most demanding task, and, when accomplished, his most fulfilling achievement. It requires technical drill based on sensitivity for good timing, and understanding of the material, and concentration, and it requires building unity and mutual respect among the cast members. When this miracle happens, individual performances blend for a unified effect in the whole production.

Rehearsing the Whole Production for Unity and Polish

The last six or seven rehearsals should be devoted to performing the whole script. This gives the cast the experience of uninterrupted rehearsals, and it

---

[1] Bacon. *The Art of Interpretation.*

gives the director the chance to look at the performance as a whole. You must ask yourself several questions. Will the story be clear to an audience hearing it for the first time? Does the theme come across? Do the scenes flow as they should, with varied tempos? Are the high points in the separate scenes and the climax of the production emphasized? Does the interplay and teamwork of the cast pull the performance together and maintain consistency of style? Because of the importance of light and music in scene changes in interpreters theatre, you should coordinate these with technical rehearsals ahead of time, so that the cast can rehearse without too many interruptions. The director usually sits in the theatre taking or dictating notes, which are used in the critique at the end of the rehearsal. If there is time, certain scenes should be repeated, so that corrections can be made before the next rehearsal. The director's goal is to have the last two rehearsals serve as preview performances for invited guests.

These rehearsals give the interpreters new impetus, and many questions of small and large concern fall into place. The interpreters begin playing together. This is the time when ensemble playing is realized—or not. During the previous rehearsals, under the director's guidance, each interpreter has been experimenting with various details of line reading and movement. In these last polishing rehearsals, the interpreters cease to experiment; no longer concerned with techniques, each cast member is free to concentrate on the story and the deeper meanings of the narration and dialogue. Preview performances with a live audience give the cast added confidence. After this, they are ready for that final spark of an opening-night audience.

Performance

The performance belongs to the cast and crew. With a cast call for warm-ups, the stage manager and crew take over backstage. The director is now a critic—of the cast's performance and of the direction. The director notes details that should be set right before the next performance, watches the audience and learns from them, and watches the performance as his or her own critic.

This chapter has charted your course as director of a production, from casting through four phases of rehearsals to the performance. Chapter 16 is a reservoir of scripts and production notes, describing how certain scripts have been or might be staged. These include *Royal Gambit,* an original play for voices, an original theatre-of-fact script, a poem, and a description of a chamber theatre production.

chapter 16

Scripts and Production Notes

Royal Gambit[1]

Hermann Gressieker
Translated by George White
Arranged for Interpreters Theatre*

SCENE I   A PROLOGUE.

**(Lights reveal the six wives kneeling next to each other, facing the
audience. As each's name is mentioned, she removes her veil; she
rises before speaking. Henry is posed on platform up center before
dimly visible crucifix. The vows are taped.)**
HENRY'S VOICE. I, Henry Tudor, take you Katarina of Aragon, to be my
 only wife and promise that I will love you and keep you unto death.
 I, Henry Tudor, king of England, take you, Anne Boleyn, to be my
 only wife and promise that I will love you and keep you unto death.
 I, Henry Tudor, take you, Jane Seymour, to be my wife, ...
 I, Henry Tudor, take you, Anna of Cleves, to be my wife, ...
 I, Henry Tudor, take you, Kathryn Howard to be my wife, ...
 I, Henry Tudor, take you Kate Parr, to be my wife, and promise that
 I will love you and keep you unto death. So help me, God!

---

 * In *Royal Gambit* and *Slatefall*, stage directions are set in *italic* type and are enclosed in
 parentheses (). Words transferred for purposes of interpreters theatre are enclosed in
 brackets []. Lines and sections omitted from the original play are represented by unspaced
 periods ... .

KATARINA. So help him, God. The truth is, I alone was his wife unto death, and I still am in our existence beyond time.

A. BOLEYN. The truth is, he gave up one world to win a new one with me, and he loved me—unto my death.

JANE S. I gave him what he cherished more than love; I presented him with the male heir.

ANNA OF C. I was the one who knew him as no other woman did, and we could have had much fun, had it only pleased him—to have me.

K. HOWARD. I found the aging man weak in his manly vigor, and I brought joy into his life again, so that he loved me murderously!

KATE PARR. I am the one he did keep unto death, although I insisted that he face up to what he was, and where it would lead, the age that he began.

[NARRATOR I]. The age that he began, he and the others ... was the age which [they] in their spirited revolt called The Modern Times.

[NARRATOR II]. The first age of the world was not to be God's, but man's.

[NARRATOR I]. It became a great age of man and of his brain.

KATARINA. The old order—it so happened—collapsed simultaneously with my marriage. It went under at that moment when he, my husband, God's great apostate, looked upon *you* (*Anne Boleyn*). (*Lights black out—music up.*)

SCENE II

(Anne and Jane are with Katarina as ladies-in-waiting. There is a royal fanfare and Henry enters pompously. onstage focus)

HENRY. Defender of the Faith! I am Defender of the Faith! It has pleased the Pope to grant me what has been long overdue.

KATARINA. My husband! The apostolic title!

HENRY. The rent due for my defense of the sacraments against that miserable Luther. Fortunate England, to have as king a great theologian!

KATARINA. Fortunate England if you preserve it as a strong island of our church.

HENRY. How could I fail, my dearest? (*He struts up and down in front of ladies-in-waiting. He takes Jane by the chin and raises her face.*) Your Jane Seymour looks pale. Could it be she, too, needs a young poet to chase her with his verses like a doe? Eh, Boleyn? ...

ANNE (*anguished*). The Queen is in audience with Your Majesty.

HENRY. Indeed you are, my love. But I don't intend to strain your patience with my confounded theology. You go—leave Boleyn here for a while. She needs a bit of advice.

KATARINA. As you wish. (*She hints a curtsy and exits with Jane. Anne maintains a guarded manner while Henry walks around her.*)

HENRY. What about you and Tom Wyatt? ... It's not proper for a lady in waiting to become involved with a poet.

ANNA. I was educated at the court of Paris, and I think I know what is proper for a lady in our days. ... Your Majesty shall not treat me as would an insignificant country squire who clings to the old order—the gothic.

208

HENRY. Girl, how dare you answer me? ... Take it as a sign of my extreme
favor that I'm not punishing you. What are you to the poet—Tom
Wyatt? ...

ANNE. It's written in his poems for all to read. He calls me the run-away
doe. ...

HENRY. Couldn't you prohibit him from calling you a doe?

ANNE. Couldn't you prohibit Luther from calling you a jackass?

HENRY. (stunned—then laughs). She has a quick wit—the doe—to my
taste. Anne, under my very eyes, you have developed more magnificently than any other woman in my kingdom. ... What can I do
to make you love me?

ANNE. Be good enough to leave me be, and I shall love you as is my duty
toward my King.

HENRY. King! King! What King? I am a man! Look at me as I stand before
you. ...

ANNE. You—Your Majesty—so—"justly famous"?

HENRY. Oh, don't listen to my boasts! I beg you to see me as I really am—a
man of thirty-five, just reaching out to put my imprint on history,
but irrevocably tied to a woman—a Spaniard, and thus incurably
afflicted with the old order, unable to follow me to a new, enlightened existence. And, what is worse, a woman not blessed to
give me the son! Just as my despair seems hopeless, my gaze falls
upon Anne Boleyn and I shudder with happiness. ... I'm yours,
Anne Boleyn. By all the saints, Anne, tell me how I may win you at
last?

ANNE. (walks to him slowly) You could if you were to belong to me, were
mine— (He reaches for her.)—in all your splendor, mine alone!

HENRY (after a pause—composed). I knew you would demand it. I could
not expect less.

ANNE. I demand nothing, Your Majesty. I merely answered your question. ... (Lights pale as he watches her leave.)

SCENE III

**(Narrators' lights on and light up on Henry in deep thought—
offstage focus)**

[NAR. I]. And so Henry Tudor begins a battle with his conscience.

[NAR. II]. And the needs of his conscience will be used as a basis for
profit—to get what he wants.

HENRY. If any man in Catholic Christendom is justified to separate from his
wife because she is barren, I am that man.

[NAR. II]. But marriage is a sacrament and as Defender of the Faith, you
cannot do it.

HENRY. I'm thinking of the peace of my soul. The thought rakes my brain.

[NAR. I]. Katarina of Aragon has been a good and faithful wife. She is your
lawful wife.

HENRY. I cannot separate from my lawful wife. The question is only—

[NAR. II]. The question is only?

HENRY. The question is only—is she my lawful wife?

[NAR. I]. Your Queen?

[NAR. II]. Your Queen?

HENRY. When we were coupled she was already a widow.

[NAR. I]. Your brother's widow.

HENRY. The Scriptures forbid marriage with a brother's wife.

[NAR. II]. The Pope has blessed it.

HENRY. But not heaven.

[NAR. I]. You have a daughter.

HENRY. One daughter and four miscarriages! Heaven frowns upon this marriage!

[NAR. II]. Henry—what are you about to do?

HENRY. What is right. ...

[NAR. II]. Could it be possible you have something in mind that could not be well intended?

HENRY. No! I must purge my conscience of this sinful marriage, put my case before the tribunal and for the sake of the realm—

[NAR. I]. For the sake of the realm?

HENRY. For the sake of the realm to enter upon another God-pleasing union.

[NAR. II]. (sarcastically). This—for all our sake and well-being— ...
(Lights out on Henry—narrators move forward.)

Transition

[NAR. I]. And so, Henry, you take your wife by the hand and inform her in a friendly fashion that your marriage is null and void. ...

[NAR. II]. You inform her of the dire need of your conscience! ...

[NAR. I]. Katarina of Aragon—her mother was the great Isabella of Spain; her nephew is the German Emperor. With his support she fights for her marriage.

[NAR. II]. The King of England becomes the laughingstock of Europe.

[NAR. I]. Spain holds him in check for three long years. At last, the Pope consents to hear Henry's lament and the tribunal is convened.

SCENE IV

KATARINA. What I have done, Jane! At last, I will act as befits me. What I have done 'til now did not. For years now, he has persecuted me according to the principles they call the spirit of the modern age. So far, I have fought them with their own weapons, with guile against guile, with force against force.

JANE. That you have, Milady, and everyone admires you for it.

KATARINA. But now, such a course seems far beneath me.

JANE. Milady! After so much effort, you're not weakening?

KATARINA. No, my dear. Do try and understand. Only now will I begin to assert myself.

JANE. What do you intend to do, Milady?

KATARINA. Whenever he fights me with arrogance, I will fight back with

210

humility. When he attacks me with rage, I will counter with cheerfulness. When he aims at me the pointed arrow of his intellect, I will fortify myself with the wisdom nature has given to us women since the beginning of time.

JANE. I'm afraid I don't understand.

KATARINA. Then listen carefully, my dear. A long time ago, my king commanded me to dispense with your services, that you might attend—the future Queen.

JANE. No, Milady. That can't be your wish.

KATARINA. It is now—accept my deepest thanks, Jane Seymour, for all your love and obedience. Obey me now for the last time and go to her. *(Jane crosses stage slowly as K. kneels)*

KATARINA. Oh Lord, guide me further upon my road, and let me travel it untroubled by the upheaval of time! *(Lights fade on K. and she moves off—lights up on left bench with Jane and Anne.)*

JANE. Ma'am—

ANNE. Jane! Are you coming to see me?

JANE. To attend you, Ma'am. Those are my orders.

ANNE. The King's?

JANE. The Queen's—ma'am.

ANNE. A good sign, but not "ma'am," Jane. What's the matter with you? Sit down beside me as my friend. ...

JANE. I must tell you, Anne—the Queen—

ANNE. The Princess of Aragon!

JANE. She's so different from what we thought. She's so much, much more.

ANNE. Enough about her—

JANE. Anne, what the King does, for your sake—aren't you afraid? I'm so afraid.

ANNE. He turns Europe upside down for my sake. That's something marvelous, Jane, something grand. But, yes—I'm afraid, but what have you to fear?

JANE. This huge castle always makes me feel uneasy. ... I'm not cut out for life at court. I'd rather have a home in the country with an earl—with children and flocks of sheep, and doves. ... That's a good way to live and to die, when the time comes.

ANNE. May God grant you your wish. I expect something different from Him—except for one thing—

JANE. What might that be?

ANNE. I am with child.

JANE. Oh, Anne! Milady—would God it be a boy.

ANNE. Don't say that. Let the man ask for that. ... *(And here is the man—)*

HENRY *(entering with great buoyancy).* Seymour here? Good! Pray tell your mistress—

ANNE. Her mistress released her that she may attend me.

HENRY. Well, well. So she has finally given in—the good woman. Be so good as to send your lady to summon the woman. I have news! *(exit Jane)*

211

ANNE. The tribunal has reached a verdict?

HENRY. Good news and bad news. ... The tribunal's careful examination of the King's marriage with Katarina of Aragon has proved it to be above reproach.

ANNE. Your tribunal! Now, I'm anxious for the good news.

HENRY. A stroke of fate that deprives lesser men of their reason, only sharpens my wits.

ANNE. Go on—

HENRY. I've been thinking, and suddenly it became clear to me. If the Pope is unable to respect the God-aroused agitation of my conscience, then he can't possibly be enlightened in Christ.

ANNE. Go on—

HENRY. ... All I could do was put my trust in God. And, lo—He enlightened me. He ordered me to ease my anguish by liberating my people from the tyranny of the Roman bishop.

ANNE. To ease your anguish by liberating your people from Rome? Your God has called upon you for that?

HENRY. You doubt it?

ANNE. No! I know your God, and I will praise Him!

HENRY. Yes, be happy, Anne. This is the hour! My Archbishop has proved his piety already by agreeing to perform the sacraments of marriage, to please God, and for our enjoyment.

ANNE. For our enjoyment, and to please God! (*Lights fade on Jane and Henry as they move off—Katarina is seen in dim light up center—narrators' lights.*)

SCENE V

[NAR. I]. Katarina of Aragon, we hereby inform you that you are not, as we believed for so many years, lawfully wed to [the King.]

KATARINA. Our marriage has been approved by the tribunal—

[NAR. II]. But not by the head of the Church of England!

KATARINA. The Church of England?

[NAR. I]. The King!

KATARINA. The Holy Father commands obedience even from the King.

[NAR. II]. Not any longer! ...

[NAR. I]. Under pain of death, the people are not to obey the Vatican, but are to recognize in their King the sole head of the Anglican Church, and the immediate representative of God on earth.

KATARINA. I can't believe it! I can't believe that at a time when our church is threatened by the Lutheran heresy, [he] would lead these souls away from the care of the Holy Father. ... Who is he? Who is he to take it upon himself to destroy the covenant? ... Who is he? Lucifer?

[NAR. I]. Who is he? ... He is the man of the modern times.

[NAR. II]. ... the man who frees his senses and becomes fully conscious of the gift God has presented to him, the all-powerful reason.

[NAR. I]. He is the man who crosses vast oceans and discovers new continents.

[NAR. II]. He is the man who is not afraid to question nature and to demand answer. ... His genius penetrates heaven and views earth as contrary to the Scriptures. ...

[NAR. I]. He is the man who understands all that really is, be it the way of the world, or the way of the heart, be it the song of the stars—

[NAR. II]. ... or the voice of conscience!

KATARINA. Oh, my Saviour, I beseech Thee, protect Thy Kingdom on earth. ... *(kneels)* My Saviour, I see it is the will of the Father to let man inherit the earth—just once, for one brief earth-hour. I can see that hour in the splendor of its high minutes and in the horror of its last seconds, and I bow my head before the wisdom of the Almighty, whom it has pleased to let this come to pass. *(She stands.)* Henry of England, how does it begin for you, this new age? You drop your pose, man of the modern times! You touch your forehead. ... You have overcome the fear of God, but with your freedom you have won anxiety. And what happens further, Henry of England?

(Narrators face front—speak as though seeing a vision with Katarina.)

[NAR. I]. Jane Seymour brings you the message that Anne has borne a child—

[NAR. II]. But Anne has borne a daughter—not a son.

[NAR. I]. You cry out against your fate. It cannot be changed.

[NAR. II]. In this matter, Henry, your God has failed to cooperate.

[NAR. I]. Embittered, you name Anne's daughter—Elizabeth.

KATARINA. Queen Elizabeth—the greatest ruler England would ever know. And further?

[NAR. II]. You must have a son!

[NAR. I]. Your gaze falls upon Jane Seymour.

[NAR. II]. Jane trembles under your examining gaze—

KATARINA. And in that moment, you have already reached your verdict about the other. *(Lights fade—a bell strikes three, and a dim light comes up on Anne in the tower.)*

SCENE VI

ANNE. Damp masonry, foul air, and a hard bedstead—that's the reverse side of the new life. And when the sun rises, my head on the block. Why? Can they do this to me? By what right? ... Because he so desires, the despot who crossed my path. And when I kneel down in the first light of dawn, I shall imagine that he is standing above me, wielding the axe. You are above me, Henry Tudor! I am yours today as in the glorious days when you and I defied an entire world, to win our lives for all times.

Now you permit them to cut me down like a crippled horse. What

213

have I done that you should let this happen? Not, as you said, committed adultery. That is not true! I did fail you by not bearing you the son and heir, and that is wicked, I realize now. For good is what pleases you; wicked, what proves troublesome. Thus I stood with you against your wife; thus you now stand against me. It is only just, Henry Tudor! It is like everything you choose to do. It is meant for the best. *(Light fades on Anne—a dim light up on F area as Jane enters with candle—a bell strikes two; Jane kneels by bench.)*

HENRY *(appearing)*. Jane! What the devil! It's an hour more till daybreak. ... Come back to sleep.

JANE.   The woman is in the Tower, waiting for the executioner. How can I sleep?

HENRY. I can.

JANE.   No! You count every stroke of the bell, too. ... Henry save the woman who was the only love of your life!

HENRY. Not another word about her! ... She was condemned after a fair trial, and it's my duty as sovereign to see to it that the verdict is carried out. ... Come, drink and don't grieve, my good girl. You mustn't for the child you're carrying. ... You who have the man and the child for the man—should be laughing! ... *(calls)* Have them make music! ... Music does for the mood what a blanket does for the body. They shall cover us with music! ... *(Music sets in.)* Ah, what lovely rhythms. Did you know, my girl, that I'm also a musician? I've enhanced many of my own verses with delicate melodies.

JANE.   Just like the Emperor Nero. He did that, too!

HENRY. Only he was a heathen, while I'm the immediate representative of God on earth. ...

JANE.   Henry, grant me one wish.

HENRY. Anything, unless it violates my good conscience.

JANE.   If your conscience prevents you from sparing Anne's life. ... I beg you, do not let the other spend her days in sorrow and need. Go to Katarina; make peace with her. She was your loyal wife. Provide for her and your daughter. ...

HENRY. This my conscience does not permit. Ask for something else. Come, let us drink to Edward, our son!

JANE.   And if it isn't a son? Will you have me tried, too? ...

HENRY. What an absurd notion that a man should be angry at his wife for not presenting him with the heir he desires! ... But it will be a son. It would be the devil's handiwork if I, with my caliber, couldn't sire a few sons.

JANE.   Yes, that's how it shall be, my terrible husband and King.

HENRY. You see, now you're happy again. It is well. And by God, we shall enjoy our lives. *(A bell sounds and music stops abruptly. Jane turns away with a cry—Henry crosses himself and drops to his knees.)*

Anne! Anne Boleyn! Oh, what have I done! *(Jane sinks down,*

214

sobbing.) You companion of my great mission, in the whole world there's no other like you, nor will there ever be. ... But it had to be; I had no choice. How can I ever atone for it? How can I make it up to you? ... Yes, upon my word, I will do what this good woman asked. I will visit Katarina, and I will care for her. It is an oath! (*exit*)

JANE. Lord! Lord! Lord! Take the poor woman unto you, and take her graciously! But oh, my God! ... what is it about this man that he destroys every woman he ever touches? (*Lights fade out; organ music.*)

SCENE VII

(Music changes to lighter tone with general lighting—Katarina walks down right to bench.)

KATARINA. It has been three months since Henry vowed to visit me. One day Jane enters confinement. And suddenly, he is in a hurry to keep his word. I await him in the garden. Here he will not see the poverty of my lodgings. ...

HENRY (*knocking and yelling from outside*). Hello there! Is no one about?

KATARINA. Yes. No one.

HENRY (*enters upstage, shouting*). Hey! Katarina!

KATARINA. I'm not hiding, and yet you can't find me. You can't hear me because you are too noisy. You can't see me because you're much too enlightened—never in all your life will you discover what you are looking for, Henry Tudor.

HENRY. Hey! Is this place enchanted? (*K. Howard has entered.*)

K. HOWARD. God's greetings, Sire. What is it you wish?

HENRY. It is enchanted. ... God's greetings, my child. (*enjoys her looks*)

K. H. Your Majesty.

HENRY. You know me? ... Who are you? How old? Still a virgin?

K. H. Kathryn Howard, Your Majesty.

HENRY. No!

K. H. Indeed, Your Majesty. Earl Edmund's daughter, if it pleases.

HENRY. It pleases!

K. H. Your Majesty, ... the princess— ...

HENRY. Are you turning a cold shoulder because I didn't recognize you?

K. H. Even the moon finds it impossible to know every star.

HENRY. A sublime answer!

K. H. The princess awaits Your Majesty.

HENRY (*moves down to Katarina, reciting mechanically*). Katarina of Aragon, greetings! ... We have discovered that you suffer a shortage of gold. ... We are willing to alleviate sundry needs. We will also visit your daughter. There is no need for you to express your gratitude. We are merely discharging our Royal obligation. (*in another tone*) How did you come by Kathryn Howard?

KATARINA. I am grateful for your kindness, yet I hardly require it, as I have enough to cover all my needs.

215

HENRY. Katarina, your voice—and the way you look! What has happened to you? You have a lover?

KATARINA. No.

HENRY. What is it, then?

KATARINA. Perhaps—freedom— ... but different from yours—less boisterous—less forced. ... Here I live and do as I please. I'm grateful to you Henry. ... It's good to sit out here. *(They sit.)* You asked about Kathryn.

HENRY. Yes!

KATARINA. She's my godchild, and an orphan. ...

HENRY. She has a quick tongue. Half humility, half wit! Sweet-sour—appeals to me—

KATARINA. She's well-read and she recites poetry beautifully, but she'll never marry. ...

HENRY. But I'm not looking for a wife.

KATARINA. Why should you!

HENRY. I have a good one, who is just facing her proudest hour. But should I need one, today it would have to be a Lutheran.

KATARINA. A Lutheran? You—the Defender of the Faith?

HENRY. ... It seems opportune now to seek a connection with the German princes in order to defend the faith, as it is guarded by England. ... I feel I can talk with you in confidence, dearest.

KATARINA. Then tell me, Henry—the age that you proclaimed in the name of reason—what is the matter with it? . . . All you see are cruel wars waged in the name of faith. Tell me, where does that leave reason?

HENRY. You see, dearest, Luther fastened ninety-five theses to the gate of modern times. But with a hammer far more powerful than his, three more were nailed to the door. They are gold—state—power. We have produced something new: the triumph of materialism.

KATARINA. Out of a great need for God—gold—state and power? That's monstrous!

HENRY. Please, dearest, I beg you, recognize in these centuries the great forward sweep of the intellect.

KATARINA. I see it, Henry, and I admire it. ... Oh, yes! I truly admire it! But the people tell it as the story of Doctor Faustus who enters into a pact with Satan in order to obtain unlimited knowledge, the most beautiful women, and the greatest power. Have you heard that fable?

HENRY. Yes. *(suddenly)* I shall tell you what I think? I think that I, Henry Tudor, am Faustus in the stage of power. ...

KATARINA. No, Henry, you're not Faustus. You're Satan's peddler.

HENRY *(with humor)*. I suppose I had that coming to me. And do you think that, in the end, Satan will push us, too, into eternal damnation? ...

KATARINA. Why Satan? You'll manage it yourself.

HENRY. Unless, of course, we find the road back to the old knowledge—Eh?

KATARINA. Yes, Henry.

216

K. H. (*enters excitedly*). Forgive me, Your Majesty! A message has arrived. Your Majesty has a healthy son.

HENRY (*deep emotion, quietly*). Oh, tell me once again, you lovely voice. Sing it out once more: Majesty, Majesty, it is a son. ... I, by God's great Grace, I have a son!

KATARINA. Henry—I'm happy that Providence has at last granted you this.

HENRY. Thank you, dearest! May heaven preserve your happy disposition. For everything else I will provide generously. And you, too, charming messenger, accept my thanks. And now, back to London!

KATARINA. How is the mother? Did the messenger say?

K. H. The mother is in danger.

HENRY. The child's baptism takes place come Wednesday, the day my astrologer selected.

KATARINA. The mother is in danger. Allow her to remain in childbed. ... To force her to get up may prove fatal.

HENRY. Only by handing the child to me can she demonstrate to the world that everything which I have done was necessary, and for the good of the realm.

KATARINA. And if this—playacting costs her life?

HENRY. God cannot want that to happen.

KATARINA. But suppose it does.

HENRY. Then it is obviously God's intention that I shall take a Lutheran. One has already been offered to me, the daughter of the Duke of Cleves. (*exit*)

KATARINA. Oh, merciful Providence, I beg thee withhold the thunderbolt this insolent spirit deserves a thousandfold. (*Lights fade on scene and come up quickly on narrators.*)

Transition

[NAR. I]. And so, Henry, you have a son—an heir! But what kind of world have you made for him? The age proclaimed in the name of reason—what did it bring?

[NAR. II]. Something new—the triumph of materialism—Modern Man —waging war in the name of peace, subjugating people in the name of freedom, contaminating nature, destroying mankind for the sake of civilization!

[NAR. I]. The winds of statesmanship blow many directions, Henry. Now you must take to wife your once sworn enemy—a Lutheran—for matters of state.

[NAR. II]. And you sanctify this action of state as you have every desire— every deed—honestly—as the true call of your conscience. You have so cleverly blended the two, Henry—conscience—the decent intention—and the decent profit!

[NAR. I]. Jane Seymour is dead. Now you bring to the altar another Anne. But how will you fare with this German Anne? (*Lights reveal Anna of Cleves and Henry meeting up center.*)

SCENE VIII

farewell

HENRY. Welcome, Anna of Cleves, my cherished bride. *(He brings her down center to sit.)* ... Was the crossing very unpleasant?

ANNA. Oh—then it was only the boat that rocked under my feet, now it's my world!

up

HENRY. Anne! I already had one with that name. She was beautiful—but contemptible. You—without a doubt, are virtuous—I mean to say—

ANNA. You meant to say: virtuous, but—ugly!

HENRY. By all the martyr's tears, how can such a thought ever occur to someone as stately as you! For example, your ears are of lovely shape—like seashells.

ANNA *(snaps)*. Are you suggesting that my ears can as readily arouse your senses as the lips of a beautiful woman? ...

HENRY. ... Your abundant charms are—how can I explain—

ANNA. You don't have to.

HENRY. You are, so God wills, just not the sort to arouse my stubborn blood.

ANNA. In short, I don't appeal to you; you don't want me.

HENRY. In short, you don't appeal to me, but I do want you. For, make no mistake, the marriage must take place! . . . You agree, don't you?

ANNA. Yes.

HENRY. All right. Then we shall submit stoically to the inevitable. Allow me, however, that in this unavoidable marriage, I—how shall I put it?—renounce once and for all the bodily comfort which you're certainly capable of offering. You won't mind? *(She shakes her head.)* You won't mind? *(He is hurt.)*

W = V

ANNA. ... If you want to deny me your bed, well, then I shall be content with throne and table.

HENRY. Good girl! ... And for your comfort, my dear— ... abstinence in marriage is a virtue of the highest order. ... In that respect, at least, you have made an advantageous marriage.

ANNA. You have a damned sly way of shaping life to suit you. You treat it like a pillow ... that you pommel into place.

HENRY. Well said, sister! You understand me! What a pity your nose isn't as straight as your speech! "Like a pillow!" ... And thus, my cherished bride, we shall keep our marriage paulistic, praise the spirit and be contemptuous of the flesh! *(Lights lower on scene—H. turns away—narrators' lights.)*

Transition

[NAR. I]. Six months, Henry Tudor. Six months of harmonious misalliance.

[NAR. II]. But time is passing, Henry Tudor. You are getting older—

[NAR. I]. Where are your many sons?

[NAR. II]. What says your conscience now? *(lights up on scene)*

HENRY. Anna of Cleves, I cordially inform you that our days together are numbered. *(Anna jumps.)* What's the matter?

ANNA. Sire, you have a favorite method of dealing with excess wives.

HENRY. What an absurd notion! Why should I do this to my virtuous German sister, my able boon companion?

ANNA. How then?

HENRY. Since you, our dear wife, according to God's will, have remained barren—

ANNA. Totally unexpected.

HENRY. We shall, for the sake of people, declare our marriage annulled. We grant you the title Sister of the King, and an estate in the country with an annual income of two thousand pounds.

ANNA. Four thousand.

HENRY. Three thousand—and worth doubly that to a Lutheran, since the money is derived from confiscated convents.

ANNA. But—

HENRY. What else?

ANNA. Must the King's sister remain faithful to her brother?

HENRY *(laughing)*. What do you take me for? A monster? Get yourself a young and strong earl, and make the most of it.

ANNA. I'll follow your advice to the best of my ability. *(She exits as light fades—light picks up Henry in thinking pose—narrators' lights.)*

Transition

[NAR. II]. What has happened to you, Henry, that you should let a woman slip from your side?

HENRY. What is happening to me? Am I getting older?

[NAR. I]. Yes, Henry, you are getting old.

[NAR. II]. You are beginning to dread being alone.

HENRY. It is a horrible sensation to have passed the peak and to be looking down at the shadowy exit—

[NAR. II]. What does the conscience say now?

HENRY. By the devil, I shall follow the dictates of my heart. That shy, young Kathryn Howard—

[NAR. I]. The Howards are Papists—

HENRY. Well, haven't I been severely punished for having tried it with a Lutheran? Is there any better way to atone than to fortify myself against the Pope with a young Papist in my bed? And I love the maiden!

[NAR. II]. This proclaims summer—not autumn. Before spreads a precious harvest.

[NAR. I]. But your summer is to be short-lived, Henry. Two short years with your young wife—and then—

[NAR. II]. As for your world, Henry—you flung a snowball and behold an avalanche. *(Lights reveal Henry, K. Howard, and Kate Parr at prayer—Henry is center on platform, facing audience; K. H. and Kate kneeling in back of him—organ under.)*

window

SCENE IX

HENRY. Lord, for thirty-two years now I've been King of England, but at the same time I see into the future; *the centuries to come have passed by me.* The age we brought about—tell me what went wrong! Lord, there are several things I'm not too happy about. For example, the war at the dawn of that late century. Now, this war to end *war!* wars could have been more noble, more useful than any other. But it defeated us all, victors and vanquished alike. Then economics! What went wrong with our cherished art of facts and figures? It assumed the role of a force of nature that haunts us with ebbs and flows as unpredictable as the tide of a fifth element. Yet you must admit that what we've accomplished in our age is almost incredible. That's it! It's not credible any more! ... Father in Heaven! Leave the world as we so magnificently completed it—leave it as it is. Leave well enough alone! I strongly advise it! Amen. *(Henry leads K. Howard to rear—they bow as if being blessed—Kate Parr comes downstage and speaks to audience.)*

KATE PARR. Fresh air—fresh air! What an odd picture we must have presented down on our knees! A self-centered monarch who chats with the God he pronounced dead like a speculator with a rich father-in-law. A frightened young Queen who beseeches her Saviour for help and a lady of the court who has studied too much to believe in anything. *(Exit Kate—Henry and K. Howard come downstage and sit.*

HENRY. Ah! It's great to have a God with whom to share your sorrows and a young wife for your joys! I'm grateful that you have made me young again.

K. H. It's my duty to bring you joy. I pray I'll never give you reason for sorrow. ... There is so much that troubles me.

HENRY. No, nothing must trouble you. I'd rather pawn my crown. Just tell the treasurer how much you need.

K. H. Thank you! If you only knew how great a favor you're granting me.

HENRY. It's only money. Throw it away! But there's one small favor I ask in turn: in your contacts with people, be more sparing of your favors.

K. H. My contacts with people?

HENRY. This note was slipped to me. *(pantomimes handing her note, which she reads aloud)*

K. H. "The Queen is exceedingly fond of the Chamberlain Culpepper."

HENRY. Think nothing of it, my child. I know what it's worth. Laugh! Laugh it off! The court is a labyrinth of jealousy—a priest sent it.

K. H. The Queen IS exceedingly fond of the Chamberlain Culpepper!

HENRY. That can't be!

K. H. It is!

HENRY. Say no more! ...

K. H. I must tell you—everything.

HENRY. Everything? Never—never tell me everything! ...

K. H.   Henry! Can't you see how man fares in your world? He suffers and you feel nothing. He looks to you, and you don't recognize him. ...

HENRY.   Yes, it's true. Great is the cold. But there's no recourse. The consequences of thought is more thinking. The consequences of power is more power. There is no other way. ...

K. H.   I don't want to end like Anne Boleyn. I'll tell you everything if you promise mercy.

HENRY.   Hush—hush! I'll grant you mercy if you tell me nothing. Hush! Don't spoil the peace of this beautiful evening. I can see a tiny cloud above—white and curved like your body. ...

K. H. *(abrupt)*. My education at Norfolk Castle was very thorough. We had a music teacher. One day during a voice lesson, he kissed me. ... He taught me much I didn't know. It frightened me at first, but I soon got used to it.

HENRY.   How old were you?

K. H.   Thirteen. Soon my cousins found out about it, and they wanted their share. There were a lot of young men at the castle—chamberlains and pages, among them Culpepper. While our aunt was asleep, we took our pleasure with each other. ... We invented games. For example: the Henraide. We reenacted the marriage comedies of our King.

HENRY.   The marriage comedies of your King? Without a stage?

K. H.   We only needed a bed. Usually I was Anne Boleyn. ... We followed your teachings.

HENRY.   What teachings?

K. H.   The teachings of the freed spirit of the modern age. You preached that the girl, too, is a human being and free to dispose of her body. We readily understood that. But I only accepted gentlemen of rank—except for the first. ...

HENRY.   Why have you told me all this?

K. H.   Now that you know, I can't be blackmailed any more. ... Now you know everything—now I can breathe again. ...

HENRY.   If anyone had dared to say evil about you, I would have had him beheaded! Now— ...

K. H.   No! ... I've confessed to have your forgiveness. I've made you young again in these two years together.

HENRY.   In two minutes, you've made me old. ... Lewdness marked your body. ...

K. H.   You approved of it. ... You said that the woman, too, was free to dispose of her body.

HENRY.   I stand before you not as a husband, nor as a philosopher, but as the supreme judge of the realm. As a judge, I must condemn you because you disgraced the King's bed.

K. H.   Disgraced your bed? I didn't know anyone could disgrace your bed. Then you might as well know how repulsive you are. ... Your bed! ...

HENRY. Kathryn! Kathryn! I need you alive! I implore you to tell me how I
    can spare your life!

K. H.   You know that is impossible. I've lied enough in my days. I don't
    want to lie any more. I can't. It is choking me!—*(Lights out—bell
    tolls.)*

Transition

[NAR. I]. One day the King appears before Parliament and announces that
    he—after the sad experience with his fifth wife—is determined
    never to marry again.

[NAR. II]. Should he, however permit himself to be swayed for the good of
    his people and take yet another wife, then anyone who suppresses
    information that the bride is unchaste shall be guilty of treason.

[NAR. II]. Four short weeks later, the bells in London ring. The King does
    marry. *(Lights up on Kate center.)*

SCENE X

KATE.   He marries, to be absolutely certain there'll be no disappointment,
    a widow. *(laughs)* He marries—Me! Kate Parr. Oh yes! The famous
    innovator has grown old. The perpetual bridegroom now desires a
    wife—to nurse his ailments. That I've done since our wedding—
    and with remarkable success. Only when he keeps bragging about
    his accomplishments in this late century, and I can't hold back my
    own ideas, does he throw a fit! *(Henry enters, in—a fit.)* ...

HENRY *(walks about blusteringly)*. Kate, I've come to a conclusion! I
    prophesy: you'll teach your tongue to stop contradicting me or our
    wedded bliss'll end most abruptly and horribly; either I'll suffer a
    heart attack or—I'll suddenly survive you! *(stiffens with a sudden
    cry of pain)* Kate! Kate!

KATE *(runs to him)*. Oh dear! What's the matter? Is it your heart? *(He
    points to leg.)* The leg! What a relief! Better ten times the leg than
    once the heart! . . . The gout—that's an honest old male disease.
    After all, you know what caused it. Think of the great, great herd of
    pigs you've eaten in your lifetime and how you enjoyed every single
    bite. *(She cares for his leg.)*

HENRY. Oh, Kate—you're such a good woman . . . such a good wife.

KATE.   Yes, I am.

HENRY. Too bad you're an old professor and against progress.

KATE.   Is it getting better?

HENRY. No! But we did make progress! Incredible progress. Around 1500
    man's lifespan was thirty-one years—not fifty-nine.

KATE.   Ah! *(still working with his leg)*

HENRY. My dear wife, these are exact figures.

222

KATE. I don't believe in figures. Figures don't tell the truth. For example: you'll go down in history as the King who had six wives. That's the figure. The truth is you had no wife—

HENRY *(howls—then blissfully)*. Quiet! There! It's going away. Ah! Bliss, bliss spreads through the poor flesh.

KATE. Didn't I promise you? Now you can straighten up again.

HENRY. Embrace me, Kate.

KATE *(throws arms around him)*. Oh, just what is it that makes everyone love you—you monster!

HENRY. Because I'm strong and pure. The people sense it—women sense it. They revere in me the spirit of humanism that at long last is bringing a lasting peace to the world. ...

KATE. Peace! When I hear peace, I see war. ...

HENRY. There won't be another.

KATE. But lately, there was a close call, when they fought for a tip of Asia and a famous general wanted to employ the ultimate weapon.

HENRY. Yes, but the president recalled him to maintain the peace of the world.

KATE. Then the life of mankind actually depended on one man.

HENRY. Wrong, Professor. Let me teach you something. Neither kings nor presidents decide any more whether there'll be war or peace—

KATE. Then who does?

HENRY. The calculating machine, the electronic brain. ...

KATE. The calculating machine, as the conscience of mankind—that is your doing—

HENRY. What? How?

KATE. Because you used your conscience as a calculating machine—

HENRY. Kate! *(advances threateningly)*

KATE *(backing away)*. With your Majesty's permission—I'm expecting a visitor.

HENRY *(takes deep breath)*. It's all right. I need time. I'm preoccupied with ideas that far overshadow what bothers you, and I don't know how much more time my God has measured out for me. ... One can become the herald of a new age just once. What to make of my heritage may have to be left to others. ... I must make plans before— ... But come over here, Kate. Don't try to change me Kate, but you, too—remain as you are. Now go and entertain your visitor. *(He releases her with a slap on the behind, following her with a clinging gaze.)* Your visitor—do I know him?

KATE. Yes—fleetingly. *(She leaves and Henry, alone, begins to pace—slowly.)*

HENRY. I must plan what words to leave so that it continues after I'm gone—so that they know what to do—hold fast to the new faith! Knowledge is power! ... Raise your eyes to the stars and colonize them! ... Much remains to be done! Plan ahead. Ah, I'm dizzy. I must—write—much remains to be done. *(He moves off unsteadily as Kate enters with Anna of Cleves.)*

KATE. I'm happy to meet my husband's former wife. *(offers seat)* I'm grateful, Anna, for this visit. But why do you stare at me? Why aren't you talking?

ANNA. Ma'am, if I'm speechless, it's because I imagined you to be— entirely different.

KATE. The King has not yet ordered coins minted with my image.

ANNA. It doesn't pay, not according to experience. Oh, do forgive me. I'm very straightforward.

KATE. I prefer it.

ANNA. How's he getting on?

KATE. He suffers from the gout. And then, his heart—

ANNA. Don't you worry! He'll outlive a few more wives. Oh, forgive me, but that's why I came. I came to warn you. You're doomed unless you escape at once! ... I've written my brother—he's arranging—

KATE. What? Warn me? What do I have to fear?

ANNA. You don't seem to understand. All right, then! I live two hours from Norfolk Castle. Kathryn, it's common gossip even among my swineherds how you used to carry on while under the care of your good aunt. Oh, please don't misunderstand! I envy you your sunny youth. ... But if the King should find out—Save your head! Escape to Cleves. I've figured everything.

KATE. Figured! Everything! Just like Henry! You mean well, Anna, but you're wrong. You've left out the one figure which he, too, often overlooks. Your mistake is one human being. The Kathryn you came to warn is Kathryn Howard, and she has already put her head on the block.

ANNA. No! Then—you are the next Katharine? ...

KATE. Yes. Thank you, Anna, for your good intentions and for your courage. It's necessary indeed that we women stick together.

ANNA. Then I can be of service to you after all? You have a past?

KATE. Oh yes. ... I was twice widowed when he married me.

ANNA. Au! That's a good one! Wonderful! Congratulations! You know, I've also plowed two under, two sturdy knights—may they rest in peace. No—no one can cope with me—except him. He's so strong, so wise, so good—so brutal!

HENRY *(a cry offstage)*. Kate! Kate!

KATE. Oh, my God—His heart! *(Kate runs off as lights fade out and Henry's weaker voice is heard calling, "Katarina!")*

Transition *(narrators' lights)*

[NAR. I]. And this time, Henry, it is the heart. *(Church bells ring.)* You, the herald of a new age. Who would have thought that you, too, would have to die. You are indispensible!

[NAR. II]. But like any other human being, you crawl away and turn into decay. And it doesn't really matter—you can see that now.

SCENE XI

(Lights reveal wives kneeling around Katarina, who is standing. Narrators look on.)

KATARINA. Here rests a man born of the weakness of the flesh, lived for the supremacy of reason, died overpowered by his own power. ... And now, sisters, ~~rise~~ and cry no longer.

ANNA *(hastily)*. Right. We had reason enough to cry while he was alive. Let our memory of him be happy, and let us share his heritage.

KATARINA. Yes, we must accept it; they are the values of his age. Kate, please!

KATE. He left it in six shares.

ANNA *(hungrily)*. What is the first?

KATE. His conscience. *(Anna retreats.)* It is the conscience that he guided his flock with.

KATARINA. Was he the shepherd?

JANE. Not the shepherd, but the sheep dog who drove ~~it~~ *the flock* from the Lord's pastures. But I will take his conscience.

KATE. Then, his gold.

ANNA. Oh, I'll be glad to take it off your hands.

KATE. *(smiles—then)*. Then, his love.

KATHRYN H. I should like to have it.

ANNE. Do you know what you're asking, my child? Don't you think I'm entitled to it?

KATHRYN. Oh, Anne Boleyn! What wouldn't he do for you! And what did he ever do for me? Nothing but fill me with fear and disgust.

ANNE. Didn't you love him?

KATHRYN. That lecherous old man?

ANNE. He was a young and handsome and strong man. I loved him.

KATHRYN *(after a pause)*. Then, it is yours. *(Anne accepts gratefully.)*

KATE. His freedom.

KATHRYN. Yes, his freedom, that is my share!

KATE. Then—the new wisdom.

KATARINA. Kate, you're entitled to it.

KATE. Because it held me enthralled?

KATARINA. Yes, but you rose above it.

KATE. Finally, his spirit.

KATARINA. It was not *his* spirit. He merely made it his own. *(slowly, lights off all women except Katarina)* It is the spirit that in eternal dissatisfaction forever cries out for more experience, but seeks only gold, state, and power. It was the forceful, restless surge of a mighty age. But that age is now near its end. It must be different, or there'll never be another for the creatures of this earth! The end of your progression away from God, the final discovery, is the discovery of God. And this, Henry Tudor, is the end of modern age. *(Light fades on Katarina—music up—cast exit slowly in dim light.)*

Slatefall[2]

Billy Edd Wheeler
A Play for Voices
Arranged for Interpreters Theatre*

SCENE I—Pay Day

VOICES *(men and women—happy, half shouting).*
> *Pay day! Pay day! Praise the Lord, it's pay day!*
> *Hot dang, bust my breeches and Good-God-A-Mighty,*
> *It's pay day! Good old pay day!*

VOICES *(men creating a beat by slapping their thighs in rhythm, women clapping).*
> There's a long line of men at the company store,
> Waiting for the pay man to open up the door.
> Been two weeks since they left this holler,
> Two long weeks since they had them a swaller of—

VOICES *(men and women).*
> Moonshine, white wine, bootleg, store-bought,
> Draft beer, bottle beer, canned beer, gin,
> Red eye, rot gut, peppermint or govermint.
> Kick up your heels, boys, Saturday's here!
> Sing a little song, boys, drinking that beer! It's pay day!
> Yonder comes Joe with a fist full of dough,
> Going down to Whitesville to see a picture show!

(guitar chords and yelling—guitar music up—Benny dances a little jig—Narrators move downstage to stools, and clapping fades out as Narrators take over, with guitar under.)

NAR. I. Pay day in Pine Ridge. Not much you can say except there's gonna be hell raised. Down at the boarding house thirty-five men are going to be out-lying, out-singing, out-fighting, and out-drinking every other man in the coal camp. Because it's pay day.

NAR. II. 'Course, some folks are sticking that money in their pockets, sad-faced and quiet-like, and some day, when their pockets get full—well, they're figuring to leave Pine Ridge. They don't trust the mountain to give coal from now on. They figure that it'll go dry. They aim to be ready.

NAR. I. They're just folks, mining town people, who want a little fun after two weeks of working. They want to make something special out of Saturday because it's the half, it's pay day. *(Guitar stops as the*

---

[2] *Slatefall* by Billy Ed Wheeler. Reprinted by permission of author. Permission to perform *Slatefall* can be obtained from the author, Billy Edd Wheeler, Box 7, Swannanoa, N.C. 28778. Permission to use the music in public performance must be obtained from the author: Sleepy Hollow Music, Box 7, Swannanoa, N.C. 28778.

Slatefall is a play in verse, but to save space much of it has been printed here as prose, by permission of the author.

*clapping of thighs begins again and voices half shout as in begin-
ning.)*

VOICES.

Pay day! Pay day! Praise the Lord, it's pay day!
Hot dang, bust my britches and Good-God-A-Mighty,
It's pay day! Good old pay day!

*(The clapping becomes muted and then dies out. As it does, two or three
chords are strummed on guitar. Chords ring into—silence.)*

NAR. I. You know when day has passed in Pine Ridge. It is about six
o'clock. *(Men and women come forward to floor and first step.)*

NAR. II. The evening crouches around you until you wonder how it could
be so grey-brown here and so yellowy, daylight-bright up there.

VOICES. That's because mountains grow high here, stranger. They hunch
their crocked spines so close together a good-sized man can stride
from ridge to ridge and not wet his toe in the valley. It's like looking
up out of a well.

NAR. I. Come up the hollow, stranger, with evening.

NAR. II. Come with young twilight's low limping light.

VOICES. Only step easy. Plant tender leather feet with care. For here are
slate streets, coal-dusted, water-washed to every grey shade. Here
are coal roads that twist you by dark houses,
Brown rotting fences and raucous creeks,
By young wet noses standing at gates,
Here roads lead you by perky old women, grey-colored and strong,
sharp-jawed and deep eye-pitted.

NAR. I. Come, wanderer. You will be at home here with Greeks, the Danes,
the Poles and the Swedes, the Negroes, the stranger Americans,
the job hunters, the drifters.

NAR. II. Come up hollows. Follow ashy streets with the mountain twilight.
*(Lights fade as light, dawn-like flute or recorder carries a simple
theme and begins a series of trills, birdlike. Group takes position
and lights pick up women grouped on steps.)*

SCENE II—High Flyin' Bird

MARY. I sit long hours and watch the birds. They're free, the little birds.

MRS. G. I love to watch them.

MARY. Used to I wouldn't sit and watch nothing. I had to be wiping dust
or straining out water rust. Couldn't sit still. Had to be jumping
around, washing clothes, building fires, canning cucumbers.
Dusting again. Always the coal dust—But that was back some
years when I counted on leaving this holler. I know now I ain't
gonna leave, lessen it's alone.

MRS. G. We've learned to sit us down to try and strain some pleasure out of
a dusty life.

MARY. Them birds yonder's what I like.

PATSY. They're happy and no-care—

LAURA. Feisty, full o' wonder.

MARY. And they're free. They fly in over the mountains. And when they're
tired out with this place, they fly out again. Yes, they fly out again.
*("High Flyin' Bird" sung by Mary or one of the girls, with guitar
accompaniment)*
There's a high flyin' bird
    Up in the sky,
And I wonder if that bird looks down
    As he flies by
Ridin' on the air so easy in the sky.

Sun comes along,
    Lights up the day,
And when he gets tired, he slides
    On over the way.
East to the West, he gets gone ev'ry day.

But, Lord, look at me here,
    Tired as can be here,
I got the sit down, can't cry,
Old fashioned gonna die blues.
(Guitar fades as Mary speaks.)

MARY. Yes, I'm a mountain woman. I'm old as the hills. But the girl in me
still runs barefoot over the rocky roads of these green, rough,
brown-beauteous mountains. The young girl in me laughs and
sings.
*(As "Red-winged Blackbird" is sung, light fades on rt. platform;
guitar strums on softly. Mary and Hiram move to center bench;
light on bench area.)*
Oh, don't you see that pretty little bird,
A-fussing with all his heart and soul.
He's got a blood-red spot on his wing;
All the rest of him's black as coal.

NAR. I. After supper at this five o'clock hour, Hiram West sits on the porch,
still in his mining clothes.

NAR. II. He listens to the creek fret and watches for a thing to happen far
up the great brown mountain. Mary, his wife, joins him.

MARY. Put ye bath water in the tub. Baby's just at that age when he wants
to crawl into everything.

HIRAM. Y'huh, he is. The rascal.

MARY. He upped today and nearly spoke. He did. Tried for the longest,
like he was straining, but the word wouldn't come.

HIRAM. Huh, now.

MARY. Nearly come, though, after I thought he 'as about to choke. Then a
rat peeped out under the sink. Scared me. But Baby just lighted up
and grinned the biggest. He tried to catch it for a plaything. Forget
about speaking a word. I gathered him back and told him, "Baby,
don't go catching after rats." *(catches her breath)* And Hiram,
Baby—Baby looked at me the happiest and said—I didn't go to

228

teach it to him, Hiram. He said "rat" as clear and plain as anything.

HIRAM. Thought I'd fixed them rats for good.

MARY. You know there ain't no fixing them permanent. The whole creek bank is dug under with rat tunnels. You'd think as much as men shoot 'em in the evenings, they'd vanish. Never happen, don't reckon, as long as there's a crumb to eat in Pine Ridge. Rats eat each other, I bet.

HIRAM. Snakes eat rats.

MARY. Hiram, Baby said "rat." I didn't go to teach him.

NAR. I. The sun hangs heavy over the hills, burning dully in the watcher's eyes who already feel cool night sliding up the creek.

NAR. II. Come, stranger, on the back of the night. It is autumn. It is September autumn.

NAR. I. By the pump in front of Hiram's house, a trunk-scarred maple stands. When it rains, the tree is shelter for water carriers. Now in September autumn, it bears the weight of wings swept down from painted hills.

MARY. Did you ever see so many birds, Hiram? I wonder where they're going?

HIRAM. Oh, they're just passing through.

MARY. But where from? Where to? Look, now they're flying. It's like a dark cloud passing over. Oh! They're circling, coming back. Don't you love to see them, Hiram?

HIRAM. Yea. In a way, I guess. They make me sad, too.

MARY. Listen to that racket! Like a thousand rusty hinges creaking and scraping. Throats must be dry from the wind to make a noise like that. I love to see their red and black wings against the sky. It's fun, ain't it, to speculate about where they been and where they're going?

HIRAM. Like I said, they're just passing through. Going south, maybe.

MARY. Wish I was a bird myself, sometimes. I wish we was all red-wings, me and you and Baby. I do, Hiram.

HIRAM. Now, that's a new way to come at me.

MARY. That's how I feel. You know I do. Before we married you said we'd go away. You said we'd plan and save and one day leave. Used to you come home from work happy and whistling, with far-off places shining in your eyes. And we talked and left this holler a hundred times in our minds. But we never done it, really. We never pulled out.

HIRAM. Have we been able, I ask ye?

MARY. We've never pulled out like many 's the one has done. When we was able we never moved. And I've seen things crumble inside of us, our plans and everything. We've sort of rotted inside, I reckon, like these houses, and leaked away at the eyes.

HIRAM. This life ain't so bad, when ye come right down to it. We got a roof over us and plenty to eat and cook for company, and Baby's got clothes a-plenty.

MARY. But what more, that humans ought to have? Some day the mountain'll give out of coal, at least some thinks so, or the company'll shut down, like they's talk of, and we'll leave ghost houses with broken windows behind and graves behind that need to be looked after. And where'll we go? What plans have we got? Why do the red wings make you sad, Hiram? What makes ye follow them with your eyes up and over them hills? Because they're going where you and me have never been—to new places, where there's a patch of grass big enough to plant something in, or to sit down in, where a body can lean on a fence without getting black dirty. *(She turns away and gazes off.)*

NAR. I. Hiram did not speak or look at Mary. But in his head, behind his tired eyes, he was thinking.

HIRAM. A woman's tongue is like a rake, that scratches and digs and rips at things that ought to go unearthed, unspoken. Bad enough to live with thoughts without having to mouth them into life so they plague you sure enough. That's a woman's way—can't hold nothing in—got to be clattering, clattering, making noise, like them damned birds yonder. Baby's learned a new word. Couldn't say something nice, like daddy, or mother, or fox, or squirrel. Got to be "rat." Coal camps do that. Baby ought to be taken off, taken to a clean, sunny place to grow up in—to talk in. I know that well as Mary. But, got to be talking. Tongue has got to keep digging, scratching, like a rake that don't wear out—that only gets white-toothed and sharp.

NAR. II. Mary spoke what every woman spoke in Pine Ridge. She feared what every woman feared.

NAR. I. The mountain was always there to be pointed at, dark and ten million years heavy.

NAR. II. Come up the slate roads—

NAR. I. Come by porch light, lamp light—

NAR. II. Far-spotted star light, winking dim and cool.

NAR. I. Hiram hears without straining his ear, all the sounds that have come to be a part of his silence. The far-off rumble and rattle of the tipple—

NAR. II. He hears guitars. Players come and go, but the music never changes. Something lonesome and nice in A minor, or an E struck with the finger nail.
(Transition: guitar chords—light fades on Mary and Hiram— new positions—music changes to something lively—lights up on group.)

SCENE III—LIFE IN PINE RIDGE

(Episode I—In the Poolroom)

NAR. I. The poolroom is the center of life in Pine Ridge. Beer hall, candy counter, movie house, dance hall, Sunday School, a workout place for boxers. Hiram sees the men drinkers leaning together singing "Precious Memories," soaping their throats for another verse.

NAR. II. And the toothless women, tip-toeing coins into slot machines. The snuff-dippers, the midwives.

PREACHER. How many babies today, Sally?

SALLY. Two bastards and one legitimate.

CLARENCE. Sally's pulled many a trick out of the box.

PREACHER. Rabbits from the hat—lined with fur.

HARRY. Listen to the bastards purr.

BENNY. Dropped me on my head. Feel that bump?

HARRY. Sin and sorrow's Sally's meat.

SALLY. Fruits of love, the bitter and the sweet. I like my work. I come by it natural. But I was late the first time! Ollie Skeens pulls me outa bed on his way to work, five damn o'clock in the morning—says he, "Maggie's ready—won't have no doctor. Go and help her, Sal, and here's a plug of tobaccer." I looked out at the snow and slept another hour. When I got there, walking around the bed, looking at her baby, cussing up a storm, there was Maggie. Vow'd I'd never be late again.

LESLIE. What about Cookie Olderson, Sally?

SALLY. She's had hers.

CLARENCE. John left town.

HARRY. I don't blame him.

SALLY. Might o' had to marry, and him a bachelor fifty years.

NAR. I. Through the blue haze of tobacco smoke, sharp smacks of pool balls echoing from the back room—

NAR. II. —the tinkle of money, the guzzle of beer down long crooked throats—

NAR. I. —a penny for licorice, a cone of cream—

NAR. II. —the silken smell of cheap perfume—and singing—

Transition: Two or three men sing "Precious Memories"—light fades on scene—group moves forward—light up on center bench area—dim.)

(Episode 2—At the Pump)

NAR. II. The night air again, damp and clear, noises from the pump where men are gathered—

NAR. I. And Clarence Withrow pumping water on the head and shoulders of his boy, Benny—the low laughter of men.

CLARENCE. I hope you drown, you—drunkard's gut, you whiskey rain worm, you—yeah, look up at your pore old man. Beg him with them whine-dog eyes, you sack of morphine and chicken puke! And you! You men! Which of ye—which of you low-down dog's hind-ends done this to Benny? I wish I knowed which of ye give red whiskey to my boy. I'd wade blood up to my knees to find the man. Come on Benny. Come on, boy. Your old man'll help ye. Pay no attention to these flat-chested women. Get up, bastard! Damn, you're greasy as a snake's tail, and it soaked in butter. ...

(Transition: Light fades on scene—group take places—light up on Mrs. Greene, Patsy, and Laura.)

(Episode 3—On Porches)

NAR. II. And Mrs. Greene, Hiram's nearest neighbor, standing on her porch talking to Laura Jean Jones and Patsy Davis.

MRS. G. How that Benny gets so drunk, I'll never know.

LAURA. He's a plumb fool.

MRS. G. Yes-s-s-s, he's a fool, all right, but I wouldn't call him a plumb fool.

PATSY. He generally gets what he wants, don't he, Mrs. Greene?

LAURA. You ought to know, Patsy.

PATSY. Just 'cause you're married, Laura Jean, don't act so angeley. I know a few things on you, I reckon.

MRS. G. Here, you hens, just smooth ye down, now.

PATSY. She started it.

LAURA. Henny-Benny!

PATSY. Angeley—Angeley!

MRS. G. Here! Benny's no fool. Oh, he does the hambone the purtiest, and he sneaks around in funny places, people laugh, but he's no out-and-out fool. He's got talent. My boy Jimmy's got talent, too. He could be singing on the radio with his voice; Hiram said so, himself. I've agged him on and agged him on, but he's scared. Won't carry his gittar offa this porch. Benny ain't scared now. People laugh, but it's a scared man can't stand a laugh. You seen who had fun at the square dance Saturday. The Skipper? Oh, he done a turn or two. Polly Day, the belle of the ball, springing around like she's a virgin? No. Benny! Benny made the devil kick up in ever'body's heel.

(Transition: Square dance music up full, hands clapping, laughter—lights fade on women—lights up on group with the clapping and laughter.)

(Episode 4—At the Square Dance)

BENNY *(jumps to center area).*

Dance, gander, dance goose!

Look out, Benny! cutting loose!

Too old to reap? Too old to sow?

Look out, devil, let me go!

(Swinging into his jig, Benny is a loose-jointed boy. He does an uninhibited dance, earthy, elemental in strength, even a little corny. He is all angles, feet and elbows, with some of the excitement of the beat coming from his own production on the floor.)

Dance all night, dance all day!

Get hot, boys, or get out the way!

(Benny dances off and the clapping fades out—music change for next scene.

SCENE IV—PINE RIDGE SAYING GOODNIGHT

(Episode 1—On the Porches)

NAR. II. Slide up slate roads,

NAR. I. Coal dusted,

NAR. II. Water washed to every grey shade.

NAR. I. Night, the black cat, grey and dark-bodied, rubs its silent fur between the twisted hollows, purring of ninety-nine thousand lives. Slate-eyed and soft, night curls up to sleep.

NAR. II. Walk softly up the patchy road in darkness, softly, and you slip by three hundred yellow lights—

NAR. I. Two hundred lights beam *(Lights up on men grouped—lights dim gradually during scene.)*

NAR. II. Softly, the voices trail to your ears.

NAR. I. Pine Ridge making an issue of saying goodnight.

HIRAM. No matter what you tell 'em, Leslie, the men'll strike. They won't take that offen the company or nobody. They know what it'll lead to. Little by little—

LESLIE. Little by little, nothing, Hiram. I know 'em as well as you do, any of you. But what do they know? Sure, they'll strike. But who're they striking against? The company? And who's the company?

PREACHER. Who's side you on anyhow, Leslie?

HARRY. Yeah, I thought you was the union leader. Damn if you don't talk like a company man. *(laughs)*

LESLIE. We're all the company. That sounds funny, but I been doing some thinking. The men say they want to get paid for riding through the mountain to work. The company says it won't pay transport time, says the men'll get money for sweating hours. The men strike, and they get paid, for setting. They go to the company store next week and pay three cents more for a slab of bacon.

HARRY. That's damn right.

LESLIE. Now, who gets the raise? And who gets hurt? Both sides. But I tell you, the miner feels it the hardest.

PREACHER. It ain't just the money. Somehow you got to show the company.

LESLIE. And somehow you got to show men. Miners get good money, and they got nothing to show for it. Twenty-five dollars a day they gets. I'm just afraid the company'll get tired and shut down. Then what would happen? And I've heard rumors—
(Transition: As lights dim, haunting recorder music comes up under. During narration, the men move to their places.)

(Episode 2—Mary and Hiram Saying Goodnight)

NAR. II. Pad quietly by grey houses. Ride on the shadow by sagging porches.

NAR. I. One hundred lights, now, and dying voices.

NAR. II. Doors close behind rusty screens. Women who still care wash little feet and tuck them, blistered and splintered, into bed.

NAR. I. Guitars find their way into molds. No music now to rival the whisper and steady tear of the creek. Only the splash of water over rocks and the transparent chink of a bottle washing in the dark stream.

VOICES. Chink!

NAR. I. The rustle of bed-springs, creaks of complaining springs.

VOICES. Chink! Chink!

NAR. II. Seventeen lights now, yellowed, shining under the cat's belly.

NAR. I. The roar of the tipple.

VOICES. Chink!

NAR. I. And Leslie.

LESLIE. Men'll strike theirselves out of work. I've seen it happen.

VOICES. Chink!

NAR. I. Clarence Withrow praying over Benny.

NAR. II. And Hiram West, snapping off the 16th light, going to bed remembering.

MARY. I wish I was a bird myself sometimes, flying, leaving this camp. Wish we was all red wings, Hiram, me and you and baby.

NAR. I. Hiram lies face-up in bed beside Mary. He speaks to her in darkness.

HIRAM. Night, Mary.

MARY. Night, Hiram. Be pretty tomorrow, I think. I seen the red clouds this evening.

NAR. II. And night, the black cat, haunches down soft and close and purrs over Pine Ridge.

VOICES. Chink-chink! Chink!

NAR. I. Everything is silent but the tipple, and the busy creek—

NAR. II. And a dog here and there nosing in damp sacks for something to eat.

(Transition: As lights dim out, night recorder music changes to light morning music—dim morning light comes up.)

SCENE V—SLATEFALL

NAR. I. Morning comes slowly in Pine Ridge. At four o'clock there is not sun or darkness, but something in between.

NAR. II. As much a morning's dream as anything. The dream a small girl has of plucking silky cobwebs out of silkier, sheenier skies and pressing to feel their nothingness, and seeing their almost invisible lines across her fingers.

NAR. I. Morning in Pine Ridge, a gauzy gown floating in the hollows—

NAR. II. —trailing the light-footed, the wandering female, Dawn.

NAR. I. Into the mist Hiram steps from his kitchen. Mary is going back to bed. It is four-thirty. *(dim figure seen up center)*

NAR. II. Hiram sucks cool pieces of fog into the warm rooms of his lungs. Across the creek he sees a flame move from a dark place, float out into mist, and bounce up the hollow.

NAR. I. That light is Jimmy Greene. He moves closer to the light and the shadow under the light.

NAR. II. They come to other flames moving through the dream of morning, drifting forward, towing each other to the bottom of the mountain where tracks run straight up and disappear into the white, lowered sky.

NAR. I. At the sand house where miners wait to be lifted up the mountain, Hiram speaks to the man who outsmiles the sun.

HIRAM. That you, Preacher?

PREACHER. Wouldn't swear to it, Hiram. Zat you? *(Black Preacher stands.)*

HIRAM. Hope to tell ye! How's the baby?

PREACHER. Which one?

HIRAM. How many ye got, anyway?

PREACHER. Lord, Hiram, las' time I counted, musta been sixteen. *(chuckles)* I believe Sam Dorsey's been chucking some of his under my porch.

HIRAM. Preacher, I feel sorry for poor old Mabel. I bet you give her a rough time.

PREACHER. Hiram, all Mabel does is have the young-uns. I got to feed what she has. That's rough. Ain't easy to feed a bunch o' crickets jumping around hungry all the time.

NAR. I. The hoist car now, men loading on—*(Hiram moves up ramp— figure seen dimly)*—sitting under hardshells, gazing down, the steady climb. Hiram looks below at Pine Ridge under gauze and wind. Miners sweeping up the hill at cable's end.

NAR. II. Men who know the sight and feel of coal, who know the sound it makes when a lump is lifted and squeezed crumbling in hand, raining pebbles on hard-toed shoes. *(Voices begin whispering the clack-clickety-clack of motor on rails.)*

NAR. I. At the top and going in, they hear the rumble of steel on popping iron rails, the fitful scratch of the motor's electric arm as it rubs along the wire above their heads. They sit bathed in noise, watching beams from their hardshells strike opposite walls of coal. Deeper and deeper into the mountain. Darkness behind, before, and yellow streaks upon a blue-black wall. *(The clacking of the rails subsides during the next narration, but it is still present at a very low volume. Dim light on group.)*

NAR. II. In the hollow of Pine Ridge, vanishing dawn—

NAR. I. Warm fires of breakfast, smells of bacon, potatoes, and coffee soaking the bright air—

NAR. II. Women rising from a second sleep, shuffling smooth feet on linoleum floors.

VOICES.
Come up the hollow, stranger.
The mountain is always there to be pointed at—
Dark, and ten million years heavy.

(Clacking begins to build again.)

NAR. I. It started with a small *crack* which nobody heard, like a distant rattling of cellophane. Then a *pop*. *(Clacking, backed with a sound of hiss and roar, begins to climb in volume, so that the next narration is almost shouted.)*

NAR. I. The motorman cuts off his machine and strikes on brakes that

screech like forty witches, jolting the men forward in the car—
(blackout—and silence—then voices in darkness)

LESLIE. Hey! What happened, Harry?

HARRY. Two or three rocks ahead of me. Almost didn't see 'em. Hiram, throw 'em off the track and take a look, will you?

HIRAM. O.K., Harry.

HARRY. Fell last night, I guess. Never seen any signs Saturday.

LESLIE *(softly)*. Watch Hiram lift them rocks. Strong.

NAR. I. Without warning, but like a piston sliding in its shaft, the first layer drops. Hiram's light goes out. His hardshell snaps from his head before he feels the blow. He jerks backwards and stumbles to get up.

HARRY. *Hiram! (special light up slowly on UC platform, where Hiram is seen dimly.)*

MEN'S VOICES. *Hiram! Hiram! Hiram!*

NAR. I. He hears no shouts. The roar stretches his ears, pulling drums out of sockets. He cannot feel or see or hear in the midst of thunder— the thunder of slatefall!

MEN *(chanting)*. Hiram—Hiram—Hiram—Hiram—Hiram—Hiram *(etc.)*

TWO WOMEN *(above the chant, crying out in a higher-pitched sing-song tone, like a mother calling her child in the distance)*. Hiiiiiiiiii- ram. Hiiiiiiiiii-rammmmmmmm.

NAR. I.
The dark of the mountain on his eyes
Removes the dream and drowns the cries of men—
(Audience sees only dim outline of Hiram standing—voices have quality of echoes.)

LAURA.
Of men I sing, and Patsy Patsy with her Henny-Penny, and

PATSY.
Angel pants with her lazy lover,
Wearing his shoes out under the cover—of—

NAR. II. Wings over Pine Ridge, dropping out of skies, dropping into dust of darkness shaken from the dandruffed flesh of coal—

NAR. I. The flash between hearing and heard, seeing and seen, breathing and

NAR. II. The flash between life and—

NAR. I. The relived life in the photograph flash between dying and being dead.

MEN *(chanting)*. Hiram—Hiram—Hiram—Hiram—Hiram—Hiram *(etc.)*

WOMEN. Hiiiiiiiiii-ram-m-m. Hiiiiiiiiii-ram-m-m.

NAR. I. Now you are the mountain's, mountain man.

NAR. II. One with root and rock and solid sand,
One with dancing mountain waves, with—

BENNY. Dance gander, dance goose,
Look out, Benny's cutting loose! Look out—

CLARENCE. Benny, you skinny bastard, wet as a worm in red whiskey rain.

LAURA. Benny's a plumb fool, ain't he, Mrs. Greene?

CLARENCE. Giggle like women, damn ye! I'd wade blood up to my knees. Come on, son—

HIRAM. Sun in its circles I see no more, but up I'll feel in fingers of green, and eyes of blossom opening on the shiver and prancing yellow quiver of sun.

MRS. G. Your life is your own business, son, but if I had your voice, I'd sing for a living, go on the radio—sing, son—

HIRAM. Sing, sun, and all the songs I didn't sing, the dances I didn't dare in dancing—

BENNY. Dance all night, dance all day,
Get hot devils, or get out of the way!

HIRAM. Dance for me, Benny, gander-necked boy—dance to life to wind and tides and fishes' tails churning—dance to the fire, the tree, the blossom, moon-pull and sun-draw, thinking and sleeping, work, life and death—dance to man and God, and dance to love.

MARY. Why do the red wings make ye sad, Hiram? What makes ye follow 'em with your eyes? Baby has learned a new word. Baby has—

SALLY. Babies of his own some day—seed in a seed. Hard to kill the common weed. Babies come and babies go—

HIRAM. Life, Sally, you pulled me through, out of the seedbed belly like an—

SALLY. Oyster—I know, with pearl teeth and slick and dripping as a calf on ice. Now look at you, back in the—

HIRAM. Dark again. In one gate and out another. You yanked me out and I walk back in. Why and where, which-what Sally can pull me out again—

SALLY. Oh, in a million years—

HIRAM. And set me dancing—

BENNY. Dropped me on my head! Feel that bump?

SALLY. Fruits of love, bitter and sweet—

BENNY. Dance gander, dance goose—

HIRAM. Dance for me, Benny. Dance to love—
(verse of "Red-Winged Blackbird" sung)
Of all the colors I ever did see,
Red and black are the two I dread,
For when a man spills blood on the coal,
They carry him down from the coal mine dead.

(During song, light on Hiram fades out—song ends with blackout, and Hiram moves off stage—song hummed as lights up on platform.)

SCENE VI—WAKING IN PINE RIDGE

NAR. II. Pine Ridge did not even hear the remote thunder, but went on waking up. Mary leaned over her baby and smiled; Mary had not heard either.

NAR. I. At the sand house, a phone rings. News trickles down the hill.

VOICE. What's that you say? Slatefall?

NAR. I. A crowd gathers and stands around the sand house. Phones ring. Men silently rush. Outside the voices—

VOICES *(low, almost whispering).*

Slatefall!

Who was it?

Don't know.

They say it was just one—

Who? Which one was it?

They say it was Hiram.

Hiram?

At number four.

Hiram West?

Yeah, that's who it was, Hiram West.

Got it quick. Didn't know what hit him.

Damn. That's too bad.

Baby just come last year, didn't he?

NAR. I. Far up, motors stop running. Bells ring keenly. Across the valley on the mountain, machines cut off. Silence creeps down the hill, as if a cloth has dropped from heaven and blots noises falling.

NAR. II. The men walk down the road to Hiram's house. They pass sagging porches where women hold babies on hips, intense, afraid to ask who it was. They pause at Hiram's gate. Mary sees—and then, she knows. *(During this speech, men and women move slowly forward—Mary moves to bench—Leslie to bench back of her.)*

LESLIE. Mary—going into number four—

MARY. I know.

LESLIE. Some rocks were on the tracks ahead, a timber cracked—

MARY *(cries out).* I know! I don't—want to hear—

MRS. G. Thank ye, Leslie. You all can go now.

LESLIE. We won't work the rest of the week. The mines'll shut down in honor of Hiram. We'll see about the funeral and all—

MRS. G. I know—like ye done for me. *(Leslie turns and joins others. All stand quiet, with heads bowed.)*

MARY. I appreciate ye coming, but you don't have to stay.

MRS. G. No, I won't.

MARY. I know how women do . . . how they're expected to do. I've heard 'em fight. I've seen 'em fight and kick at the truth until it wore 'em out.

MRS. G. We all have. Yes.

MARY. I've already cried, Mrs. Greene, a hundred times before. Now that it's really happened, I don't have tears left for it. I've cried in my mind 'til I've washed my insides out. Death never disappoints us, does he? He worries us while we live with promising to come, and we don't dare laugh at him and say we've beat him. And by the time he comes, we're half dead already. But he comes. He don't disappoint.

MRS. G. I know there's nothing I can say, Mary. You got to work it out yourself. But ye got to *work* at it and not give up—you can't go sour.

You've got to look for new strength and try to understand. And wait. The Lord gives and . . .

MARY. The Lord takes away? The Lord took Hiram, did he? I wish I could believe that. It would be easier. It would drain some hate out of me. You know why I can't cry? Look out the window. Look out the door. Look anywhere in Pine Ridge and you'll see the reason. The mountain! The mountain! That's what I hate. I'm so full of hate I can't breathe. Or full of the mountain. They're both the same to me. That's what took Hiram. I see a big, brown glutton of a thing that feeds on miners' bones, that mashes 'em flat and sucks their bloody juices. They're tombstones!

MRS. G. I know how ye feel. I know. Time alone can help us get along. We just got to wait on time to pass. We got to wait.

MARY. Just one man this time, and that one Hiram. Why? Why did that one have to be Hiram?

MRS. G. Maybe you ought to lay down on the bed and rest some, Mary.

MARY. Maybe I'll cry after all, when evenin' comes . . . the sun goes down. *(Lights fade as one verse of "High Flyin' Bird" is sung—Mary moves off—others to position—lights up on group.)*
There's a high flyin' bird
  Up in the sky,
And I wonder if that bird looks down
  As he flies by,
Riding on the air so easy in the sky. . . .

PATSY. Where will she live now? Will she move away?

MRS. G. Maybe, by and by.

LAURA. I'd hate to see her move away, wouldn't you?

MRS. G. Yes. Yes, I would.

LAURA. Do you think she will?

MRS. G. I guess we all will, sooner or later.

LAURA. I don't want to ever leave the mountain, Mrs. Greene. I don't think I could be happy anywhere else.

PATSY. I'd hate to see Mary leave. It'd make me sad. As much as she's dreamed of leaving, I'd still hate to see her leave—go away.

MRS. G. I would, too—she would, too—but maybe she's already gone. *(sung)* Red-winged birds fly over the hill,
  Leave behind the miner's wife;
She'll dream about you when you're gone,
  She'll dream about you all her life . . .

NAR. I. Come sit with her, stranger, under scar of maple . . .

NAR. II. Evening's wings, frail red and beating.

W. VOICE. Sit by Mary and her baby.

NAR. II. Young they sit, under wind-bright skies . . .

M. VOICE. Between deep mountains, by a constant creek.

NAR. I. Come by the shady roads of slate and twilight . . .

M. VOICE. Coal-dusted—

M. VOICE. —cool, to leaden-topped bannisters.

NAR. II. Hear her speak of a noise beyond hearing

M. VOICE. Of earth, a darkness deeper than breathing
WOMEN. Chink!
ALL (chanting softly). Hiram-Hiram-Hiram-Hiram-Hiram-Hiram.
TWO WOMEN. Hiiii-ram. Hiiii-ram.
NAR. II. You know when day has passed in Pine Ridge.
WOMAN. Chink! Chink!
NAR. I. Look to mountains, mountain man.
NAR. II. Red wings circle and fall from sight.
MEN AND WOMEN. The west is jagged, brown against blood.
WOMEN. Follow the red wings with your eyes.
(Music: "High Flyin' Bird" up as group moves off and house lights come up.
Light guitar music and birdlike trills carried by recorder under.)

Production Notes

What values within this play help shape the director's production concept?
Regarding *Slatefall* and its production, the author has said:

> With *Slatefall* I am trying simply to paint a portrait of a coal-mining town, the people and the landscape, as it is before and during a tragedy, the likes of which happen every year in Kentucky and West Virginia. I would like for the people to seem universal rather than mountain, but with many hints at the mountain character—not pronouncing the "ings," tearing into passages with gusto and flavor, then backing into reticence and reserve. I would rather see it understated, if anything.

The author has given us two clues to guide the production concept: keep it simple, like a group portrait, and beware of overplaying it.

This play, published here for the first time, reveals much about the author: his love of the sounds and mysteries of nature; his love of the mountains; his understanding of the mountain people's courage, despairs, and longings. And here, too, is his talent for poetry and song. The writing of this inspired the ballad, "High Flying Bird," a favorite among recording artists.

Generally, the director might carry out the author's intentions by keeping the group portrait concept in mind and by using an abstract style with multiple casting, offstage focus, stylized movement, and other alienation effects. But let us suggest a few specific answers.

How can a director use visual and aural elements to highlight the author's intention?

Casting

The group nature of the interpretation should be highlighted by chorus voices and multiple casting. The chorus might consist of the full cast, six men and five women, plus two narrators. Each individual could be assigned one of the eleven identified character roles, as well as being one of the unidentified voices.

Set

To provide aesthetic distancing and effective lighting, three-quarter round (thrust) or proscenium staging is suggested (See Figure 16–1 below).

The three-step platform should provide a good grouping for the cast. Area F, a small higher platform, is reached by a ramp from area E. This helps provide aesthetic distance and allows special lighting for suggesting Hiram within the mine. The downstage area A, with a bench, is used for dialogue and action scenes and possibly forward placement of the chorus. The two narrators can be placed on low revolving stools DL and DR, from which they move to observe scenes or join the others for group scenes.

Focus and Scripts

To give emphasis to the alienation effect, offstage focus should be predominant throughout. However, some changes in focus are called for. In the pump scene, Clarence imagines his drunk son on the ground at his feet, and he turns to face the group upstage as he accuses them. Lively physical response is called for in the pay-day and poolroom scenes, with an exchange of glances suggesting relationships as the characters clap their

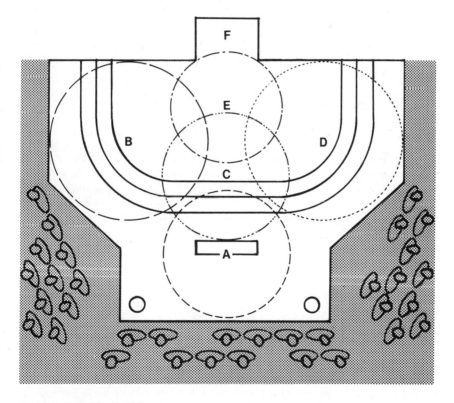

Fig. 16–1 Staging for *Slatefall*

hands and lean together while they sing. But the relationships in these scenes should be suggested rather than made too obvious.

The narrators hold their scripts, contributing to the desired alienation effect. However, both in identified character roles and as voices in the chorus, the cast must have their lines memorized.

Movement and Costuming

The cast should have basic platform positions. Lights pick up small group scenes. Changes in positioning suggested in the script should be kept to a minimum.

Each of the characters expresses his or her own personal tempo in movement as well as speech, and the mood changes of the scenes are made evident by the interpreters' body tension. Throughout, their eyes move to look at the mountains surrounding them, creating constant awareness of place. To further highlight the group, movement in certain scenes can be stylized; for example, the group coming forward after Hiram's death might give the illusion of slow motion.

In keeping with the presentational style of *Slatefall,* no attempt should be made to literalize the costumes. Simple casual dress with a few selected clothing props (caps, shawls, etc.) give the appropriate suggestion.

Lighting

Lighting plays an important part in setting mood, giving emphasis to the group, and changing scenes. The special light on Hiram in the mine has an eerie cast, removing him from reality. Special lighting is needed in various scenes, such as when Hiram moves up the ramp to enter the mine in the early morning mist.

Music

Two cast members should be able to sing and play the guitar. The recorder or oboe music can be taped or supplied by someone offstage. The square-dance music may be either taped or played by guitarists onstage.

Taped music, live guitar music, and ballad singing helps create focus on the group and establish mood change. The music here is important, beautiful, and deserving of special consideration.

Lest We Forget: Kent State[3]

A Theatre-of-Fact Script
compiled by Dan Robinette

> . . . there is a disposition in the human heart to attribute moral character to the symbol of the community. For if that symbol is acknowledged to be as tainted as it actually is, the very meaning of man's social existence is called into question.[4]
> Reinhold Niebuhr

---

[3] *Lest We Forget: Kent State* by Dan Robinette. Reprinted by permission of author.

[4] Reinhold Niebuhr. "Limits of Liberty," *Nation,* January 24, 1943, p. 87.

NARRATOR 1. It is now Monday, May 4, 1970, and there will be firing on the hill that overlooks the Commons. Before it starts—a rain of fifty-five steel-jacketed bullets which could kill at a range of two miles—let us find out more about the background of two of the students. The first of the victims is Carol Meyer, a freshman at Kent State; she enjoyed every aspect of life as her Hebrew name implies—"goodness, kindness, all the joy one can think of in life." This zest for life was noted by her friends:

GEORGE. If you were really down and out, the first person you'd want to see was Carol. Man, she had a laugh like you haven't heard. Makes you feel good inside just to hear her. Within ten minutes I guarantee, you'd be up on top again. There wasn't anything Carol wouldn't do for you. She cared.

NARRATOR 2. Like many young students, Carol was idealistic and very socially conscious. She once said:

CAROL. I think the way to help people is to work individually and gradually rather than just sit around and talk about how unjust things are. I just can't buy these people who beat their chest and then do nothing. Why aren't they in the ghettos, or doing inner-city work?

NARRATOR 1. Certainly, the Vietnam War was one of her concerns, but she seldom showed it. Says her roommate, Libby:

LIBBY. Some of the guys who came over to the house were pretty much into politics and would rap for hours about the economics of the war, U.S. imperialism—the standard topics. But not Carol. She'd just as soon be out in the kitchen fixing something for everyone to eat. Sure, she was against the war, but who isn't? I guess the best way to explain it is this: she cared because people were dying, not because of the military-industrial complex.

NARRATOR 2. In one of her courses, Carol had been required to write an essay about the war and had started with the phrase:

CAROL. Who is to say?

NARRATOR 2. One of her friends, noting this, had kidded Carol about it, and the rest of their group used it as a constant gag, mournfully exclaiming:

STUDENT 1. *Who* is to say?

STUDENT 2. Who *is* to say?

STUDENT 3. Who is to *say?*

NARRATOR 1. On Sunday night, only eight hours before the shooting would begin, when asked her opinion about the weekend riots, Carol replied:

CAROL. Who *is* to say?

STUDENT. If you were making one of the old style rah-rah college movies, Kevin would have to be the star. You know the type: good build, easy smile, the campus hero.

STUDENT 1. But there was a hell of a lot more to him than that. He wasn't your party boy; he was a real thinker.

STUDENT 2. Kevin didn't have to search for an identity, like the rest of us.

He was so sound in the head. He knew himself and what he was capable of.

NARRATOR 2. Kevin Muller was a studious person who devoted his spare time to sports and ROTC. He once said—

KEVIN. When I first got the ROTC scholarship, I thought it wouldn't be such a bad trip. But now I just can't justify our being in Vietnam and I don't think I could ever fight there. And the worst part of it is having killing drilled into you day after day. And what can I say when people are constantly hammering at you for being in ROTC? Like the other day when I happened to be in uniform, one of my professors said to me, "What are you, some kind of fascist or something?" I know he was kidding, but it really gets to you after a while.

NARRATOR 1. These are only two of the four students who lost their lives. Ironically, however, these students do not represent our major concern; they were objects, consequences of a conflict with roots much deeper than Kevin and Carol, and boundaries which transcend the battlefield of Kent State.

NARRATOR 2. The problem that culminated in the deaths of four students, then, is not a drama which concerns only the youth at Kent State, but a drama with action that encompasses a conflict of life styles across the world.

NARRATOR 1. Thus, our concern is not with people, but with symbols— specifically how men align themselves under certain symbols— radical and liberal, conservative and hippy, hawk and dove, peace and war, pigs, imperialists, and warmongers.

NARRATOR 2. A point is reached when people no longer are manipulators of symbols, but become the manipulated.

MAN 1. The symbols close off discussion.

MAN 2. They forbid problem-solving.

WOMAN 1. They dictate life styles.

WOMAN 2. In effect, they create a society in which man is depersonalized.

ALL.   Unimportant. *(pause)* Inconsequential.

NARRATOR 1. Paradoxically, the turn toward violence at Kent State was not inspired by the war or politics, in the opinion of some people. The first rocks thrown in anger were hurled through the muggy Friday night of May 1 by beery students who could not resist the urge to dance on a Kent street. Hundreds of students were drinking at the bull-and-beer spots that flourish in most college towns.

WOMAN 2. Spirits were light. A crowd swarmed into the warm night, blocking busy North Water Street, responding to the rock beat.

MAN 3. An irate motorist gunned his car's engine as if to drive through the dancers. Some students climbed atop the car, jumped on it, then yelled.

STUDENTS. One, two, three, four, we don't want your fucking war!

NARRATOR 1. A drunk on a balcony hurled a bottle into the street—and suddenly the mood turned ugly.

STUDENT 1. The revolution is here!

STUDENT 2. Fuck the pigs!

STUDENT 3. To hell with the fascist state!

STUDENT 4. Fuck you, Agnew!

STUDENT 3. Power to the people!

STUDENT 2. Nixon sucks!

STUDENT 3. Cambodia is a disgrace; burn the damn town!

ALL.   Capitalist pigs! Imperialists! Motherfuckers!

NARRATOR 1. Students smashed the car's windows, set fires in trash cans and began to smash store fronts. Police were called. The Kent mayor ordered a curfew, but few students were aware of it. Police stormed into bars after midnight, turning up the lights, shouting:

NARRATOR 2. O.K. The party's over. Get your ass out! You've had your fun for the night.

NARRATOR 1. Police and sheriff's deputies pushed the youths back toward the campus, then fired tear gas to disperse them.

NARRATOR 2. Finally, it was quiet. Many people had reasons why it had started in the first place:

BARTENDER. It wasn't alcohol.

NARRATOR 1. The bartender at Big Daddy's.

BARTENDER. That's for sure. A couple of years ago the students used to drink a lot more than they do now. If the riot had occurred in 1968, I'd said it was booze. This time, impossible. You want my opinion? Spring. Something like this happens every spring, but this one was bigger.

RICK.   It was Cambodia.

NARRATOR 2. Says Rick Rollins, a secondary ed. major from South Euclid and a strong liberal.

RICK.   Nixon's Thursday night speech was the cause of it all. What other reason could there be?

BILL.   It wasn't Cambodia—

NARRATOR 1. Said Bill Manic, a Kent State student who sat down immediately after the events were over and typed out firsthand recollections of the events.

BILL.   —at least not with the kids I saw. I saw no evidence of malice over Nixon's Cambodian announcement.

STUDENT 1. It wasn't police brutality, because no police were in sight when it started. As a matter of fact, the police behaved well, considering.

STUDENT 2. It was the weather. First nice Friday night of the year, you know, the panty-raid spirit.

NARRATOR 2. David Withers, who has a keen feeling for these matters, says:

DAVID. Who's looking around deep for reasons? I was sitting in Orville's having a beer. Everything normal. I hear a crash out in the street and somebody runs in shouting: "Guys are throwing bottles out there!" All I could think to say was, "Wow, man. That's pretty far out!"

NARRATOR 2. The students got administrative approval to hold a rally that evening on the Commons at the center of the campus. There, militant war protesters managed to take complete charge of a crowd of about eight hundred, many still smarting from the conflict of the night before. They disrupted a dance in one university hall, then attacked the one-story Army ROTC building facing the Commons. They smashed windows and threw lighted flares.

NARRATOR 1. The building caught fire.

NARRATOR 2. When firemen arrived, students threw rocks at them and cut their hoses with machetes until police interceded with tear gas.

NARRATOR 1. Without bothering to consult Kent State authorities, the mayor of Kent asked for help from the National Guard.

NARRATOR 2. The governor quickly ordered Guardsmen transferred to Kent.

GOVERNOR. We've seen here in the city of Kent probably the most vicious form of campus-oriented violence. Now it ceases to be a problem of the colleges in Ohio. This is now the problem of the state of Ohio. We're going to put a stop to this. They have one thing in mind and that is to destroy higher education in Ohio. Those people just move from one campus to the other and terrorize the community. They're worse than the Brown Shirts and Communist element, the night riders or the vigilantes. These people who are causing the trouble are not all the students at Kent State University. They are the freaks—the worst type of people that we harbor in America. We are going to eradicate the problem. It's over with in Ohio.

NARRATOR 1. In like manner, with equal rhetoric and passion, the speeches for the opposition were being delivered, too, only blocks from the comments of the governor.

TERRY SMITH. The war is on at Kent State University. Two weeks of intense struggle have seen the SDS lead several major actions, rallies, marches, and raise the political consciousness of thousands on the campus, while the thug administration has responded with swift and heavy repression. A struggle has begun and will continue on Kent's campus. War at Kent State!

NARRATOR 2. Gradually, the intensity increased.

JIM HOUBEN. We're no longer asking you to come and help us make a revolution. We're telling you that the revolution has begun, and the only choice you have to make is which side you're on. And we're also telling you that if you get in the way of the revolution, it's going to run right over you.

NARRATOR 2. Until the voices reached a crescendo:

A STUDENT. They used guns at Cornell, and they got what they wanted. It will come to that here.

A STUDENT. We'll take a machine gun and kill every bastard there!

ANOTHER. We'll start blowing up buildings; we'll start buying guns.

NARRATOR 1. Within an hour, about five hundred Guardsmen, already weary from three nights of duty, arrived with fully loaded M-1 semiautomatic rifles, pistols, and tear gas. They were in time to help police block the students from charging into the downtown area.

NARRATOR 2. Students reacted by dousing trees with gasoline, then setting them afire. Order was restored before midnight.

NARRATOR 1. On Monday, the campus seemed to calm down. In the bright sunshine, tired young Guardsmen flirted with leggy co-eds under the tall oaks.

NARRATOR 2. Classes continued throughout the morning. But the ban against mass assemblies was still in effect, and some students decided to test it again.

NARRATOR 1. At high noon, youngsters began ringing the school's victory bell—normally used to celebrate a football triumph.

NARRATOR 2. A bell which was later to peal anything but a victory.

NARRATOR 1. About a thousand students, some nervous but many joking, gathered on the Commons. Another two thousand ringed the walks and buildings to watch.

NARRATOR 2. From their staging area, the burned-out ROTC building, officers in two jeeps rolled across the grass to address the students with bullhorns:

NARRATOR 1. Evacuate the Commons area! You have no right to assemble!

NARRATOR 2. Back came shouts:

VOICE 2. Pigs off campus! We don't want your war!

VOICE 3. Students hurled insults.

NARRATOR 2. The jeeps pulled back. A formation of fewer than a hundred Guardsmen pursued fleeing students between the two buildings.

NARRATOR 1. Then the outnumbered and partially encircled contingent of Guardsmen ran out of tear gas.

STUDENT 1. Suddenly, they seemed frightened.

STUDENT 2. They began retreating up the hill toward Taylor Hall, most of them walking backward to keep their eyes on the threatening students below.

GUARDSMAN 1. Some of the troops held their rifles pointed skyward.

GUARDSMAN 2. Several times a few of them turned, pointed their M-1s threateningly at the crowd, and continued their retreat.

NARRATOR 2. When the compact formation reached the top of the hill, some Guardsmen knelt quickly and aimed at the students who were hurling rocks from below.

NARRATOR 1. A handful of demonstrators kept moving toward the troops. Other Guardsmen stood behind the kneeling troops, pointing their rifles down the hill.

NARRATOR 2. A few aimed over the students' heads.

NARRATOR 1. Within seconds—

ALL.   A sickening staccato of rifle fire—

NARRATOR 2. A Kent State journalism professor could not believe—

PROFESSOR. They are shooting blanks—they are shooting blanks! Then I heard a chipping sound and a ping; my God, this is for real!

NARRATOR 1. The campus was suddenly still. Horrified students flung themselves to the ground, ran for cover behind buildings and parked cars, or just stood stunned.

NARRATOR 2. Then screams broke out.

VOICE 1. My God, they're killing us!

NARRATOR 1. A river of blood ran from the hand of one boy, saturating his school books.

STUDENT 1. One youth held a cloth against the abdomen of another, futilely trying to check the bleeding.

WOMAN 1. Guardsmen made no move to help the victims.

NARRATOR 1. In that brief volley, four young people—none of whom was a protest leader or even a radical—were killed.

NARRATOR 2. Ten students were wounded, three seriously.

NARRATOR 1. Many seemed driven to find a reason which would provide relief from their shock and fear.

NARRATOR 2. Fear to the point of panic was certainly one of the chief reactions to the weekend of May 1 through 4.

NARRATOR 1. The fear of a shopkeeper threatened with destruction of his business unless he displayed a peace symbol.

NARRATOR 2. Or perhaps the fear of a student who went home to find himself reviled by a formerly friendly neighborhood, and even his parents. No case of parental rejection equaled that of a family living in a small town near the Virginia border, with three good-looking, well-behaved moderate sons at the University.

NARRATOR 1. Without any record of participation in protest, the boys found themselves inadvertently involved at the vortex.

NARRATOR 2. The middle son was photographed standing beside one of the students who was shot.

NARRATOR 1. The youngest was arrested for trespassing and his picture appeared in the home-town paper, to the embarrassment of his family.

NARRATOR 2. The family spoke to one of the researchers for a newspaper.

MOTHER. Anyone who appears on the streets of a city like Kent with long hair, wearing dirty clothes, or barefooted deserves to be shot.

RESEARCHER. Have I your permission to quote that?

MOTHER. You sure do. It would have been better if the Guard had shot the whole lot of them that morning.

RESEARCHER. But you had three sons there.

MOTHER. If they didn't do what the Guards told them, they should have been mowed down.

RESEARCHER. Is long hair a justification for shooting anyone?

MOTHER. Yes. We have got to clean up this nation. And we'll start with the long-hairs.

RESEARCHER. Where do you get such ideas?

MOTHER. I teach at the local high school.

RESEARCHER. You mean you are teaching your students such things?

MOTHER. Yes, I teach them the truth. That the lazy, the dirty, the ones you see walking the streets and doing nothing ought to be shot.

RESEARCHER. Or perhaps the fear that impelled thousands to cry out on radio open-line programs, in letters to the editor, in conversations, obsessed with making sense out of the senselessness of death.

NARRATOR 2. From a North Olmsted, Ohio, man to the President of Kent, May 12, 1970:

VOICE 1. As a taxpayer I am fed up with your lack of control of minority radicals on your campus. We pay your salary to see that all students are taught the good old American traditions. We do not expect you to employ free thinking socialists to corrupt all the years of training we have given our children, before sending them to our university. We expect you to back our President and American principles before the students, regardless of your personal feelings or opinions. If you and your staff are not capable of controlling the students or if your teachings have caused them to riot—don't complain about the National Guard killing them.

NARRATOR 1. From a Richmond, Virginia, woman to the President of Kent, May 20, 1970:

VOICE 2. I should think that now you and all the students who attend Kent State would take a good look at yourselves. All of you are responsible for the lives of the four kids who died on your campus. They were there of their own free will, and they took part in what is a criminal offense. If you are afraid of a bunch of radical, selfish, spoiled kids and cannot stay in control of the situation, resign and let someone who can do the job. . . .

NARRATOR 2. From a reader of the Akron *Journal:*

VOICE 3. When a soldier of the United States, under orders and in uniform, is attacked in any way, this constitutes an act of treason. Every country in the world specifies death as the penalty for treason. Let Kent radicals realize they were, in fact, in violation of the law of the land, like it or not. It is too bad that death must be the price of preservation of the law. The price of freedom from anarchy is high.

NARRATOR 1. From an Akron, Ohio, man:

VOICE 4. Based upon total costs, college students are about one-fifth as expensive to kill as Viet Cong. Perhaps soon we will be able to murder as economically as Adolf Hitler.

NARRATOR 1. Written communications alone do not give a full awareness of the extreme violence of some responses to the deaths at Kent. For obvious reasons, most of these responses never reach print.

NARRATOR 2. Resulting often from real panic, and leading often to more panic, such statements should be mentioned. Every statement given was heard in varying forms:

VOICE 1. One Guardsman was killed by the students, but his body was smuggled away because the authorities are leftists and are afraid to antagonize the students.

VOICE 2. President Nixon gave orders to have some students killed because of fear of the youth culture's political force.

VOICE 3. SDS members were converging on Kent from all over the country to burn it to the ground as the signal for a Communist revolution.

249

VOICE 4. It is deeply meaningful that three of the four dead students were Jewish.

VOICE 5. Ohio students are patriotic; the out-of-state students make all the trouble.

VOICE 4. The older faculty is patriotic; the teaching assistants make all the trouble.

VOICE 2. Students are forced to read un-American history and pornographic literature by faculty members who are traitors.

VOICE 3. The leftist news media tried to create sympathy for the slain students by printing high school portraits, not photos showing that they had become hippies.

VOICE 5. The University should be blown up and started with real Americans.

VOICE 1. All the Guardsmen were members of the Ku Klux Klan, the John Birch Society, or both.

VOICE 4. Students were stockpiling weapons for a take-over of the University when the fall term began.

NARRATOR 1. The shots fired on the campus Commons that day still echo in the divided American psyche, for this was one of the events by which a nation's citizens define and divide themselves—

NARRATOR 2. But the events that followed have spread until the paranoia is everywhere. Nowadays everybody and everything is the cause of the trouble.

NARRATOR 1. Here are some blacks who know for a certainty that all the trouble flows from a plot among white liberals to make genocide official.

NARRATOR 2. Here is a warlike old man with a Bible. He knows who is making all the trouble.

VOICE 1. Hippies, Doctor Spock, unwashed bums.

NARRATOR 1. The hippies know better. When a hippy baby cries in the night, it is because—

VOICE 2. —he has been dreaming of the establishment.

NARRATOR 2. This brings a smile of scorn to lips of men high in government—

VOICE 3. —men close to the President and vice president—

VOICE 4. —men close to the brilliant, hard-nosed, tough-minded young White House staff aides;

BOTH. They know all too well where all the trouble comes from:

ALL. The media.

VOICE 1. Congressmen are not sure.

VOICE 2. Some know that the White House is right about the media.

VOICE 3. Others know for a certainty that all the trouble is caused by the FBI,

VOICE 4. The New Left,

VOICE 2. The Black Panthers,

VOICE 1. The memory of Martin Luther King,

VOICE 3. The Supreme Court under Earl Warren,

VOICE 1. The Supreme Court under Warren Burger,

VOICE 4. Governor Brown,

VOICE 2. Ronald Reagan,

VOICE 4. deficit spendings,

VOICE 3. and lots more.

NARRATOR 2. In this situation, the division was based on pro-student or pro-Guard.

NARRATOR 1. Pro-student meant a passionate commitment to saintly, peace-loving, sexually honest flower-power fighters for a better world against repression in all its forms.

NARRATOR 2. Pro-Guard meant a commitment, equally passionate, to national honor seen in terms of Washington praying at Valley Forge, Old Glory raised on Mount Surabachi, fascism defeated by men devoted to hard work and decency, which is now threatened by an immoral, corrupt generation.

NARRATOR 1. Yes, the events of May 4, though not symbolically neat, are not to be minimized, for, in an awful way, the Kent deaths had everything:

NARRATOR 2. The well-publicized generation gap;

NARRATOR 1. The new life style of the young, as expressed aggressively or casually in speech and personal appearance;

NARRATOR 2. The conflict over American involvement in Indochina; over the power of the President;

NARRATOR 1. Over the influence of the military;

NARRATOR 2. Over the choice of working within the system or smashing the state.

NARRATOR 1. With the pervasive presence of the news media and its ambiguous power to create news by reporting news.

NARRATOR 2. Yes, the University would have preferred to be known for its Ph.D. program, its connection with the Cleveland Orchestra through Blossom Center, its library with a collection soon exceeding a million volumes.

NARRATOR 1. It became best known, instead, for the events of May 1970.

Production Notes

What values within the play help shape the director's production concept?

Lest We Forget: Kent State is about symbols, about a dehumanizing process common to our society that is gradually vaccinating individuals against human qualities. The author feels Kent State was simply the normal extension of this process. One finds it increasingly difficult to relate to people as people, for they have become objects hiding behind symbols, marks which prevent one from addressing the real person. In effect, this is a world of alienation. Any staging of this play must emphasize this alienation, the prime cause for the Kent State affair.

How can a director use visual and aural elements to highlight the author's intention and realize the production concept?

Casting

The script calls for eight performers, four men and four women; however, the cast can be reduced or expanded. Multiple casting is essential, however. The fact of performers becoming Guardsmen, townspeople, and students emphasizes the theme of the production: the play concerns a conflict of symbols, not people. Especially effective is the irony of a performer playing diametrically opposed roles.

Set

The set is not important. Perhaps only the minimum is needed to reinforce the presentational style of the performance. The number of scene changes further reinforces the presentational approach.

An ideal set might provide three levels. There could be three platforms with steps leading up to either end, and a ramp connecting the higher middle one with the stage. This should provide at least three acting areas. The floor space between the platform and the edge of the stage should provide three other acting areas. If possible, steps on either stage, leading into the audience, would provide acting areas for the two stationary narrators and would increase the intimacy between the audience and the narrators.

Focus and Scripts

The focus is predominantly offstage, to increase the alienation, while at the same time elevating the scene from one specific occurrence. Naturally, the narrators maintain visual contact with the audience and the interpreters to reinforce the liaison concept.

Scripts should be used by the narrators to connect the presentation with the story and, equally important, to emphasize the text in a physically symbolic way. The alienation techniques and the simple staging help call attention to the text. Scripts for the actors are probably unnecessary.

Movement and Costuming

Costumes, setting, and property should be simple, in keeping with the traditional view of interpreters theatre, but also in order to give the desired effect of *Lest We Forget: Kent State*. Costumes would be everyday student dress with some elements of suggestion, such as symbols that reinforce the theme—peace symbols, Guardsman hats, etc. No props would be used, since most of the staging is suggestive by nature.

Movements should be minimal. The crucial element in this production is the director's use of space. The director should keep in mind that this incident was prompted by a failure of communication among the participants. By grouping the interpreters into opposing forces, by maintaining marked distance among the people in individual scenes, by utilizing offstage focus, by eliminating any form of physical contact, the director can reinforce the concept of alienation.

Setting and Lighting

The setting can be greatly enhanced through the use of slides. Slides for this production might easily be procured from newspaper clippings. A blank cyclorama serves as the background for projections.

Lighting can aid this production greatly, providing blackouts while the interpreters regroup, illuminating areas that require particular emphasis, and reinforcing the mood and atmosphere. The sound could be created largely by the performers. Here is an excellent opportunity to let the protest songs of the period provide an added dimension. The act is so dramatic and the pace so quick that the music could be used as the audience enters, while the performers wander about onstage, as students might do during a typical school day.

The War Prayer [5]

by Mark Twain
Adapted for a Chorus in Interpreters Theatre

ALL.   It was a time of great and exalting excitement.
INT. 2. The country was up in arms,
INT. 3. The war was on,
INT. 4. in every breast burned the holy fire of patriotism;
INT. 5. the drums were beating,
INT. 6. the bands playing,
INT. 2. the toy pistols popping,
INT. 4. the bunched firecrackers hissing
INT. 3.   and spluttering;
INT. 5. on every hand and far down the receding and fading
         spread of roofs and balconies
         a fluttering wilderness of flags flashed in the sun;
INT. 2. daily the young volunteers marched down the wide avenue,
INT. 3. gay and fine in their new uniforms,
INT. 2. the proud fathers
INT. 4, 5, 6.   and mothers
INT. 4. and sisters
INT. 4, 5, 6.   and sweethearts
INT. 5. cheering them
INT. 4, 5, 6.   with voices
         choked with happy emotion as they swung by;
INT. 2. nightly the packed mass meetings listened,
ALL.   panting,
INT. 3.   to patriot oratory
         which stirred the deepest deeps of their hearts

INT. 4. and which they interrupted
at briefest intervals with cyclones of applause,
INT. 6. the tears running down their cheeks the while;
INT. 3. in the churches the pastors
INT. 2.   preached devotion to the flag
INT. 3.   and country
INT. 2. and invoked the God of Battles,
INT. 3. beseeching His aid in our good cause
INT. 4. in outpourings of fervid eloquence which moved every listener.
ALL. It was indeed a glad and gracious time,
INT. 5. and the half-dozen rash spirits that ventured to disapprove of the
war and cast a doubt upon its righteousness
ALL. straightway
INT. 3.   got such a stern and angry warning
INT. 5. that for their personal safety's sake they quickly shrank out of sight
and offended no more in that way.
ALL. Sunday morning came—
INT. 2. next day the battalions would leave for the front;
INT. 4. the church was filled;
INT. 3. the volunteers were there,
INT. 2. their young faces alight with martial dreams—
INT. 3. visions of the stern advance,
INT. 2. the gathering momentum,
INT. 3. the rushing charge,
INT. 2.   the flashing sabers,
INT. 3. the flight of the foe,
INT. 2.   the tumult,
INT. 3. the enveloping smoke,
INT. 2.   the fierce pursuit,
ALL MEN. the surrender!—
INT. 6. then home from the war,
INT. 2. bronzed heroes,
INT. 3.   welcomed,
INT. 2.   adored,
ALL MEN. submerged in golden seas of glory!
ALL WOMEN. With the volunteers sat their dear ones,
INT. 4. proud,
INT. 5.   happy,
INT. 6.   and envied by the neighbors and friends
who had no sons and brothers to send forth to the field of honor,
there to win for the flag or failing,
die the noblest of noble deaths.
ALL. The service proceeded;
INT. 5. a war chapter from the Old Testament was read;
INT. 4. the first prayer was said;
INT. 6. it was followed by an organ burst that shook the building,
INT. 3. and with one impulse the house rose,
with glowing eyes and beating hearts,
and poured out that tremendous invocation—

ALL.   God the all-terrible! Thou who ordainest,
                Thunder thy clarion and lightning thy sword!
INT. 2. Then came the "long" prayer.
INT. 3. None could remember the like of it for passionate pleading
        and moving and beautiful language.
INT. 4. The burden of its supplication was
        that an ever-merciful
INT. 5.   and benignant
        Father of us all would watch over our noble young soldiers
INT. 6. and aid,
INT. 2.   comfort,
INT. 3. and encourage them in their patriotic work;
INT. 4. bless them,
INT. 5. shield them in the day of battle and the hour of peril,
INT. 6. bear them in His mighty hand,
INT. 2. make them strong and confident,
INT. 3. invincible in the bloody onset;
INT. 4. help them to crush the foe,
INT. 2. grant to them
INT. 3. and to their flag and country
INT. 2. imperishable honor and glory—
INT. 1. An aged stranger entered and moved
        with slow and noiseless step up the main aisle,
        his eyes fixed upon the minister,
INT. 4. his long body clothed in a robe that reached to his feet,
INT. 5.   his head bare,
INT. 6. his white hair descending in a frothy cataract to his shoulders,
INT. 4. his seamy face unnaturally pale, pale even to ghastliness.
ALL.   With all eyes following him
INT. 5. and wondering,
INT. 1. he made his silent way;
ALL.   without pausing,
INT. 1. he ascended to the preacher's side
        and stood there,
ALL.   waiting.
INT. 3. With shut lids the preacher, unconscious of his presence,
        continued his moving prayer,
INT. 5. and at last finished it with the words,
        uttered in fervent appeal,
INT. 3. "Bless our arms, grant us the victory,
        O Lord our God,
        Father and Protector of our land and flag!"
INT. 6. The stranger touched his arm, motioned him to step aside—
        which the startled minister did—and took his place.
INT. 1. During some moments he surveyed the spellbound audience
        with solemn eyes in which burned an uncanny light;
INT. 5. then in a deep voice he said:
INT. 1. "I come from the Throne—bearing a message from Almighty
        God!"

ALL. The words smote the house with a shock;
INT. 4. if the stranger perceived it he gave no attention.
INT. 1. "He has heard the prayer of His servant your shepherd
and will grant it if such shall be your desire
after I, His messenger, shall have explained to you its import—
that is to say, its full import.
For it is like unto many of the prayers of men,
in that it asks for more than he who utters it is aware of—
except he pause and think.

"God's servant and yours has prayed his prayer.
Has he paused and taken thought?
Is it one prayer?
No, it is two—one uttered, the other not.
Both have reached the ear
of Him who heareth all supplications,
the spoken and the unspoken.
Ponder this—keep it in mind.
If you would beseech a blessing upon yourself, beware!
lest without intent
you invoke a curse upon a neighbor
at the same time.
If you pray for the blessing of rain
upon your crop which needs it,
by that act you are possibly praying for a curse upon some neighbor's crop
which may not need rain and can be injured by it.

"You have heard your servant's prayer—
the uttered part of it.
I am commissioned of God
to put into words the other part of it—
that part which the pastor,
and also you in your hearts,
fervently prayed silently.
And ignorantly and unthinkingly?
God grant that it was so!
You heard these words:
'Grant us the victory, O Lord our God?'
That is sufficient.
The whole of the uttered prayer
is compact into those pregnant words.
Elaborations were not necessary.
When you have prayed for victory,
you have prayed for many unmentioned results
which follow victory—must follow it,
cannot help but follow it.

Upon the listening spirit
of God the Father fell also
the unspoken part of the prayer.
He commandeth me to put it into words.
                    Listen!

"O Lord our Father,
our young patriots,
idols of our hearts,
go forth to battle—
be Thou near them!
With them, in spirit,
we also go forth
from the sweet peace
of our beloved firesides
to smite the foe.

"O Lord our God,

INT. 2, 3, 4, 5. help us
INT. 1.   to tear their soldiers
          to bloody shreds
          with our shells;

INT. 2.   help us
INT. 1.   to cover their smiling fields
          with the pale forms
          of their patriot dead;

INT. 2, 3. help us

INT. 1.   to drown the thunder
          of the guns
          with the shrieks
          of their wounded,
          writhing in pain;

INT. 2, 3, 4. help us

INT. 1.   to lay waste
          their humble homes
          with a hurricane of fire;

INT. 2, 3, 4, 5. help us

INT. 1.   to wring the hearts
          of their unoffending widows
          with unavailing grief;

INT. 2, 3, 4, 5, 6. help us

INT. 1. to turn them out roofless
with their little children
to wander unfriended the wastes
of their desolated land
in rags and hunger and thirst,
sports of the sun flames of summer
and the icy winds of winter,
broken in spirit, worn with travail,
imploring Thee
for the refuge of the grave
and denied it—
for our sakes
who adore Thee, Lord,
blast their hopes,
blight their lives,
protract their bitter pilgrimage,
make heavy their steps,
water their way with their tears,
stain the white snow with the blood
of their wounded feet!
We ask it,
in the spirit of love,
of Him Who is the Source of Love,
and Who is the ever-faithful
refuge and friend
of all that are sore beset.
and seek His aid
with humble and contrite hearts.

ALL. Amen"

INT. 4. After a pause:
INT. 1. Ye have prayed it;
if ye still desire it,
speak!
The Messenger of the Most High waits!

INT. 2. It was believed afterward
that the man was a lunatic,

ALL. because there was no sense
in what he said.

Production Notes

**What values within this piece of literature help shape the director's
production concept?**

Mark Twain's "War Prayer" is an excellent study in dramatic irony; this could become the director's production concept. Twain acidly reminds us of the tragedy of war while poking fun at the all-consuming spirit of jingoism which permits, even encourages, people to lose their individuality, rallying around a "holy" cause which is never questioned. The zeal of the "patriots" is made even more poignant when juxtaposed with the prophetic prayer uttered by the hoary visitor. It is climaxed by the subtle irony of the concluding understatement.

In what manner can the director use visual and aural elements to highlight the author's intention?

Casting

The poem itself offers myriad possibilities for the creative director. The preceding adaptation was used in class to demonstrate the flexibility of the form. The adaptation maintains the narrative effect by consistently assigning to a select group of interpreters certain lines which are obviously narrative. This aids in reinforcing the story effect. Other line assignments are intended to support the choral effect or are simply the adaptor's effort to reveal the psychological motivations of the "patriots" by permitting them to speak the sort of lines usually given to a narrator.

The arrangement here calls for three men and three women, who serve as narrators, characters, and chorus. This arbitrary number of interpreters could be expanded without difficulty. Of chief importance is an effective blend of the male and female voices. It is suggested, however, that all the interpreters have multiple roles, except the one who plays the messenger of God.

Staging and Movement

The presentational staging emphasizes alienation through the use of offstage focus and multiple casting of unidentified voices. Thus, the movement should be suggestive rather than literal. Stylized movement will help the audience use imagination to create the appropriate picture: a fist raised in fervor suggests the zealous commitment of the crowd; a figure standing gravely erect suggests the marching soldiers; a small group in neat rows on benches suggests an entire congregation.

Focus and Scripts

All scenes are played with offstage focus. Naturally, the interpreters use facial expressions and stylized movement to suggest characterization. The concluding lines should be delivered with onstage focus—that is, for the first time, the interpreters establish eye contact with one another. This would suggest that, even though they are aware of each other, they still never understand the impact of the messenger's prayer.

Production Notes for Chamber Theatre

"Why I Live at the P.O."
a short story by Eudora Welty
planned and directed for chamber theatre
by Charlotte Nolan.*

Here we are describing a particular dramatization of this story to demonstrate chamber theatre style. The story, which can be found in *Selected Stories of Eudora Welty*, was used as written.

What values within the story help shape the director's production concept?

Though Miss Welty's method of storytelling appears direct and simple, the theme and tone of the story are quite complex. It appears to be comedy, but something grim lurks close to the surface, for it contains innuendoes of cruelty that reveal the false pride and jealousies of the human condition. Though we know that most of the leading character's (Sister's) persecution is of her own making and we smile at the comic effect of her situation, we believe that Miss Welty intended for us to sense Sister's alienation, the pain of her aloneness. The characters appear to be caricatures, and yet they are very real—nothing is false. They are both funny and sad. Miss Nolan described the characters and the story's meaning in this way:

> Early in the game we begin to understand "Sister," who tells her own story. She is a self-righteous spinster who is suffering from a persecution complex. What she says happened is not what we see happening and this gives her away. Stella Rondo is not a "fluzzy," but a self-centered country girl who enjoys her power to make Sister squirm. The rivalry between the sisters has been going on for years. Mama is a traditionalist, a peacemaker, soft, sentimental—and not very bright. Uncle Rondo is not an old rip of a drunk; he is hung over and sick. It's his day off—the Fourth of July, a day for celebrating. Now, trying to sober up, his family gets in his way. Papa Daddy is a hard old nut to crack, but, for the most part, he just wants to be let alone.
>
> Perhaps the most important clue Miss Welty gives us for directing a chamber theatre production of this story is the incongruity of her leading character's words and actions. For example, when Sister is ready to leave for the P.O., no one is lifting a finger to keep her from it. In a stunned moment, when she has recognized this fact, she declares loudly, "It's too late to stop me now." To interpret Sister in a truly joyous mood at the end would be to miss the author's point of the story.[6]

In what manner did the director use visual elements to highlight the story's meaning and values?

---

* Miss Nolan was a student of Dr. Robert Breen at Northwestern University when he first began his experimental work with chamber theatre. With other Northwestern students, Miss Nolan later set up an experimental loft theatre in New York, where they continued to work with Dr. Breen's new medium. After fifteen years in professional theatre, Miss Nolan is once again involved with chamber theatre, using it to open up the world of literature for young people in her native Southeastern Kentucky.

[6] Interview with Charlotte Nolan, December 1976.

Setting

Miss Nolan's staging (Figure 16–2) was planned in an open area, with the audience in three-quarter.
Set pieces suggested in the above figure include a platform with a step unit, metal chairs, typing tables, a high stool, a rocker, and a suitcase.

Various areas represent rooms inside and outside the house; on the platform are two bedroom areas; the step area is the hall; the living-dining room is center; the kitchen is left area; and right stage and across the front are the outside.

Use of Costumes and Props

The women wore black skirts (Sister's to the knees, Mama's below the knees, Stella Rondo's above the knees) and colored blouses (Sister's red in a prim style, Mama's pink with a brooch, Stella Rondo's purple with a scoop neck). The men wore black pants and some color above the waist: Uncle Rondo's shirt was orange and Papa Daddy wore green suspenders. The suitcase was the only hand prop used; it was literalized because of its importance in the situation. Through pantomine, Uncle Rondo made the audience see him change into a long flowing robe, and Papa Daddy's long beard became evident through suggestion. Two costume props were added: Sister wore horn-rimmed glasses, and spectacles rested low on Papa Daddy's nose.

Movement

An introduction was used to bring the actors on as themselves: as each character's name was called, the interpreter entered briskly, abruptly

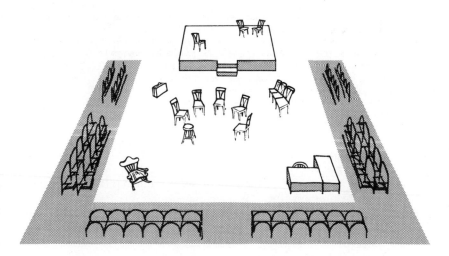

Fig. 16–2   Staging for "Why I Live at the P.O."

freezing in the appropriate character pose. The tableau was held only for a second: then each person moved into position: Stella Rondo to pick up the suitcase and hold an imaginary child by the hand; Uncle Rondo to the right upstairs bedroom area, to sit with his back to the audience; Papa Daddy to the couch; Mama to the kitchen area; and Sister to the step area. The characters eased out of the freeze and came alive at a signal, the suitcase dropped to the floor.

These actions were pantomimed before a word was spoken: hearing the sound, Mama comes to the door, embraces Stella, and reacts to Shirley T, the imagined child; Stella Rondo takes the child to meet Papa Daddy, who inspects her before nodding off again; Uncle Rondo pantomimes loosening his tie, drinking from a bottle, taking his shoes off, etc.; Mama takes the suitcase upstairs, followed by Stella with the child after Stella and Sister have exchanged hostile glances; Mama puts the child on the bed and makes over her. Only then does Sister, as the narrator, move forward and talk directly to the audience. Her shifts in focus continue throughout.

When asked what advice she would offer for directing chamber theatre, Miss Nolan replied:

> For the continuous small actions performed throughout, each director must supply his own creative details. An awareness of certain devices is helpful in coordinating words and actions. There should be preparation cues for movements coming up as well as cues for the actual movements. Each interpreter should know the precise moment when he should begin preparing for transitional movements, so he can appear motivated and natural. There should be no rushing of movement in order to get to the next line. The "holding" of lines becomes natural only when the actors sense the general tempo and are able to concentrate on the inner motivations of their characters. At certain points, a director may use the freeze as an aid in focusing attention and in coordinating words and actions. The tendency to want to rush the pantomimed action and to forget the imagined child's presence are two problems likely to require careful attention in directing this particular script.
>
> Our simple suggestive staging allowed viewers to become involved in the story through their imaginations. It also allowed the story to be performed in whatever space was available, proving that all the conventions and facilities aren't necessary in order to dramatize fictional stories well—anywhere.[7]

Suggested Readings

Abel, Leslie, and Robert Post. "Towards a Poor Readers Theatre," *The Quarterly Journal of Speech*, December 1973, pp. 436–442.

Adams, William J. *Readers Theatre News*, San Diego, California: San Diego State University.

Pickering, Jerry V. *Readers Theatre*. Belmont, California: Dickenson Publishing Company, Inc., 1975.

Breen, Robert S. *Chamber Theatre*. Englewood Cliffs, N. J.: Prentice-Hall, 1978.

---

[7] Ibid.

Coger, Leslie, and Sharon Pelham. "Kinesics Applied to Interpreters Theatre," *Communication Education*, March 1975, pp. 91–99.

Coger, Leslie, and Melvin R. White. *Readers Theatre Handbook*. Glenview, Illinois: Scott, Foresman and Company, 1973.

Forrest, William, and Cornelius Novelli. *Oral English*. Syracuse, New York: Le Moyne College.

Haas, Richard. *Theatres of Interpretation*. Ann Arbor, Michigan: Roberts-Burton Publications, 1976.

Hirschfeld, Adeline. "Stylized Movement in Interpreters Theatre," *Communication Education*, March 1976, pp. 111–120.

Hudson, Lee. "Oral Interpretation as Metaphorical Expression," *The Speech Teacher*, January 1973, pp. 27–31.

Issues in Interpretation. Ann Arbor, Michigan: Department of Speech Communication and Theatre, University of Michigan.

Kleinau, Marion and Marvin. "Scene Location in Readers Theatre: Static or Dynamic," *The Speech Teacher*, September 1965, pp. 193–199.

Long, Beverly Whitaker, et al. *Group Performance of Literature*. Englewood Cliffs, N. J.: Prentice-Hall, Inc., 1977.

Long, Chester Clayton. "Three Kinds of Theatre," *The Liberal Art of Interpretation*. New York: Harper and Row, Publishers, 1974, pp. 390–406.

Maclay, Joanna H. *Readers Theatre: Toward a Grammar of Practice*. New York: Random House, 1971.

Rienstra, Phyllis. "Resurrecting the Past: Historical Documents as Materials for Readers Theatre," *The Speech Teacher*, November 1972, pp. 310–315.

Schneider, Raymond. "The Visible Metaphor," *Communication Education*, March 1976, pp. 121–126.

Index

270